D1042053

Accounting and Budgeting in Public and Nonprofit Organizations

Accounting and Budgeting in Public and Nonprofit Organizations

A Manager's Guide

C. William Garner

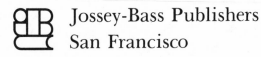
Jossey-Bass Publishers
San Francisco

ACCOUNTING AND BUDGETING IN PUBLIC AND NONPROFIT ORGANIZATIONS
A Manager's Guide
by C. William Garner

Copyright © 1991 by: Jossey-Bass Inc., Publishers
350 Sansome Street
San Francisco, California 94104

Library of Congress Cataloging-in-Publication Data

Garner, C. William.
  Accounting and budgeting in public and nonprofit organizations: a
manager's guide / C. William Garner. — 1st ed.
    p.   cm.—(The Jossey-Bass public administration series)
(The Jossey-Bass nonprofit sector series)
  Includes bibliographical references and index.
  ISBN 1-55542-336-1
  1. Finance, Public—United States—Accounting.   2. Corporations,
Nonprofit—United States—Acounting.   3. Financial statements.
4. Program budgeting—United States.   I. Title.   II. Series.
III. Series: The Jossey-Bass nonprofit sector series.
HJ9801.G37   1991
658.15'11—dc20   91-8376
                                                           CIP

Manufactured in the United States of America

The paper used in this book is acid-free and meets the
State of California requirements for recycled paper
(50 percent recycled waste, including 10 percent
postconsumer waste), which are the strictest guidelines
for recycled paper currently in use in the United States.

JACKET DESIGN BY WILLI BAUM

FIRST EDITION

HB Printing   10 9 8 7 6 5 4 3 2

Code 9139

**The Jossey-Bass
 Public
Administration
 Series
and
 The Jossey-Bass
Nonprofit
 Sector
Series**

Contents

Preface

Accounting and Budgeting in Public and Nonprofit Organizations, unlike most books on accounting and budgeting, is for people with no formal preparation in accounting. In recent years dramatic changes have taken place in the accounting standards set forth for public organizations and for nonprofit organizations that come under some governmental oversight. The primary purpose of this book is to help those in, or preparing for, leadership positions to work efficiently and effectively with the business operations within the framework of the standards. Although the information is at times complex, it is a comprehensive presentation essential to understanding the many facets of accounting and budgeting operations.

Another important feature is that this book presents accounting and budgeting practices as two separate systems that must formally interact with each other. The failure of accounting and budgeting systems to interact appropriately can be their greatest weakness. To counteract this, I describe how these two systems can interact with each other at six specific points.

Throughout this book, I describe the procedures used to implement the accounting and budgeting systems in the context of the evolution of accounting practices and standards. The descriptions of these procedures correspond to the Generally Accepted Accounting Practices (GAAP) of the Governmental Accounting Standards Board (GASB). (The standards and principles of the GASB are applicable to state and local governments and nonprofit organizations that are subject to some degree of control by a government unit; nonprofit organizations not subject to such control should follow the standards set forth by the Financial Accounting Standards Board.)

This book will help managers and others understand accounting language and practices so that they can work with their financial program and business officials to ensure that the ac-

counting and budgeting systems support each other, to interpret
accounting and budget reports, to control organizational resources,
to make sure that legal requirements are met, and to fulfill their
ultimate responsibility—to maintain the financial integrity of their
organization. At the same time, the book is designed to provide
managers and others with an understanding of their organization's
accounting and budgeting systems so that they can integrate their
philosophy, goals, views of the economy, and priorities with their
organization's financial plans and influence the direction their organization's resources should take. And with the book's outline for
developing a financial analysis program, they will be able to examine and interpret their organization's financial records and statements to plan for the future and prepare reports to enable organizational stakeholders—boards, taxpayers, contributors, or dues-paying
members—to understand how their money is being spent.

Overview of the Contents

This book focuses on the operational level of accounting and
budgeting systems rather than the specific details of accounting
practices or theory. It is intended to help managers and others to
answer questions such as these: Are the budget records accurate? Are
the budgets being recorded into the accounting system to the best
advantage of the organization? Is the most appropriate budget preparation method being used by the organization? Are the budgeting
and accounting procedures appropriate for the different funds in
the organization? What forms should be used to process expenditures? Are budget allocations, supplements, and amendments being
properly approved and recorded? Are the methods and records used
to manage the budget appropriate for the different budget units in
the different funds? Can the expenditures be justified in terms of
these activities and services? How are the excesses in the funds
handled? What is the condition of fund reserves in a debt fund,
investment fund, or endowment fund, and how are they being used?

Chapter One begins with a brief history of accounting and
budgeting, which leads into the current standards being applied to
public and nonprofit organizations. It then provides definitions of
some of the key terms used throughout the book, such as *public,*

nonprofit, accounting, and *budgeting.* Finally, the chapter sets forth an overview of the accounting and budgeting subsystems described throughout the book and an outline of the six points where the two systems interact.

The structure for the accounting and budgeting systems in a public or nonprofit organization is created by the use of entities called "funds." Funds are what make public and nonprofit organizations different from other types of organizations as well as different from each other. Chapter Two explains what fund entities are and why they are important to the financial operations and to the accounting and budgeting systems of an organization. The chapter describes six types of funds that are typically used in public and nonprofit organizations and presents an outline of the fund structure presentèd by the GAAP. It explains how the funds formally interact with each other through the accounting and budgeting systems, and provides a simple method for categorizing and recognizing these interactions in the accounting records.

The activities of a budgeting system are divided into three subsystems, which are called the AAA subsystems: approval, adoption, and allocation. Chapters Three, Four, and Five concentrate on these subsystems. Each of these subsystems has three components: input, process, and output.

Chapter Three describes the first two subsystems, approval and adoption. The input to the approval subsystem is the budget proposal, which may be prepared through the use of one of several budget methods described in the chapter; the process is the systematic review of the proposals for approval; the output is the approved budget. The approved budget is then the input to the second subsystem, in which the budget is presented for adoption and a budget award. In these two subsystems, the budget calendar plays an important role in processing the budget through the reviews, filings, and actions needed to produce the output of the second subsystem: the adopted budget. Adoption of the budget informs the organization that it will receive a revenue award.

The approved and adopted budgets provide the input to the third subsystem, allocation. Chapter Four explains how a budget is allocated, how a budget numbering format is developed and why it is so important to the allocations, how budget reports are used, and how budget modifications are managed.

After the budget allocations are made and the budget is adopted, the budget must be properly managed if the system is to work. Chapter Five explains the budget control process with respect to the receipt and expenditure of money and the management of the reports and office records that ensure the accuracy of budget reports. It includes a description of the different types of budget forms and a management technique called "red light/green light."

Chapter Six introduces the language of accounting and explains its application to the information and processes used in the accounting system. The chapter discusses the accrual and cash basis methods as well as the double-entry accounting formula. Chapter Six also describes the different types of accounts, the accounting numbering system called the "chart of accounts," and the importance of debit and credit entries to the double-entry accounting formula.

Chapter Seven describes the input and processing of information in the accounting system. It begins with the entry of information into a journal through the use of debits and credits. From there the chapter follows the information through the system to the trial balance, which is used to check the accuracy of the accounting system. Because this part of the accounting system is the core of regular accounting activities, the chapter describes how various journals and additional forms are used in an accounting operation. It also introduces the key to the interactions between the accounting and budgeting systems—the use of the subsidiary ledger to generate the budget reports.

Financial statements, the accounting system's output, are presented in Chapter Eight. The chapter describes three basic financial statements, as well as a combined format that allows the statements of the different fund entities to be shown on one form. It also includes descriptions of the fiscal year, the accounting cycle, and the closing of the books.

Chapter Nine brings the accounting and budgeting systems together by looking at the six points where they interact. These six points are important if the two systems are to be integrated from the beginning of the year to the preparation of the financial statements.

An accounting and budgeting system should not be seen as a series of annual events but rather as a set of activities that span the life of the organization. This is the purpose of the adjustments that are discussed in Chapter Ten. At the beginning of the chapter, the specific differences between cash and accrual methods of accounting are set forth, particularly as they relate to the accounting adjustments, and the chapter continues by presenting three types of adjustments—expenses and revenues, inventory, and depreciation—and the different methods that may be used to calculate inventories and depreciation.

Chapter Eleven focuses on auditing and the analysis of financial information. It recommends, in addition to the formal external audit, an internal audit by a team or committee as well as a manager. The chapter goes on to describe the areas to be included in an audit, the techniques to follow, the final report, and the follow-through. It explains the purpose of a financial analysis, points out the benefits of a quantitative study that uses a statistical approach, with a particular focus on the issues of equity, efficiency, and effectiveness, and stresses the importance of reliable and valid financial information.

When conditions change for an organization, some managers seem to have difficulty in adjusting their systems to accommodate the changes. This is often because the systems do not follow a basic accounting and budgeting design but have grown up piecemeal around the management structure and programs of the organization. Thus, the organization may lack flexibility or become bogged down in detail and not be able to expand its operations as needed. For an organization to successfully adopt and plan for the future, it must have a strong set of accounting and budgeting systems, integrated from the beginning of the year to the end of the year and linked from the beginning of the life of the organization to the present. It is the purpose of this book to help the managers and others concerned with the future of a public or nonprofit organization achieve that end.

Acknowledgments

I wish to express my appreciation to the people who provided valuable assistance in the preparation of this book. First and foremost is my wife, Karyl, who served as my critic and tirelessly read and reread the material. I also wish to thank the graduate students who read the draft material and provided helpful comments and encouragement. Last, but not least, I wish to thank Alan Shrader of Jossey-Bass for his seemingly unlimited patience, confidence, advice, and willingness to work with me on a very different accounting book. Of course, at this time, I fondly remember the many teachers who made this work possible.

New Brunswick, New Jersey   C. William Garner
February 1991

The Author

C. William Garner is associate professor and program coordinator of education administration in the Graduate School of Education at Rutgers University. At the university level he has served as a staff administrator with responsibilities for accounting and budgeting, as an administrator for an off-campus facility, as chair for two different academic departments, as a continuing education director, as a dean, and as a director of a resource center. He has also served on several public boards.

To my wife and best friend, Karyl,
for her support over the many years
—from the day long ago
when the student nurse met the sailor

Also to my children, Ron and Juliet,
who always know Dad can do it

Accounting and Budgeting in Public and Nonprofit Organizations

1

The Origins and Purposes of Accounting and Budgeting

The premise of this book is that accounting and budgeting must be recognized as separate systems that must interact in a complementary manner if managers are to exercise control over the financial resources of their organizations. This chapter provides a brief introduction to the development of accounting and budgeting practices, describes current efforts to establish uniformity in the accounting practices of public and nonprofit organizations, and offers an overview of the two systems.

The book does not describe the systems in terms of bookkeeping entries and does not delve into the individual processes and procedures used by various types of public and nonprofit organizations (hospitals, state and local governments, colleges and universities, and so on). Rather, in describing the two systems, the book follows the guidelines known as the governmental Generally Accepted Accounting Principles (GAAP) and other standards set forth for public and nonprofit organizations by the recently created Governmental Accounting Standards Board (1987), which is referred to as the GASB.

A factor of increasing importance to those responsible for managing their organizations' financial resources is the extensive changes occurring in computer software. Through the use of computers, an organization may hire data-entry clerks rather than bookkeepers to maintain its business records or, in some cases, may utilize a centralized computer service to process records, prepare the payroll, and provide monthly budget reports and annual financial statements. Computers, of course, offer several advantages, such as reducing turnaround time, costs, and manual bookkeeping errors. However, the use of computers and data-entry clerks often means that managers may not have a knowledgeable business adviser to provide daily insights into the business process or recognize when the systems are in jeopardy of being compromised. Thus, this book's focus is on the need for managers to develop an understanding of accounting and budgeting systems (not bookkeeping entries and procedures used by the computer) if they are to be sure that the financial resources of their organizations are secure and effectively and efficiently utilized.

The Origins of Accounting and Budgeting

In establishing an understanding of accounting and budgeting systems, managers need to have some knowledge of the creation and evolution of these systems in order to relieve any possible confusion about their origins; for example, some people do not realize how many years accounting and budgeting practices have been in use in the public sector or that they are international in nature. In addition, managers must recognize the efforts currently being made to establish uniformity in the accounting and budgeting practices of public and nonprofit organizations in the United States. What was in vogue a short 10 or even 5 years ago may no longer be current; but at the same time, some practices that were in vogue nearly 500 years ago are still applicable. This may sound like a contradiction, but it is not. Rather, it is the reason why the origins of accounting and budgeting are important to practices today. Each has a rich and interesting history and is the subject of considerable current reform.

Accounting. With respect to the evolution of accounting, there is evidence that efforts were made to keep records of money, goods, and taxes in early Egypt, Babylonia, Greece, and Rome; fragments from Florentine bank ledgers from the year 1211 are the earliest records that researchers have found related to the use or attempted use of double-entry bookkeeping (Lee, 1984c). The first complete record of a double-entry bookkeeping system was discovered in the Massari (treasurer's) books for the city of Genoa for the year 1340 (Chatfield, 1974; Kam, 1986; and Yamey, 1984). Because double-entry bookkeeping is believed to have been created in Italy, in one early reference to double-entry bookkeeping, Wardaugh Thompson, in 1777, called it the "Italian method" (Yamey, 1984).

Theorists have argued about why double-entry bookkeeping evolved in Italy when it did. According to one theory, after the Crusades opened up the trade routes between the Middle East and Europe, there was a need to have a records system in Florence to deal with the increased volume of trade. Another theory holds that although the opening of trade was important, it was only after the Hindu-Arabic numbering system had come to Europe that the double-entry mathematical system could be developed. Others do not agree with this position but argue that the Roman numeral system was in use when the double-entry system was initially being created (Williams, 1984). Regardless of the theories, it is universally accepted that the double-entry method was created in Italy in the thirteenth century, expanded throughout Europe, and then eventually proceeded around the world.

A major reason given for the spread of the double-entry accounting method was the publication in 1494 of a book by Luca Pacioli, *Summa de Arithmetica Geometria Proportioni et Propro-tionalita* (Review of arithmetic, geometry, and proportions), which was published in Venice and gave double-entry accounting a formal reference. Pacioli did not design or ever claim to have designed the double-entry system but simply reported what had been used in Venice for nearly 200 years. As a result of his work, the double-entry method became popularly known as the "Method of Venice," and his book served as the authority for bookkeepers for more than 100 years and as a reference into the twentieth century (Chatfield, 1974; Kam, 1986). Interestingly, the same basic double-entry algebraic equation reported by Pacioli 500 years ago continues to be used today by both for-profit companies and public and nonprofit organizations as well as computer software accounting programs.

Current Accounting Principles. In the early years of the twentieth century in the United States (as well as in other countries), there began to be a growing concern about the need for uniformity of accounting practices and financial statements in private businesses and public organizations. This was evidenced in the United States by two events. The first was the granting of authority to the

Securities and Exchange Commission (SEC) to oversee the financial reporting activities of private businesses and to set accounting and reporting standards for them via legislative acts in 1933 and 1934. The second event, which also took place in the 1930s, was the establishment of the first professional accounting standards boards for for-profit and public organizations. One board was created to set standards for private businesses, and then other professional groups assumed the responsibility for setting standards for public and nonprofit organizations (except for the federal government, which is under the jurisdiction of the U.S. comptroller general). Over the years, the SEC has relied on the professional boards or associations to set forth the accounting standards for private businesses so long as they represented the best interests of the public (Freeman, Shoulders, and Lynn, 1988).

The actions taken in the 1930s set the stage for the legal governmental oversight of private business but not of public organizations. This led to the establishment of accounting standards by professional associations for private businesses and public and nonprofit organizations but not by the federal government. The standards-setting associations or their names have changed as new associations have evolved. These associations have attempted to provide clearer guidelines and to refine practices to coincide with the changes taking place in society; however, in the public and nonprofit sector, the efforts of the standards associations have gone unheeded by many state and local governments and other public and nonprofit organizations. The reason for this lack of recognition has been the right of the individual states in the United States to establish their own laws and related practices, including the accounting practices of the state and local governments and the public organizations associated with these governments. Nonprofit organizations, which do not have any relationships with a governmental body, typically are not compelled to conform to any accounting or budgeting standards except those demanded by their members or contributors.

Consequently, the accounting and budgeting practices of public and nonprofit organizations within a state have not had to follow any standards unless the state laws required them to do so. Recognizing the need for a uniform set of accounting standards for public and nonprofit organizations, as well as the need to be cautious in order to protect the legal rights of the individual states, professional associations continued their efforts to establish a more uniform set of practices. Even so, in some states, the governmental bodies and organizations continued to use a simple cash-basis accounting method with customized local variations, while other states had a sophisticated double-entry system with adjustments, inventories, depreciation, and formal financial statements. Although the federal government required that the use of federal money be reported according to standards, this simply meant that the expenditure reports had to conform to specified guidelines. Thus, a point to be recognized is that generalizations regarding past as well as present accounting practices of public and nonprofit organizations have to be made very carefully, since uniformity of these practices on a national scale does not exist.

As of 1980, governmental, public, and nonprofit organizations basically fell into five groups, each with a different set of accounting standards or guidelines set forth by different professional groups: (1) colleges and universities, with practices recommended by the National Association of College and University Business Officers (NACUBO), the American Council on Education (ACE), and the American Institute of Certified Public Accountants (AICPA) (National Association of College and University Business Officers, 1975, 1982; American Institute of Certified Public Accountants, 1986); (2 & 3) hospitals and voluntary health and welfare organizations, with guides provided by the American Hospital Association, the Health Care Financial Association, and the AICPA; (4) nonprofit organizations, with guidelines set forth by the AICPA; and (5) state and local governments, with standards established by the National Council on Governmental Accounting (NCGA) and the AICPA.

A new arrangement was instituted in April 1984 when the Governmental Accounting Standards Boards (GASB) was formed and immediately succeeded the NCGA. This succession meant that the accounting principles of the NCGA were now under the GASB and were to be used as its guidelines until it revised or revoked those principles. In addition, the Financial Accounting Foundation (FAF), sponsored by several associations, agreed to oversee two independent accounting standards boards: the Financial Accounting Standards Board (FASB), established in 1973 for for-profit companies; and the Governmental Accounting Standards Board (GASB), established for state and local governments. Then, in 1986, the AICPA granted the GASB the authority to include the AICPA accounting standards, which broadened the base of the GASB (Bailey, 1989; Freeman, Shoulders, and Lynn, 1988).

Therefore, after considerable effort and compromise, the GASB became responsible for setting forth broad accounting standards for state and local government units, including hospitals, colleges and universities, and nonprofit organizations subject to some degree of oversight or control by a governmental unit (it must be emphasized that this text recognizes that this does not include those nonprofit organizations that do not come under any oversight or control of a governmental unit). The meaning behind "some degree of oversight" regards five criteria: financial interdependency, selection of governing authority, designation of management, ability to significantly influence operations, and accountability for fiscal matters (Bailey, 1989; Freeman, Shoulders, and Lynn, 1988). The FASB sets forth the accounting standards for all other entities, including those nonprofit organizations that do not come under any oversight or control by a state or local government.

At this time the GASB pronouncements include (until revised or revoked by the GASB) the GASB Statements, Interpretations, Technical Bulletins, Exposure Drafts, Discussion Memoranda, and Concept Statements; the NCGA Statements, including the twelve Generally Accepted Accounting Principles (GAAP), the NCGA Interpretations, and the NCGA Concept Statements; and the AICPA Statements of Position and Audit Guides (Bailey, 1989). The FAF agreement established an accounting hierarchy for organizations to follow in determining their accounting practices; if a practice is not described at one level of the hierarchy, then the organization should move to the next lower level for guidance. These hierarchical levels are:

1.   Pronouncements of the GASB
2.   Pronouncements of the FASB

3. Pronouncements of other expert accounting bodies that follow a due process
4. Practices or pronouncements that are widely recognized
5. Other accounting literature

   Principle 1 of the GAAP states that an organization's accounting system is to present that organization's financial position and the results of its financial operations and that this accounting system is to conform to the GAAP as well as to all financially related legal and contractual provisions. As Bailey (1989, p. 1.04) points out, in those states whose laws do not follow the principles set forth by the GASB or the FASB, the state and local governments and other required organizations (such as nonprofit organizations under some form of governmental oversight) may use a non-GAAP basis to maintain their records and to prepare their financial statements. In such cases, a government or organization will also have "to adopt a supplementary accounting system that will enable it to report on a GAAP basis." In order to refrain from using two accounting methods, one as set out by state law and one to comply with the GAAP, many states are changing their laws to institute the GAAP.

   The twelve principles of the GAAP are the focal point of this book and provide the basis of its description of accounting and budgeting systems for state or local governments, colleges and universities, hospitals, and nonprofit organizations subject to oversight by a state and local government. This book will not attempt to present, explain, or even mention all of the numerous standards, statements, principles, guides, and so on that have been promulgated by the GASB or the myriad applications used by different governmental bodies and public and nonprofit organizations. Rather, it refers to the principles and other selected standards in describing the basic, ideal accounting and budgeting systems that should be implemented by public and nonprofit organizations, including those that do not have to abide by the GAAP but wish to have more responsible accounting and budgeting systems.

   Consequently, the changes that took place in 1984 point to a new era in public and nonprofit accounting, but they are just a start. With the long list of principles and guidelines that have been placed under the GASB, there is a need to refine, coordinate, and organize the standards into a single coherent body of information. In addition, because there is no legal requirement for public and nonprofit organizations to join the GASB, a means must be found to appeal to all organizations to follow a uniform set of standards.

The institution of sound accounting and budgeting systems governed by the uniform guidelines provided by the GAAP offers numerous benefits to organizations and managers. For example, a team of auditors will be able to review the accounting and budgeting systems and the related policies and practices of an organization in an orderly and efficient manner (perhaps within one week), and then to provide a clear and concise report about the financial operations of the organization. A clear and positive public report by a team of auditors will go a long way with the public and will give a sense of confidence in the management of the organization that cannot be bought by a public relations program. Another benefit is the ability to publish a set of financial statements. When the public is provided with a full set of statements that disclose the annual financial operations of a well-managed organization, the managers will be viewed as professionals and the organization will be supported (assuming that the reports can be comprehended by the average citizen). Finally, when managers or governing boards need to tighten up operations, they must have the necessary information in the reports that they are given. When uniform and proper guidelines are followed, the accounting and budgeting systems will produce reliable and comparable financial information, making possible a revenue, cost, or cost-benefit analysis that is needed to make important operational decisions.

Budgeting. Budgeting in the public sector, at least in England, is considered by Chatfield (1974) to have started as a result of the twelfth article of the Magna Carta (1215), which placed restraints on the king's right to tax nobility—the first successful attempt to have some form of budget control over the revenue to be collected by the government. Later, in 1689, the English Bill of Rights declared that only Parliament had the authority to tax the people. This eventually led to Parliament requiring the king to present an estimate of expenditures. In the eighteenth century, the customary process was for the king, through the chancellor of the exchequer, to provide an accounting of expenditures for the past year, an estimate of expenditures for the coming year, and a recommendation for a tax levy. This is quite similar to the process followed by organizations today.

When the U.S. Treasury was established on September 2, 1789, the secretary of the treasury was required by Congress to develop an estimate of revenues and expenditures. Alexander Hamilton, the first secretary of the treasury, decided to work with Congress in the same manner as the chancellor of the exchequer worked with the English Parliament. In the early years of the nineteenth century, Congress passed a law that required the secretary of the treasury to present the budget as Hamilton had done. Over the next century, the use of budgets by organizations and governments increased. Then, between 1910 and 1920, the public interest in governmental budgeting grew, as evidenced by the passing of budget laws in forty-four states. In 1921, the National Accounting and Budgeting Act moved the responsibility for presenting the country's budget to the president (Chatfield, 1974).

In recent years, the concentration has been on the development of budget methods for public and nonprofit organizations. The most important differences between these methods have been in the reasoning and objectives behind the design of the methodology. As discussed in Chapter Three, there are three primary types of budget methods: line-item, performance, and program budgeting. However, organizations do not usually implement one particular budget method but rather customize the methods to meet their individual needs; for example, the line-item method may be supported by some elements of the program and performance methods. As computers have become less expensive and more popular and with the advent of the personal computer, these customizations of budget methods have become easier to implement.

Because of the importance of budgets, they are also an expressed concern of the GASB, which presents a three-part budget guideline in Principle 9 of the GAAP: First, an annual budget should be adopted; second, the accounting system is the basis for budget control; and third, the financial statements should show budget comparisons for each budget that has been adopted for the organization.

Conclusion. Accounting and budgeting are not recent developments; each has an interesting history. The initial efforts to use double-entry accounting were made more than 700 years ago, and the use of budgets by the public sector has evolved over the past 700 years. In more recent years, accounting and budgeting activities in the public and nonprofit sector have become more interdependent as they interact to provide greater protection of and control over the revenue and resources of organizations. The recognition of this interaction between accounting and budgeting is particularly important as public and nonprofit organizations become larger and more complex, and an understanding of this interaction by managers becomes more critical as computers assume the responsibilities of bookkeepers.

Definition of Terms

As this book addresses accounting and budgeting for public and nonprofit organizations, terms such as *public, nonprofit, accounting,* and *budgeting* and others must be understood as intended by the author. This is critical as often the popular use of these words has a variety of contexts. For example, the terms *public* and *nonprofit* are used in their broadest sense, but *accounting* and *budgeting* are used as specific technical business terms, not in a broad planning, management, or decision-making context. This section provides definitions of some of the terms used in the discussion of accounting and budgeting systems throughout this book.

Accounting. Accounting is often confused with bookkeeping, or the two words are used interchangeably. However, these terms have distinct meanings. Very simply put, bookkeeping is the act of recording business transactions; accounting then uses the bookkeeping records in a planned system designed to protect the revenue and resources of the organization and to create financial reports and statements. Meigs and Meigs (1984) describe accounting as a system that is used to record, classify, and summarize business activity. Some definitions of accounting include the analysis of financial reports, but in this text, the analysis of the information generated by the accounting system is considered as a part of financial management. That is, *accounting* and *financial management* are not synonymous; rather, the accounting system is a critical component, or tool, utilized in a financial management program.

Double-entry accounting is a process in which an algebraic method is used to ensure that an accounting system is self-balancing. Skousen, Langenderfer, and Albrecht (1983) explain that the double-entry method provides for the equality of the accounting equation. The equality of the equation creates the self-balancing feature, which is critical to the protection of the revenue and resources of the organization. In other words, if certain totals in reports and statements are not equal, there is an error that must be identified (and that may take hours to find).

The self-balancing feature of the double-entry method is also important in ensuring the accuracy of the statements that form a financial picture of an organization and provide the data needed for the analyses that managers conduct in order to make business and financial decisions. This accuracy is dependent on correct bookkeeping entries being made to input information into the system, the processing of this information from the initial entries through the system without error (which may be done via a computer software program), and, finally, the proper output of the information in the financial statements.

Budgeting. Budgeting has been defined and described in many ways; for example, as a political decision-making process (Cope, 1989); as a program description with estimates of the expenditures and revenues needed by an organization (Hartman, 1988); as an activity related to planning and controlling (Welsch, Hilton, and Gordon, 1988); as a process of allocating scarce resources (Freeman, Shoulders, and Lynn, 1988); as a plan of action (Gross and Jablonsky, 1979); and as a plan of financial operations (Bailey, 1989). Looking at the budgeting process from a historical perspective, one can describe it as a process that evolved from an effort to provide people with some form of control over the amount of money they had to give to a governing body through taxes (Chatfield, 1974).

In this book, the budgeting system is discussed in relation to the business operations of a public or nonprofit organization and is thus presented as consisting of three subsystems, which may be thought of as the *AAA* subsystems: the first subsystem focuses on the internal approval (first A) of the budget, the second subsystem concerns the external adoption (second A) of the budget, and the third subsystem revolves around the allocation (third A) of the budget award.

Revenue, Income, and Resources. When the accounting and budgeting systems complement each other, an organization can truly manage its revenue, income, and resources. Thus distinctions must be made among the words *revenue, income,* and *resources,* as they, too, are often used interchangeably.

Resources refers to cash and any property (assets) that can be converted into cash (supplies, equipment, buildings, and so on) or used to earn cash. While revenue may be considered to be a resource, in this book the term *revenue* denotes money received from some form of assessment, such as taxes or membership fees, or from donations. Income, which may at times also be placed within the broad category called resources, here means money that is earned from the sale of goods or services, such as tuition, dorm rent, bookstore sales, license fees, rental of pumps at a fire station, and so on.

Public and Nonprofit. This book is concerned with the design of ideal, basic accounting and budgeting systems. These systems should be the same in all public and nonprofit organizations under the oversight or control of a governmental unit. While the basic accounting and budgeting principles presented by the GASB are not prescriptive, and their applications may vary from one organization to another, in these applications the accounting and budgeting systems should follow the same basic design, should interact properly, and should follow the GAAP principles.

A major reason for uniformity in the recognition of the GAAP principles and the institution of the basic, interacting accounting and budgeting systems is the common threads that tie all public and nonprofit organizations together. One common thread is the lack of a profit motive (Meigs and Meigs, 1984). Another (Henke, 1977) is the fact that public and nonprofit organizations do not have any equity interests and, thus cannot be owned, bought, or sold by any individual or individuals. These commonalities dictate the necessity for uniform practices and systems for a variety of reasons, including protection of public interests.

Governing Boards. Because a public or nonprofit organization is not owned by any private party or parties, it is either directed by a board (for example, a board of governors for a university) or supervised by an elected body (such as a state legislature, city council, or school board). The boards for these organizations may be elected by a membership that pay fees to the organization, be elected by the public, be appointed by a public official, be appointed by an official of a nonprofit organization, be a mixture of elected and appointed people, and so on. The differences among these types of bodies are not critical for the purposes of this text (although the differences are extremely important); they all play a key role in the accounting and budgeting processes of public and nonprofit organizations.

Boards and supervising bodies set laws, rules, goals, objectives, and policies to be followed to achieve the mission of the organization and approve the budgets that are used to request needed revenue or to propose a spending plan for anticipated earned income. Most boards and elected bodies have the constituted authority to make operational decisions; however, rather than engaging in the clumsy practice of trying to have daily operational decisions made by a group of people who meet periodically, boards and elected bodies hire managers to direct the operations of an organization. These managers are then directed by the mission, laws, rules, goals, objectives, and policies of the organization as well as the approved annual budget. This description of a governance structure is admittedly oversimplified, as there are numerous details and issues associated with it, as Oakerson (1989) explains. However, the important point here is that many of the decisions made by managers of public organizations are subject to laws, rules, and regulations (Robbins, 1976).

At the end of an operating year, managers must report the accomplishments of their organizations to their boards or governing bodies.They must also be prepared to defend their reports on expenditures and/or financial audits. This is terribly difficult to do when the accounting and budgeting systems are not properly implemented, do not comply with the GAAP, or are not fully compre-hended by a manager or board member. When an organization does not use proper systems or the manager does not have an adequate knowledge of the systems, an audit or examination of the financial operations places that manager in the position of playing a form of financial Russian roulette—the records and reports are presented with the hope that there is no live round in them for the firing pin (auditor) to hit. If the firing pin should hit a chamber with a live round in it, tragedy strikes, and often careers and even organizations are killed. For example, if an audit reveals improper expenditures or errors in the system, a manager must either defend the improper expenditures or practices or conduct an internal investigation. This is a lose-lose situation, as the evidence of errors or improper expen-ditures can only lead the governing body to conclude that there has been either improper behavior or poor supervision. When the amount of money lost has been so great that minimum services have been rendered by an organization, questions may be raised as to whether there is a need for the organization to continue. Such sit-uations are not hypothetical, as evidenced by frequent newspaper accounts of such incidents in countries around the world.

System. A system is an entity composed of interacting parts that attempt to achieve a multiplicity of goals or objectives (Mos-cove and Simkin, 1987, p. 4). If a system is to function efficiently and effectively, the parts must interact properly. This interaction is achieved through the transmission of information between the parts whereby a change in one part of the system affects the other parts (Coombs and Hallak, 1987; Moscove and Simkin, 1987). The parts of a system are described differently by different authors; in this text, each system and subsystem is viewed as being composed of three parts: input, process, and output.

There are two ways in which the accounting and budgeting operation of an organization could be viewed: as a financial system in which there is an accounting subsystem and a budgeting subsys-tem with information transmitted between the two subsystems or as two separate systems that interact in the financial operation of the organization. This text prefers the latter view, because accounting and budgeting activities are often separate and conducted by different staffs, even though they may be under one manager. It should be noted that this separation is preferred for control purposes, as discussed later in the text; however, the idea of separate systems should not imply that the two do not interact.

Accounting and Budgeting Systems
for Public and Nonprofit Organizations

In the functioning of a system or subsystem, the input of information is processed to produce an output. A change in any one part of the system—input, process, or output—will affect the other parts. For instance, the type of input that is needed depends on what type of output is appropriate to the objectives of the system. That input must be accurate and processed properly if the proper output is to be obtained; accurate input is meaningless if it is not processed properly.

When accounting and budgeting operations are placed in a systems format, that format must clearly specify their outputs, as well as the process and inputs used to produce them. The format for the accounting system is presented as a flow diagram in Figure 1. As the diagram shows, the accounting inputs come from the business activities of the organization, such as revenue awards, payments of cash, budget expenditures, budget revisions, payments of invoices, payments of salaries, and so on. A record of the input, which is called a journal entry, should be made from a hard (paper) copy of the activity, such as a copy of the budget, a deposit slip, a purchase order form, a memo with the approved budget revision, an invoice from a vendor, a signed salary contract, and so on. For control purposes, direct input should not be made into a computer

Figure 1. Accounting System.

INPUTS Records of Business Activity	→	PROCESS Classification and Summary of Entries	→	OUTPUTS Budgets Reports and Financial Statements

without a hard copy with an approval signature, as discussed in Chapter Five. After the input data are recorded, they are processed by the ledger and possibly a subsidiary ledger and then summarized by a trial balance. After this summarization, the budget reports and financial statements may be prepared.

The budgeting system is graphically presented as three subsystems in Figures 2, 3, and 4. In the first subsystem (Figure 2), the input consists of an estimate of the revenue or income to be received

Figure 2. Budgeting Subsystem 1.

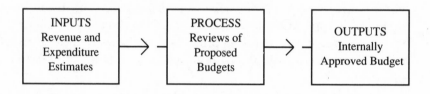

Figure 3. Budgeting Subsystem 2.

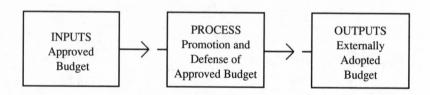

Figure 4. Budgeting Subsystem 3.

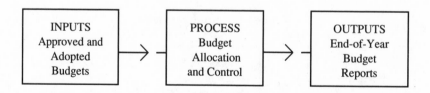

and the estimated expenditures made by each budget unit. With one of the budget methods discussed in Chapter Three, proposals are prepared, reviewed, and revised. The desired output for this subsystem is a budget approved internally by the CEO and, if applicable, by a governing board.

In the second subsystem (Figure 3), the input is the approved budget from subsystem 1. This approved budget must be promoted and defended so that it will be adopted by a body or official external to the organization, such as a legislative body, voter, agency, administrative official, board, and so on. The method of promoting and defending an approved budget for adoption varies tremendously from one organization to another. When the process follows a set of scheduled deadlines, a budget calendar may be created.

The input for the third subsystem (Figure 4) is the approved and adopted budgets. The process in this subsystem involves three specific activities: the budget allocations to the units within the organization (approved budget), control over the receipt of revenue (adopted budget), and control of expenditures. The output for this subsystem is the end-of-the-year budget report.

Simply establishing accounting and budgeting systems for an organization is not sufficient; they must formally interact with each other. When two separate accounting and budgeting systems do not interact, their inherent advantages are considerably lessened. As noted previously, Principle 9, part b, of the GAAP explains that the accounting system is to provide the basis needed for budgetary control. This is not possible if the two systems do not interact in a planned program.

As detailed in Chapter Nine, there are six points at which the accounting and budgeting systems formally interact with each other. The first three points of interaction are initiated by the budget system, as follows:

	Budget System	*Accounting System*
Point 1.	Budget is approved.	Formal record is made.
Point 2.	Budget is adopted.	Formal record is made.
Point 3.	Revenue is received and budget expenditures made.	Formal record is made.

The next three points of interaction are provided by the accounting system as follows:

	Accounting System	*Budget System*
Point 4.	Accounts are summarized.	Budget reports are prepared.
Point 5.	Accounting books are closed at end of year.	Budget is closed.
Point 6.	Accounting financial statements are prepared.	Annual budget report is prepared.

Summary

For managers to ensure that the financial resources of their organizations are used effectively and efficiently, they must, first, be able to work with the accounting and budgeting systems of their organizations and, second, ensure that their accounting and budgeting systems are designed in a manner that allows them to maximize their resources, are properly implemented and operated according to the principles of the GAAP, and formally interact with each other.

The objective of the accounting system is to record, classify, and summarize business activity. To ensure that the information recorded, classified, and summarized by the accounting system is accurate, the double-entry accounting method should be used. This check on the accuracy of the process enhances the protection of the revenue and resources of the organization as well as the validity of the organization's financial statements. The accounting practices of state and local governments, colleges and universities, hospitals, and other nonprofit organizations, subject to oversight by a state or local government, should comply with the Generally Accepted Accounting Principles (GAAP) set forth by the GASB.

The budgeting system is a separate system that should be designed to meet several objectives of the business operation of an organization. It can be divided into three subsystems: internal approval, external adoption, and allocation, which provides the end-of-year budget report.

Describing the accounting and budgeting operations in a systems format means that each is composed of interacting parts that are designed to achieve an objective, or output. The accounting system and each of the three budgeting subsystems can be described in terms of their input, the procedures used to process that input, and their output.

Finally, the three parts of the accounting system and budgeting subsystems must interact properly, the budgeting subsystems must complement each other, and the accounting and budgeting systems must formally interact with each other at six specific points.

2

Accounting and Budgeting Systems in Public and Nonprofit Organizations

The Role of Funds

The structure by which accounting and budgeting systems operate is created by putting together units called funds, as recommended by Principle 2 of the GAAP. Basically, funds are formal entities that allow organizations to divide their activities into separate business operations. Two examples of a fund are a general fund (the name used by the GAAP as per Principle 3), which is used to place the revenue and charge expenditures for the general operations of the organization, and a self-support fund (called an enterprise fund as per the GAAP, Principle 3), which is for income receipts and corresponding expenditures related to a self-supporting business run by an organization. An organization using these two funds could be assured that the activities related to the general operation of the organization could be run through a general fund, while the activities of a self-supporting business run by the organization could be handled through a self-support fund (also called an enterprise fund). Thus, these operations could be run almost as if they were two different organizations, except that they both provide activities designed to achieve or complement the primary mission of the organization.

An organization uses different fund entities to meet different needs. In doing so, the funds build a financial structure; within each fund, there is an accounting system and a budgeting system. Be-

Purpose of Funds

cause the needs of organizations differ, the funds they use to build the structure will differ, and although the basic designs of the accounting and budgeting systems will be similar, they will not be identical.

Essentially, because fund entities act as small business units and permit the financial activities of the organization to be incrementalized. This, in turn, is helpful to the manager who is responsible for the supervision and financial integrity of an activity, as well as to the CEO who is in charge of a multiplicity of activities. As an organization grows or modifies its mission, the fund structure and the funds can be modified accordingly.

Fund Entities

The use of funds by public and nonprofit organizations is not a recent phenomenon. Rather formal descriptions have been given for funds by the National Committee on Governmental Accounting (1951, 1968), the Municipal Finance Officers Association of the United States and Canada (1968), and the Governmental Accounting Standards Board (1987). These descriptions are all similar, which is understandable given the evolution of these organizations as described by Freeman, Shoulders, and Lynn (1988). As Principle 2 of the GAAP describes it, a fund is a fiscal entity with a set of self-balancing accounts that enable it to segregate its resources for specific activities and objectives and that provide a record of the financial activities, budget reports, and financial statements for the entity. In other words, a fund (1) has a separate accounting and budgeting system, (2) uses the double-entry accounting method, (3) prepares a separate set of records, reports, and statements through the accounting system, and (4) segregates resources for specific activities and objectives.

Thus, each fund has specific activities and objectives for which budget proposals are prepared for approval and adoption. When revenue or income is received, it is placed in a fund's accounting system and allocated by the budget system, and then expenditures are processed by the accounting system against the revenue or income. Throughout the year, budget reports are prepared to disclose the amount of revenue or income received by the fund, the amount of the fund's expenditures, and the difference between the receipts and expenditures. If a residual balance remains for the revenue or income at the end of the year, this will be shown in the accounting system and reported by the fund's set of accounting statements, which also disclose the total receipts and expenditures as well as the remaining resources and debts of the fund. In addition, at the end of the year, a combined accounting statement is prepared for each kind of statement in order to exhibit the same statements for all of the funds in the organization on one form (described further in Chapter Eight).

A note of caution must be inserted here. Communication problems often occur with the use of the term *fund*. For example, the word *funds* is frequently used to refer to a sum of money; it is not used to mean money in this text. Also, a fund entity may be called a "fund account"; a "fund account" is actually a specific account within the fund entity, such as a fund account for cash. Further, because of its use of fund entities, the accounting system used by public and nonprofit organizations is often referred to as "fund accounting." This is appropriate if the above criteria for a fund entity are properly understood. Too often, however, *fund accounting* is used to describe the use of a budget without any funds or a double-entry accounting system. When an organization operates with only a budget, this system is correctly referred to as the single-entry or checkbook method of accounting, not fund accounting.

Types of Fund Entities

As the heading for this section indicates, "types" of fund entities are described below, which means that the funds presented are not to be considered *the ones* that have to be used by all organizations. Each organization should use the types of funds that meet its individual needs. As Henke (1970) recommends, names given to funds should identify how the resources in a fund may be used by the organization. Thus, the names used in the descriptions of types of funds below are presented merely as suggestions. Organizations may and should provide names for their funds that clearly denote the purpose or use of the funds.

The description below includes six types of funds that will essentially meet the needs of most organizations. A financial structure may contain only one fund or all six. Within a fund, accounts may be set up in order to segregate activities. For example, an organization may set up accounts for different income-producing activities within a self-support fund, or it may have more than one self-support fund.

Principle 4 of the GAAP recommends that an organization should use the minimum number of funds legally required of the organization and necessary for it to institute a sound financial program. The appropriate number varies from one organization to another and is a subjective decision made by the board. The application of the accounting and budgeting systems within the funds should be appropriate to the principles set forth by the GAAP. Creative arrangements in order to use funds to manipulate, rather than manage, the resources of an organization should not be considered. Principle 11 of the GAAP explains that an organization is expected to be consistent in the use of terms and the classification of information in its budgets, accounts, and reports for each of the funds.

The fund structure set forth by Principle 3 of the GAAP consists of ten funds, which are placed into three groups. In the simplified format presented in this section, six types of funds are described. The following list presents the GAAP classifications and the corresponding designations used in this text:

GAAP Funds	*Text Funds*
Governmental Funds	
General fund	General fund
Special revenue fund	Restricted fund
Capital projects fund	Fixed-asset fund
Debt service fund	Debt fund
Proprietary funds	
Enterprise fund	Self-support fund
Internal service fund	Internal fund
Fiduciary funds	
Expendable trust fund	Restricted fund
Nonexpendable trust fund	Restricted fund

Pension trust fund   Restricted fund
Agency fund   Restricted fund

General Fund. The general fund is the primary fund used by an organization. The resources in this fund are used to provide the activities and services required of the organization to achieve its primary mission. This is the fund in which the annual allotments for operations are placed. A popular name for this fund is "operating fund," because the budget for this fund is often referred to as the "operating budget." It is also called an "unrestricted fund" to indicate that the revenue in this fund may be used as deemed necessary by the board or supervising body for general operations and is not restricted for special use. In fact, some organizations, including some hospitals, use only two funds: an "unrestricted fund" and a "restricted fund."

Typically, the revenue received for the general fund must be spent within the fiscal year or time period specified by law or the bylaws of the organization. If this revenue is transferred from the general fund to another fund, it must be spent within the time period specified unless otherwise permitted. For example, an organization may transfer revenue that must be spent by the end of the year from the general fund into a savings account in another fund in order to earn interest income until the money is needed for operations. The interest earned in the other fund may then be carried over to the next year, while the revenue from the general fund must be returned to the general fund and spent by the end of the fiscal year.

Self-Support Fund. Many public and nonprofit organizations offer services that are not fully or partially supported by the revenue received for operations. When these services are provided, a fee is charged and income is earned. The fee is called a cost recovery charge, and the income received is typically placed in the type of fund referred to here as the "self-support fund." The names of self-support funds vary from organization to organization. For example, an organization may simply call it the "income fund" or may provide a name that represents the activities or services provided through the fund, such as the "clinic fund."

The GAAP suggests the use of two types of self-support funds under a category called "proprietary funds": the enterprise funds, which serve the purpose of the self-support funds described here, and internal service funds (described here as internal funds), which are for self-support activities operating only within the organization.

A fund structure may include more than one of the same type of fund, particularly in organizations with two or more major income-producing operations. In order to provide a separate set of accounts, budget reports, and financial statements for each major activity, an organization could create separate funds with different names for these activities, such as a clinic fund and a food service fund, or it could simply create one self-support fund with separate accounts for the clinic and for food services.

In some organizations, a small amount of money may be earned by a service that is an integral part of the primary mission of the organization and is heavily supported by revenue in the general fund. In these situations, the income may be placed in separate accounts in the general fund rather than a separate self-support fund being created. In these arrangements, separate budgets would be prepared and approved by the governing board for that income and for the annual allotment. An example of such an operation is a nonprofit clinic that receives annual revenue allotments from the state and local governments to provide services to people with low incomes. Occasionally, a person whose income is above the amount prescribed may request services. Rather than turning such a person away, the clinic would charge a fee, with the amount based on a graduated fee schedule related to personal income. The income received would then be placed in and managed through a special group of accounts in the general fund. This would require that a budget be prepared for the clinic account in addition to the budget for the annual revenue allotment.

Should a self-support operation have an income residual (profit) after expenses are paid, the profit can usually be carried over to the next year. (A full discussion of the reporting of this excess as profit is presented in Chapter Eight.) When a profit is earned, the managers should formally (through the use of the accounting statements) report the excess to the board so that it can decide officially how the excess will be used. This ensures that the legal authority of the board is recognized and the spirit in which such services are offered is protected. (Unfortunately, managers of income operations often have inappropriate proprietary feelings about the profits generated by their activities.)

Managers should be particularly sensitive to the handling of profits because of the numerous controversies that are emerging as public and nonprofit organizations become more aggressive. Some boards and managers see self-supporting activities and related profits as opportunities for institutions to be creative, to meet needs for which money is not available, to hire personnel, to extend their services, and so on. A good example is the use of income earned by football or basketball teams at large universities. In many cases, this income is used to support the non-income-producing athletic teams and an intramural program for the student body. Some people believe that profits should be used to supplant the revenue provided to an organization in order to lower taxes. Others feel that if money is to supplement the activities offered by an organization, the properly elected body or official (not the governing board) through whom the annual revenue is provided should approve the way the profits are used.

Another controversy surrounding self-support income concerns the offering of services that compete with those of private businesses, such as a university, library, or nonprofit organization providing photocopy services for a fee in direct competition with a private company across the street. Private businesses must pay for the use of their business space through rent payments or mortgage payments and property taxes, and must pay taxes on their profits as well as sales taxes. On the other hand, the same operation run by a public or nonprofit organization is not charged rent for the building space unless an overhead fee is levied against the income, it does not pay taxes on the profits, it does not pay local property taxes, and, in some cases, it does not pay sales tax. Some states have recently taken action either to curtail such operations, to tax the profits, or to charge sales taxes, and a number of other states are presently considering such legislation.

Still another controversy concerns the use of self-support income by professional employees. For example, assume that several professionals in an organization put on a conference that earns income. After the conference, personnel, who may or may not have worked on the program, then use the income to attend a convention. Should the money used to attend the convention be treated as taxable income by the professionals? The answer hinges on whether such self-supporting operations are being used by professionals as a means to provide services and avoid income taxes.

Because there is a lack of clear guidelines regarding such operations, managers should exercise caution with respect to the use of self-support funds. Too often, operations are neither condemned nor condoned, and unofficial permission or the failure to disapprove past practices is taken to mean that the practice has approval. When an operation is questioned, the answer is often that "no one has said anything yet" or "there is precedent for doing this" or "it has always been done this way." However, so often in the public domain, what appears to be an acceptable practice today may not be acceptable tomorrow. One tragic example is practices regarding the receipt and use of money by members of Congress thirty years ago, that today have come back to haunt many of them, particularly those who were not sensitive to the changes taking place over the years and continued to follow the same practices. Thus, because the current guidelines related to the collection and use of the profits generated by self-supporting activities are quite vague, this money should be handled cautiously.

Restricted Fund. A restricted fund is used when there are provisions on how money or the interest earned on it may be spent; this includes money that the board wishes to temporarily invest to earn interest. This type of fund may also be given the name of donor fund, endowment fund, investment fund, savings fund, or some other title that indicates that there are restrictions on how the resources in the fund may be used.

Fiduciary funds, a group of funds suggested by the GAAP in Principle 3, are for resources being held in a trustee capacity. Within this group, the GAAP suggests four Funds: expendable trust funds, nonexpendable trust funds, pension trust funds, and agency funds. Under the category of governmental funds, the GAAP includes a special revenue fund for government revenue that is restricted for a specific purpose. Should an organization use the fund structure suggested by the GAAP, a sophisticated arrangement for handling restricted resources would be provided (as compared to the use of one restricted fund, which is presented here for the sake of simplicity and also because many organizations need only one fund).

When money is donated to an organization and placed in a restricted fund, there are four basic arrangements that can be made governing its use. One is that the money can only be invested, not spent, and how the return on the investment can be spent is restricted. With this type of arrangement, the contributions are called endowments, and an organization may create a separate endowment or trust fund to segregate such donations. There are a variety of conditions under which an endowment may be created, with different legal and tax benefits to the donor and to the organization. When an organization receives several endowments, a board may set up one endowment fund with a set of accounts for each endowment, such as the "Mary Smith Account" and the "Ace Company Account." However, if a large or special endowment is received, a separate endowment fund may be set up solely for that contribution and be named for the person making the donation and the activity for which it is to be used, such as the "Mary Smith Endowment Fund for the Arts."

With the second type of arrangement, donations are made for investment purposes only but there are no restrictions on how the returns on the investment may be used. In this case, the board may spend the money earned from the investments as it best sees fit. With the third type of arrangement, the money donated may be spent, but only as specified by the donor or the organization. Finally, a fourth type of donation may be given to an institution to be used at the discretion of the board.

Two miscellaneous comments need to be made about donations. First, if an organization is given an asset other than cash, such as a building or an expensive piece of art, the fair market value of the asset should be established and used to record a dollar value in the accounts of a fund, as recommended by Principle 6 of the GAAP. Second, in most cases, any costs incurred in receiving donations or money earned by donations (such as shipping costs) or in managing them (such as secretarial costs) can be charged against them. If such charges are levied, this must be understood and agreed upon by the donor at the time the contribution is made. Such understandings are important, since how donations are handled reflects on the organization.

The importance of setting up a fund for donations with proper accounts and budget units cannot be stressed enough. As an illustration of this point, consider a donation to a city for a park. Because the money is only for the park, it should be placed in a restricted fund and protected under a special budget unit called "City Park" rather than being entered into the general fund. Should the money be placed in the general fund under a budget category for miscellaneous improvements, the city manager could be terribly embarrassed if the park donation were accidentally spent to repair potholes in the streets. At the end of the year, when the money in the general fund has been expended, the manager would have fewer potholes but would not be able to show either the park improvements or the money donated for the park.

As noted above, a restricted fund may also be used for investment purposes or to serve as a trust for another fund. There are numerous occasions when an organization has to set cash aside for a period of time. For example, an organization that receives its revenue in quarterly or semiannual payments may use a large portion of this revenue for salaries and wages while retaining part of it for the quarterly payment of taxes and benefits. Rather than having this money sit in the checking account in the general fund, the organization should temporarily transfer this money into a restricted fund. The money would then be invested until it had to be returned to the general fund for the payroll or for payment of the taxes or benefits. The interest earned would be retained in the restricted fund to be used at the discretion of the board, which might continue to invest it, spend it, or transfer it to another fund. Such investments have become an important component of a comprehensive financial management program, which, in turn, is quite dependent on a properly designed fund structure as well as accurate information recorded and produced by the accounting and budgeting systems.

Fixed-Asset Fund. Fixed-asset funds should be used for land, buildings, equipment, and other large assets that are owned and used over a long period of time. Money for the maintenance of fixed assets should not be placed in this fund, although if the repairs or improvements increase the value of the asset, the change should be noted in the accounts of the fund, as discussed in Chapter Nine. An organization determines what equipment, furnishings, or other large assets it considers fixed assets (assets that are depreciated) by establishing a minimum dollar amount to be spent. For example, depending on the size of the organization, a fixed asset could be any item that costs more than $500 or possibly more than $1,000.

When money is provided to purchase a fixed asset, it may be bought either through the fixed-asset fund or through any other fund except the general fund. If the asset is purchased through another fund, it should be transferred into the fixed-asset fund after being purchased. For example, if money is donated to an organization to buy a mainframe computer, the money would be placed in the restricted fund, the purchase would be made from that fund, and the computer would be transferred into the fixed-asset fund. Thus, a permanent record of the purchase would exist in the restricted fund, and the computer would be accounted for in the fixed-asset fund, where it would be depreciated by the accounting system.

On the other hand, if money is awarded for the computer and the revenue allotment is placed in the general fund, the revenue would then be transferred to the fixed-asset fund, and the computer would be purchased out of that fund. Should the computer be purchased through the general fund, the large expenditure would be shown against the budget in the general fund at the end of the year. A board member, elected official, executive, or voting member in the community reading the financial statements at the end of the year might question why the total amount spent through the general fund was so much greater than in previous years. Even if the reader of the statements were aware of the reason for the larger totals, it would be difficult to compare year-to-year annual revenue and expenditure totals (and the reason might be noted only in a small footnote at the bottom of the report along with numerous other footnotes).

When revenue is transferred from the general fund to the

fixed-asset fund for the purchase of the fixed asset, the amount spent by the general budget is reduced, and an exceptionally large expenditure for the year is eliminated, while the cash account and the residual balance of the fixed-asset fund are increased. When the equipment is purchased, the cash balance in the fund is reduced. When the equipment is depreciated each year (see Chapter Nine), the depreciation decreases the value shown for the computer in the accounting records (the book value) and reduces the residual balance in the fixed-asset fund. With this arrangement, the fixed-asset fund shows the individual book values of the land, buildings, equipment, and other large assets owned by the organization, and the residual balance of the fixed-asset fund equals the total book value of all of the fixed assets held by the organization. In addition, the purchase of the equipment and the depreciation expenses do not appear in the general fund as annual expenses against the general operating budget of the organization.

The reason for the above discussion of processing revenue, purchasing fixed assets, and recording depreciation is twofold. First, an understanding of this process is critical to managers, as it is a change that must take place in the accounting systems in public and nonprofit organizations. Second, this is one of the few cases in which the recommendations in this book differ from those set forth by the GAAP. Principle 3 of the GAAP proposes that a capital projects fund be used for the acquisition of land, equipment, and other large assets and for the construction of buildings, but only for those assets that are bought with government revenue. Principle 7 provides that, after acquisition or construction, the asset should appear in a general fixed-assets account group (meaning general fixed-assets fund) for depreciation. In these regards, there is no major disparity between the recommendations made here and by the GAAP except for the name of the fund.

However, with respect to those assets acquired from money placed in the Proprietary or fiduciary funds, Principle 7 of the GAAP recommends that the purchase be made through those funds and that the item remain in the Fund for depreciation. This differs from the recommendation of this text that the assets be transferred to the fixed-asset fund, where they would be depreciated. The reason the GAAP makes its recommendation that these assets not be placed in the capital projects fund is that this fund comes under the GAAP category of governmental funds and is therefore precluded from registering any assets or expenditures not made from government money. This, in turn, means that all government fixed assets are shown in one account group, while other fixed assets are shown in the funds through which the assets were purchased. Although that may be the best arrangement for some governmental bodies and government auditors, many organizations may be better off showing all their fixed assets—not just those purchased from government money—in the fixed-asset fund for the reasons given above. (Note that in both arrangements set forth by the GAAP and those recommended in this text, fixed assets are not to be shown in the general fund.)

Debt Fund. The debt fund (called the debt service fund by the GAAP) is for money to be set aside to pay the interest and principal on long-term debts, such as bond issues, long-term notes, or mortgages. As money is placed in the debt fund, it is invested to earn interest. The money set aside and the interest income are then used to pay interest on the loan and to retire the debt. This process, called debt management, is an important component of the financial management process of a public or nonprofit organization.

When a restricted fund is used for investments and a debt fund is used to set money aside to retire long-term debts, the fund structure establishes a separate accounting and budgeting operation for each activity. This ensures that the activities of each fund will be managed according to its intended objectives and that the budget reports and financial statements will provide separate and important information necessary to each of the investment plans.

Some organizations do not use debt funds but instead include in the general fund a set of accounts to set aside money to pay off debts and another set of accounts to set aside investments. This procedure creates complications in the management of the general fund and a complex financial picture. For example, the financial statements for the general fund could be misunderstood if they exhibit a large unexpended investment balance (set up to retire a long-term debt) in addition to interest earned on other investments (from money waiting to be spent on salaries and benefits) as well as the regular revenue awarded for operations, which could have a residual balance. Footnotes have to appear at the bottom of such statements to explain the accounts, which give the appearance that exceptions were made. Long-term debts and investments should be shown in a straightforward manner in the funds created solely for retiring long-term debt and for investments, and the general fund should be used for operations.

Internal Funds. Principle 3 of the GAAP suggests that internal service funds be used when a cost-recovery operation is run within an organization. This means that a department such as a physical plant department or a supplies department would charge another department in the organization for the goods or services it renders. If the goods or services are rendered to someone outside the organization, then a self-support fund would be used.

An example of an internal operation is a physical plant department moving furniture or painting a room for another department in the organization. The department receiving the service transfers money from its budget to the physical plant fund to pay for the service. In turn, the physical plant fund pays the salaries of the managers, staff, and workers and the costs of the materials used in the job. Other arrangements are possible; for example, the general fund might pay the salaries of the personnel in the physical plant and the department receiving the services pay only for the materials used on the job, or the general fund might transfer money for all administrative costs and the department receiving the services then pay for labor and materials. There is no set procedure that should be followed; it may vary from organization to organization as well as among different internal operations within an organization.

Setting up an internal fund for services provides numerous advantages for an organization, such as having specialized people on staff to perform the work and, in some cases, the ability of the organization to save money. For example, a large institution that uses a large number of brochures and forms would possibly be better off financially if it set up its own graphic arts and print shop operation with a separate internal fund. A word of caution is in order, however: The money transferred into internal funds must be carefully recorded and presented in the financial statements. Otherwise, the transfers may appear to be a means to set aside money in order to circumvent the requirement that all revenue be spent before the end of the budget year.

Transferring Resources and Money Between Funds

Transfers of money or resources from one fund to another must be properly executed via the accounting system in each fund in order to ensure that the legal guidelines or policies associated with a revenue award will not be violated. For example, because of the importance of the time limitations placed on the use of a revenue allotment, a manager would want to be sure that the money is spent as planned before the end of the year. It would be terribly distressing if, at the time the books were closed, the board realized that a large sum of money had been transferred from the general fund into the restricted fund and forgotten.

This section provides some insights for managers who wish to guard against errors related to transfers between funds within the organization. There are three basic types of transfers: (1) transfers of money or resources that must be spent, used, and repaid within the year or shortly thereafter; (2) transfers that will be repaid sometime after the current year; and (3) permanent transfers of money or resources. By being able to identify the kind of transfer that has been made, a manager can determine whether the money will be returned to a fund to meet current expenditures, the transfer will not be available for some time, or money has been shifted permanently from one fund to another fund.

The GAAP addresses the importance of transfers in Principle 10, part a, which explains that transfers are to be classified separately from the revenues and expenditures of a fund. That is, when money is transferred between funds, the accounting system is to ensure that the transfers are not mistaken for revenue receipts or expenditures. One method to accomplish this is the use by the accounting system of special account names for the different types of transfers.

Transfers of Resources for the Current Period. Transfers of money or resources that must be spent and repaid by the end of the current year or shortly thereafter appear on the accounting records and budget reports for each of the funds involved. In the fund from which the money or resource was transferred, an account called Due from (name of other) Fund should appear; the fund into which the money or resource was transferred should show an account called Due to (name of other) Fund, meaning that this fund now owes the other fund.

An example of such a transfer between funds is a computer repair order from the general fund to the physical plant fund. When the repair is made, the general fund owes the physical plant fund for the repair and shows a record of the debt by using an account named Due to Physical Plant Fund. At the same time, the physical plant fund records the transaction in an account named Due from the General Fund. When the general fund pays the physical plant fund for the repair, these "Due to/Due from" accounts are canceled. The expense for the repair is then recorded against the budget in the general fund, not the physical plant fund.

The physical plant fund shows the payment as a revenue receipt. It must be noted that this receipt must not be recorded or reported like revenue received by the general fund, which is one of the concerns of the GAAP. For example, rather than an account named "revenue" or "income," the name recorded by the physical plant fund accounting system might be "revenues—charges for services." Managers usually would not want "due to/due from" accounts on the records when the books are closed at the end of the fiscal year.

A different example of a current period transfer would be the loan of money from the general fund to the restricted fund in order to invest money. When the loan is made, the general fund shows a record of the loan in the account Due from Restricted Fund; the restricted fund shows a record in the account Due to General Fund. When the general fund needs the money, the money (and not necessarily the interest earned) is transferred from the restricted fund back to the general fund, and the "due to/due from" accounts are canceled.

Advance of Resources Beyond the Current Year. For a variety of reasons, an organization may transfer revenue or resources from one fund to another for a period beyond the current year. In these cases, the name of the account used to record the transfer would be Advance to (name) Fund, and the account in the fund receiving the transfer would be Advance from (name) Fund. Because the loan may be repaid or eliminated in any future period, the account names "advance to/advance from" may appear in a fund's financial statements at the end of the fiscal year.

An example of a case in which a long term-loan is made by one fund to another is a board authorizing a transfer of interest income from the restricted fund to buy a computer in an internal fund, which for the purposes of this example will be called the Computer Services Fund. At the time of the transfer, the amount is recorded in the restricted fund under an account named Advance to Computer Services Fund, indicating that the Computer Services Fund must repay the restricted fund the amount loaned. In the Computer Services Fund, an entry in the account Advance from Restricted Fund shows the obligation to repay the restricted fund. These accounts appear in the accounting records and on the financial statements of the two funds until the loan is repaid. If in two years the Computer Services Fund has accumulated sufficient cash to repay the restricted fund, a transfer is made, and the "advance to/ advance from" accounts are canceled and removed from the records.

Permanent Transfers. Transfers of money or resources that will not be repaid to the fund making the transfer are of two types. The first type is a transfer made at the time the revenue is provided to the organization. The budget award may require that a portion of the revenue be used in one fund and another portion in a different fund. This requires a permanent revenue transfer from one fund to another upon receipt. For example, a portion of the operations budget may be targeted to retire a bond issue and have to be permanently transferred to the debt fund after the award is received. The second type is a transfer made when a board approves a transfer for a specific purpose; for example, the permanent transfer of a computer from the computer services fund to the fixed-asset fund.

Colleges and universities (and some other organizations) sometimes make permanent transfers from the general fund to another fund because the transfer is specified contractually; a popular term for this kind of transfer is *mandatory transfer*. When the board specifies that a transfer must be made, the transfer is labeled a *nonmandatory transfer*. (This is mentioned because these terms tend to be used in general conversations and can be confusing to the uninformed.)

When permanent transfers are made, the accounts are named Transfer to (name) Fund and Transfer from (name) Fund. For example, when a computer is transferred from the computer services fund to the fixed-asset fund, the account used in the computer services fund is the Transfer to Fixed-Asset Fund. At the end of the year, these entries may be removed from the records when the closing entries are made and their amount permanently added to or deducted from the residual balance of the fund, or the accounts may be retained and then added to or deducted from the residual balance on the financial statements.

Accounting and Budgeting Systems and the Fund Structure

The accounting and budgeting systems introduced in Chapter One are instituted in reference to the fund structure. When a fund structure consists of multiple fund entities, each will have its own accounting and budgeting systems. As shown in Figure 5, when there is a transfer between Fund A and Fund B, this is executed through the accounting systems in the two funds. After the transfer, the information is transmitted by the accounting systems to the budgeting reports for each fund.

Revenue Receipts. Revenue and income accounts are given names that identify the sources of the money—state tax revenue, local tax revenue, tuition income, and so on. When revenue is received and placed into more than one fund, the same account name may be used for the revenue source in each of the funds, because each fund has a separate set of self-balancing accounts. Thus, if an organization has two funds and places state tax revenue in each of them, the name of the revenue account in each fund is State Tax.

When a revenue award is placed in two or more funds, the budget that accompanies the award must be split accordingly. For

Figure 5. Multiple-Fund Structure.

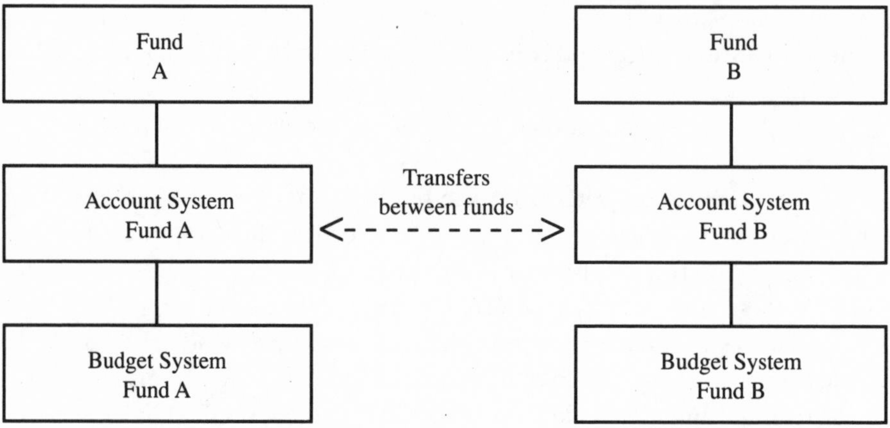

example, assume that an SPCA uses a general fund for operations and a fixed-asset fund for buildings and equipment. This organization received $100,000, of which $85,000 is awarded for operations and $15,000 for building renovations; specifically, $10,000 for asbestos removal in administrative offices and $5,000 for a new personal computer to keep animal-care records. The manager should place $85,000 in the general fund and use the budget related to that amount as the expenditure plan (such as salaries, supplies, animal food and so on), and $15,000 should go into the fixed-asset fund, with the budget allocation showing that the organization is to spend $10,000 for permanent building improvements (under the heading "miscellaneous: asbestos removal") and $5,000 for equipment (under the heading "equipment: computer equipment"). The operations money should be spent through the set of accounts in the general fund, and the money for the building and equipment should be spent through the set of accounts in the fixed-asset fund. If the manager decided to spend the money otherwise—for example, to install a $15,000 central air conditioning unit in the administrative offices instead of buying the computer equipment and having the asbestos removed—the audit would reveal the improper expenditure through a comparison of the allocated budget with the actual purchase orders, invoices, and canceled checks. Since the air conditioning equipment may not be able to be removed from the building and returned, it is likely that the manager would be.

As discussed later, if a manager wishes to make any changes in a budget, he or she should file a budget amendment to show the budget revision, which is usually accompanied by a statement of justification. The amendment should then be approved by the appropriate managers in the organization and then by the board. In some cases, the amendment may have to be approved by the source that provided the revenue.

Multiple Account Sets. If an organization receives two or more revenue allotments and wants to have them shown separately on the financial statements of the general fund, two sets of accounts are set up. For example, if a school receives revenue for a special education program and needs to account for this money in a separate financial report at the end of the year, one set of accounts would be used for the special education money and another for the other revenue received. Separate revenue and expenditure records and budget reports are maintained for each set. The financial statements at the end of the year are then able to report the revenue, expenditures, and balance for each set of accounts.

If the special education money did not have to be accounted for separately at the end of the year, the revenue allocation would be made to the budget for special education. The expenditures by the special education program would be recorded against that budget. Although the financial statements generated through the accounting system would show the revenue for the special education program in a separate account, the expenditures would be combined with the other expenditures in the fund and any residual would not be shown (it would be combined with others on the budget report).

Managing a Fund Structure

The Fund structure is critical to the effective management of the financial resources of an organization. In building and maintaining a fund structure, managers must be sure to take into consideration the different activities of the organization as well as their size in relation to the overall operation. Having too many funds can create problems in maintaining the accounting systems and interpreting the overall financial standing of an organization (Gross and Jablonsky, 1979; Gross and Warshauer, 1979; Henke, 1977). When a fund structure becomes too complex, it is inevitable that black holes appear in sections of the accounting and budgeting systems, and records disappear into them. In order to avoid these black holes, managers should ensure that when a fund is created by their organization, it is warranted, well defined, and properly staffed.

Problems can also be created when a fund has too many sets of accounts and budget units; for example, when a large university uses one fund with one set of self-balancing accounts containing multiple revenue, income, and expense accounts and budget units for tuition and fees, government appropriations, grants and contracts, gifts, endowment income, income generated through such activities as dining services and cafeterias, dorm rent, student activities, athletic events, and any other miscellaneous income that comes along, this arrangement also creates black holes. Such a fund should be split into several funds.

As noted earlier, a fund is a defined entity with resources that are to be used for specific activities and objectives. From a management perspective, then, a fund should be viewed in terms of the tasks required to perform and manage the fund activities and achieve fund objectives. This means that the purpose and objectives of the fund should define the personnel needed to manage its operation. For example, two funds—the general fund and the self-support fund—usually involve activities directly related to the mission of the organization, such as the offering of instructional classes by a public school or security patrols by a police department. Consequently, the managers of these funds should have backgrounds appropriate to the activities and objectives to ensure that the resources will be effectively and efficiently used to provide the expected services.

In contrast, the restricted fund, the debt fund, and the fixed-asset fund are not used to provide services directly to people inside or outside the organization. They each require personnel with an expertise different from that required of the personnel who provide the services related to the primary mission of the organization.

Finally, internal funds require personnel with entirely different abilities from those required for the activities associated with the other funds. These funds require managers and personnel with backgrounds in construction, printing, supply management, or whatever is provided to departments within the organization.

By recognizing the objectives of and type of activities provided through a fund, an organization may identify the tasks and expertise needed by the personnel and managers in that fund. Too often, professional personnel without the proper credentials are hired; for example, a person with a professional background in the services provided by the organization is typically not prepared to assume the responsibilities of an investments manager without extended formal preparation. Likewise, a person without any knowledge of or experience in the delivery of the services related to the primary mission of the organization cannot be expected to be aware of or appreciate the priorities of the professionals. The CEO, managers, and personnel who must work with and supervise all of the funds in the structure must have a broad formal and informal background that relates to the multiplicity of activities of all funds.

Summary

Funds are entities used to segregate revenue, income, and resources within an organization for specific activities and objectives. The use of a set of funds establishes a structure of smaller business entities with different activities and objectives within an organization. Through their separate sets of accounts, funds formally interact with each other just as separate private companies interact with each other.

With the establishment of smaller business entities within an organization, the accounting system is able to provide a set of financial statements for each fund, and the budget system can be designed to allow more direct control over the collection and expenditure of revenue and income. Only when the fund structure, the use of the funds, and the accounting and budgeting systems follow the principles promulgated in the GAAP can an operation ensure that an organization's resources are as secure as possible.

The six basic types of funds that may be used by an organization are (1) the general fund, for revenue that is used at the discretion of the board to provide activities related to the primary mission of the organization; (2) the self-support fund, for income earned from offering services and used to pay the expenses generated by the activities; (3) the restricted fund, for revenue and investment income that must be spent according to the stipulations placed upon it by a donor or the governing body; (4) the fixed-asset fund, for the purchase of fixed assets, such as buildings and equipment; (5) the debt fund, to set aside money to retire a debt, such as a bond issue or mortgage; and (6) the internal fund, to provide services within the organization.

Transfers between funds can be involved and complicated from an accounting point of view. However, such transfers can be classified in three categories: (1) transfers of resources to be used, spent, or repaid within or shortly after the current operating period (using account names "due to/due from"), (2) transfers that are used, spent, or repaid in a future period (using account names "advance to/advance from"), and (3) transfers that are permanent (using account names "transfer to/transfer from").

3

The First Two A's of Budgeting

Approval And Adoption

As noted in Chapter One, the budgeting system described in this text consists of three subsystems, referred to as the *AAA* subsystems. The first *A* represents the approval of the budget, the second *A* denotes its adoption, and the third *A* stands for the allocation of the budget award. All three subsystems may be used by an organization; however, as noted below, some organizations may use only one or two of them. This chapter is concerned with the first two subsystems.

Principle 9, part a, of the GAAP calls for each organization to have an annual budget. Budgeting by public and nonprofit organizations follows no uniform practice. This is understandable, since professional associations cannot get public and nonprofit organizations to comply with uniform accounting standards, let alone budgeting practices. Organizations jealously guard their right to implement their own particular budget procedures; yet many mistakenly assume that the same or similar budget procedures are followed by all other organizations and that a common terminology exists. This creates difficulties when a manager moves from one organization to another, when one organization tries to work with the budgets in several other organizations, and when authors try to describe the budget process. A good analogy is that the budget process is like painting pictures; there are a variety of techniques that include a range of features from artistic style to the texture of the paints. No one technique works for everyone. There are, however, some common denominators that cut across all painting techniques, as well as all budget processes. This book focuses on the common denominators of budgeting.

The terms *approval, adoption,* and *allocation,* like many others used in the public and nonprofit domain, may be used differently in different organizations; in this text, they have the following meanings:

Budget approval—the internal approval by the CEO and governing board of the estimated budget expenditures and estimated revenue receipts

Budget adoption—the action of an external body (such as government officials, an elected body, registered voters, dues-paying members, and so on) on an approved budget to award revenue to an organization

Budget allocation—distribution of the revenue received to the budget units within the organization by expenditure categories

Of course, some public and nonprofit organizations are not required to have their approved budgets adopted by an external body or membership. For example, a nonprofit organization may simply have a proposed budget approved by an advisory board and, because it does not come under any governmental oversight or membership body, not need to have the budget adopted. Further, because some organizations are small and do not have any operational units in a hierarchical structure, they do not allocate their budgets to units, although they may make informal allocations to activities or events. Even so, these organizations should still prepare a budget for approval, the budget should interact with an accounting system, and the organizations should prepare end-of-year budget reports.

On the other hand, some organizations may have to include an additional step in the budget process. In one state, the school districts are required to have their budgets approved by their school boards, adopted by the voters in a public election, and then further approved by a state government official. Thus, the subsystems presented by this text are not intended to be prescriptive but rather are to serve as a guide that may be modified for a complex operation as well as for smaller organizations.

Budgeting Subsystem 1: Approval

As noted in Chapter One the input to the first budgeting subsystem is the estimate of the revenue or income to be received and the

Figure 6. Budgeting Subsystem 1.

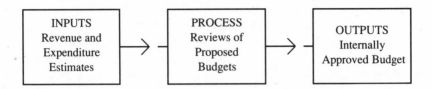

estimated expenditures submitted by each budget unit. The expenditure proposals are prepared and processed by one or a combination of the budget methods discussed in this section, and the revenue estimates are made by personnel who are familiar with the revenue source or sources. The process for this subsystem then should lead to the desired output, which is budget approval internally by the CEO and, if applicable, by a governing board (see Figure 6).

Components of the Budget

Estimated Revenue. Estimated potential revenue to be received is a topic that is covered in depth under public finance (rather than in a book on accounting and budgeting). Revenue estimates should be prepared by a business official, administrator, or adviser who is knowledgeable about public finance: about how revenue estimates are made for different tax sources and contributions, how the amount of the tax revenue and contributions may be estimated by a study of economic indicators, how revenue is influenced by local business activities, where new sources of revenue may be found and how to attract them, how estimates of revenue generated by a bond sale must relate to present values and annuity calculations, how estimates of revenue from investments must consider the different pros and cons of the means available to invest money, what the effects of elasticity are on a tax source, and so on. For example, if an organization has a tax source that is not responsive to economic growth or is adversely affected by a lack of growth or a decline, then tax options must be considered in terms of revenue sources along with expenditure options. When money becomes tight, an organization too often considers only expenditure cuts or increases in assessments, rates, or dues rather than seeking alternatives related to peculiar economic characteristics, the market for the services of the organization, or alternative revenue sources.

Basically, public finance officers should recognize money as a commodity. Revenue estimates do not have to be as exact when there is a large supply of it as when the supply is scarce. Public and nonprofit organizations must continually monitor situations that affect the supply of money, particularly situations that have a direct relationship to their source of revenue or that affect their immediate geographical area. They must question whether their methods of raising revenue, its sources, or their tax bases have become outdated as a result of changes taking place in the country or in their own area.

One activity affecting the money supply is the change taking place in the international marketplace. A negative trade balance has an important impact on the supply of money in the country, and this, in turn, has an influence on the amount of revenue available to public and nonprofit organizations. When the United States had a positive trade balance, money was more plentiful. When money is not scarce and the economy is expanding, revenue estimates can be more liberal and based loosely on previous years' receipts.

On the other hand, a trade deficit decreases the supply of money (assuming that the government does not print more of it and cause unnecessary inflation), and an organization must consider the possibility that less public revenue will be available than in the past. Over a long period of time, this deficit can be expected to have an important impact on public revenue for more and more organizations because the wealth of the country is gradually being displaced. Less money means that the overall per capita income will likely decline, particularly when inflation is recognized as a variable in the formula. This requires more conservative revenue estimates. This topic will become more relevant as international business activities are affected by the move from a world divided by a cold war to one in which free trade promises to create a new set of international practices and procedures. Will the wealth of the world be redistributed?

Another influence on the money supply for public and nonprofit organizations is the triple whammy being dealt to them by the federal deficit. First, the deficit requires the government to borrow money, which further increases the deficit and reduces the supply of money in the banks; second, the attempt to reduce the deficit by reducing services and support offered by the federal government transfers the costs and problems to national, state, and local public and nonprofit organizations; and, third, the increase in tax receipts by the federal government to cover the deficit reduces the proportion of the money supply available to public and nonprofit organizations. Can we be a competitor in the international market with a federal government in debt?

A third factor affecting the revenue of public and nonprofit organizations is the change in the median age of the population. This shift in median age and the increasing number of retired citizens on lower incomes influence how much money is available in a local area, as well as creating changes in the needs for services. As the median age shifts from younger to older, the distribution of public revenue to different organizations must change in response to the change in the demand for services; for example, many communities have fewer students in public schools but an increasing demand for services by senior citizens. Thus, some communities are realizing that their public revenue bases are shifting or possibly declining and that this requires a coordination of efforts, a redesign of tax structures, and a review of public services. Unfortunately, these efforts require a different data base and research at the state and local level than are now available.

States and communities are also aware that people who are at the low end of the economic scale are unlikely to participate in industrial production. As the numbers of low-income people grow and production declines, the amount of goods to sell is reduced. This, in turn, affects the money supply in a community. The decline in production is also affected by a national shift from an industrial-based to a service-based economy; more and more people earn money from providing services rather than producing goods for sale. When these two situations have an impact on industrial production in more and more communities, how much impact is felt on the money supply in the community, the state, and the country? Can the United States be a world competitor by moving from a production to a service economy? This is possible only if it can sell services to other countries.

In sum, public finance is a complex topic to be studied seriously, with the use of all the tools available, including information produced by the accounting and budgeting systems. A person making revenue estimates needs to be very sensitive to all of the variables discussed above, as well as others too numerous to mention, and their impact on the potential to collect money for an organization.

Estimated Expenditures. With respect to the input regarding estimated expenditures, each of an organization's operational units with a budget should present an estimate of the money to be spent in the coming year, along with an expenditure plan prepared according to one of the methods described below. This should include, for example, how much a department will need for salaries, wages, supplies, travel, and equipment. One way to look at the purpose of a proposed budget is offered by McCaffery (1989, p. 290), who describes it as a "formal calculation of what needs to be done and how much it will cost." A proposed budget may also include expenditure outlines, program descriptions, an evaluation plan, quantitative performance data, and other statements required by the board or an agency, such as a sex-equity guarantee.

Preparing the Budget

The importance of getting budgeting managers ready to prepare their budget proposals cannot be stressed enough. In this stage, there should be meetings of the managers who prepare the unit budgets in order to ensure uniformity and to eliminate misunderstandings. Budget forms should be designed to save time, and managers need to be instructed on how to complete them. A budget plan should outline the process to be followed from the originating unit up through the organization to the CEO and the governing board. This plan should specify the review and decision-making process followed by the organization for each budget in each fund. The criteria for evaluating the budget proposals should be provided in writing, not only to the evaluators but also to the budget managers who are preparing the proposals. Finally, strict timetables should be set for the preparation of the proposals, for their evaluation at each level, for the decisions by the top management, and for the approval by the board. Nothing should be left to chance.

One or a combination of budget methods may be used for the preparation of the proposals. The same method should be used for a fund, although different funds may use different methods. For example, managers whose budgets come under the general fund and the self-support fund would use the same method and forms, while the managers of the restricted fund and debt fund might use a different method and forms.

A variety of budget methods have been designed to prepare an estimate of the amount of money an organization will need to provide the services necessary for it to achieve its intended mission. These budget methods can be categorized into three groups: line-item budgeting, performance budgeting, and program budgeting. However, organizations may use a number of variations in each method or arrangements that combine parts of different ones. The customized budget options are too numerous to describe; it is doubtful whether many organizations follow any one method without variations.

Practitioners often refer to budgets as being divided into two sections: "above-the-line" and "below-the-line" expenses. Although this division was not created by any official or legal action and is not even discussed in most books, its use is quite common. It is created by an imaginary line that runs between the budget categories for regular personnel (salaries and wages) and the other budget categories (such as costs for supplies, consultants, travel, equipment, telephone, rental of equipment, and so on). Personnel costs are usually listed in a budget first and, therefore, are referred to as "above the line," while the other expenses are referred to as "below-the-line" expenses. The reason for this division is that, in many cases, budget awards and allocations are made in terms of one amount for personnel and another amount for all other budget categories. In some situations, a manager or board can move money from above to below the line; in other cases, permission must be obtained from the granting agency; in still others, the proportion is fixed by law. Another way of looking at above-the-line/below-the-line categories is that above-the-line costs involve tax deductions and fringe benefits, such as Social Security, health insurance, unemployment, and so on. In addition, in terms of overhead charges for grants, many organizations charge a percentage rate based on the amount of money above the line.

This division is important to budget planners for several reasons. First of all, the items above the line often account for the greatest percentage of the budget; for example, in public schools and many other public organizations, the above-the-line budget sometimes accounts for as much as 80 percent of the total budget. This can have important implications for budget strategies; a budget cannot be easily cut by firing people or reducing their salaries when such a move would lead to a drastic reduction in services. In a budget crunch, the public does not appreciate a proposal to reduce the size of the police force, although this is often a threat made by city officials when revenue is short and taxes must be increased. Thus, the below-the-line budget often receives the greatest attention when budget adjustments are being considered, but it has the least promise for solving financial problems, because it is typically a small percentage of the total budget.

Line-Item Budgeting. The line-item budgeting method is the easiest procedure for making cost estimates and is probably the oldest of the methods used today. Hartman (1988) explains that in line-item budgeting, the focus is on the item to be purchased and not on the purpose for its purchase. This method is also sometimes referred to as the *object-of-expenditure* or the *traditional* method, although there is a slight difference among these methods. Cope (1989) describes object of expenditure as a method in which a line-item format is used and the budget proposes objects to be purchased. Technically, a line-item budget simply shows the expected expenditures for each budget-line category—for example, salaries, supplies, and so on. Some organizations may include a narrative with the line-item budget describing a plan for the use of money, but this is not a "pure" line-item budget.

In her research, Cope (1986) found that one-third of the local governments that she surveyed used the line-item method, while another 43 percent used this budget method with other, supporting information. Cope (1989, p. 282) believes that the use of "the line item format as the only budget presentation" seems to be growing and that this may be a result of the increased use of computer spreadsheet programs.

A major advantage of the line-item method is that it is control-oriented. With this method, an organization requests specific amounts for specific expenditures, the governing body or official approves the expenditures, and then the end-of-year audit checks to see whether the specific expenditures were made. For example, in a line-item budget, the above-the-line budget presents the specific salary for each individual. In one case this was a problem because the organization granted salary increases for all employees as per a union agreement but a granting agency did not wish to recognize the increase shown on the budget proposal for one person being paid through a grant. The increase, which was set with the collective bargaining agent, had to be upheld. The granting agency argued that the line-item budget method gave it control over the amount to be paid and that the time being worked by the employee should be decreased in order to match the awarded salaries.

In another example of the use of a line-item budget, one granting agency required that the object of expenditure be used in the travel category in the budget proposal. In this strict line-item budget format, the travel allocations had to be shown by person per trip. In other words, assume that an organization submitting a proposal has a coordinator, Ivan Goalot, whose job requires him to travel frequently. In the line-item budget under the travel category, the request for Goalot's travel appears as follows:

Travel:
    I. Goalot—8,000 miles @ .20 per mile;
    68 days per diem @ $25 per day, 47 days
    hotel room @ $55 per day $5,885

If Goalot were to spend $5,885, or a little less but not much less, on travel, his performance would be deemed appropriate. If he were to spend more, the organization would have to pay the excess amount; if he were to spend significantly less, he would likely receive less than he requests for the coming year. As Freeman, Shoulders, and

Lynn (1988) point out, some drawbacks of line-item budgets are that decision makers are not provided any supporting information, planning is neglected, past activities are perpetuated, effectiveness is not considered, and the performance evaluation is based on spending.

Performance Budgeting. Some people may use the budget terms *performance budgeting* and *program budgeting* interchangeably, or mean *performance budgeting* when using the words *program budgeting* and then use the term *program budgeting* to mean only "planning, programming, budgeting systems" (PPBS), which is discussed next. However, to be technically and historically correct, performance and program budgeting are not the same. In the most elementary case, performance budgeting uses the line-item method format to present the financial request and then describes what will be accomplished with the money (not why).

Freeman, Shoulders, and Lynn (1988) identify performance budgeting as a method in which the activities and the work program are described in a proposed budget so that performance is measurable. As compared to the line-item budget, they point out, it shifts the emphasis from objects of expenditure to activities, much like a performance contract. Thus, a more complex definition of performance budgeting is the preparation of a budget with a supporting narrative that describes in measurable terms the proposed performances of the organization in the delivery of a program, activity, and/or service. Because of this feature, Cope (1989) takes the position that this budgeting method is more relevant to management needs than for making policy decisions.

At the end of the year a formal evaluation is conducted in relation to the performances proposed in the narrative submitted with the budget. For example, a performance budget narrative would describe what activity the personnel would accomplish and how the below-the-line money would be spent to support the activity. The emphasis is on efficiency, and the evaluation concerns a comparison of unit costs, work loads, and outputs (Cope, 1989; Freeman, Shoulders, and Lynn, 1988). However, the cost for the quantitative documentation, analysis of data, and the corresponding interpretation for the appraisal is a major problem.

Program Budgeting. Program budgeting, as Hartman (1988) points out, is meant to answer the "why"; it explains the objective of the expenditure in relation to the proposed financial budget. Matkin (1985) feels the explanation for the expenditures in a program budget overcomes the major disadvantage of the line-item budgeting method. Although the performance budget concentrates on the "what," this does not imply that a program budget may not also address "what." In fact, this is why some people refer to their budget method as a "performance program" budget. A program budget may use a line-item budget format or a broader format, using budget categories rather than object of expenditure.

By providing the "why," a program budget describes the reason the program will be delivered. For example, a program may be described in terms of goals and objectives and then a plan is presented to illustrate how they will be achieved, by whom, and when. If the performance component is included, the plan describes in measurable terms the work to be accomplished by each person to meet the objectives, possibly with time lines. This type of program budget has become known as the planning programming budget (PPB) method.

PPB in turn led to the planning, programming, budgeting system (PPBS), which consists of numerous elements, including a cost-benefit analysis and a systems component (which is why they added the *S* to PPB). Although PPBS became well known in the 1960s, experts point out that the elements used in PPBS originated years before it was created. Merewitz and Sosnick (1971) note that a cost-benefit analysis procedure was used in 1844 by a French engineer, Jules Dupuit, in a public works project. Novick (1968) discusses the important work by Bell Laboratories on the use of systems analysis and also points out that General Motors used a form of PPBS in 1924. However, regardless of the variety of influences on the development of PPBS and how this involved process evolved over a considerable period of time, the specific format known as PPBS did not originate until recent years.

The first attempt to test a PPBS method was made by the U.S. Air Force in the 1950s. In 1961, Secretary of Defense Robert McNamara brought the use of PPBS into the federal government; it was implemented in fiscal 1963 by Charles Hitch, assistant secretary of defense (Merewitz and Sosnick, 1971). In August 1965, President Johnson formally announced the introduction of PPBS into all levels of the federal government, and on October 12, 1965, Bulletin 66-3, concerning the establishment of PPBS, was sent to the heads of the federal executive departments (Knezevich, 1973). In his book *The Essence of Security*, McNamara (1968, p. 95) claims that the new planning system allowed the Department of Defense "to achieve a true unification of effort."

In June 1971, according to Merewitz and Sosnick (1971, p. 301), "the U.S. government quietly abandoned its compulsive version of PPB." This meant that the Office of Management and Budget (OMB) discontinued the requirement for "program accounting, detailed description of activities, and zero-based budgeting and . . . restricted multi-year costing and benefit-cost analysis to expenditures that would represent new policy decisions" (p. 302). In September 1971, the director of OMB "called for a significant revision in many of the components of PPB" (Knezevich, 1973, p. 15).

Several reasons have been given for the decline in the popularity of PPBS. Matkin (1985, p. 12) feels that the method was too expensive, that it "increased dissension and discord between program staffs," and that staffs saw "each other as rivals for the same pot of money." Chatfield (1974) believes that it was due to misuse and misunderstanding and that, unless a strong proponent such as McNamara is behind it, it will not work. Freeman, Shoulders, and Lynn (1988) discuss the difficulties related to presenting clear goals that everyone can agree on, creating an adequate data base, having a staff with a high level of technical ability, and developing objective measures of performance, as well as the threat to power bases that is created by those holding the purse strings.

In a planning, programming, budgeting system, the objectives of the program are described along with the activities and a plan to be implemented to meet the objectives. The costs of the objectives and activities are then presented in a budget. Preferably, several alternative plans and corresponding budgets are proposed to achieve the objectives. As the proposals are considered at successively higher levels of the organization's hierarchy, each level conducts an analysis of the potential effectiveness, benefits, and costs of the program alternatives. The higher administrative officials in the organization then decide which programs or combination of programs to recommend. The following is a brief outline of the PPBS components:

> Planning—set short-term and long-term objectives
> Programming—provide alternative approaches to achieve the objectives
> Budgeting—propose costs for program alternatives
> System—design a structure with procedures to review the plans, programs, and budgets

Thus, the budget should focus on the organization's objectives, with quantitative data and a supporting narrative. When a budget is presented, a review of the effectiveness of the current program should be included in the evaluation.

Another well-known program budgeting method is zero-based budgeting (ZBB). As Knezevich (1973) explains, the U.S. Department of Agriculture began to formulate the ZBB method in 1962 and implemented it in 1964. President Carter introduced its use on a large scale throughout the federal government in 1977; its use was discontinued when President Reagan took office (Cope, 1989).

In the ZBB process, every budget in an organization starts at a zero amount each year, and the budgets for all existing programs, as well as proposed new programs, must be approved for the coming year. The manager of each decision unit (that is, each unit with a budget) in the organization prepares a proposal for existing and new programs. The proposal includes a set of alternative designs and budgets for each program and a recommendation that either ranks the programs or describes which are the most efficient alternatives. The proposals, which are called *decision packages,* are processed through the organizational hierarchy and ranked at each level. The recommendations and proposals (or summaries of them) are then given to the CEO for the preparation of the organization's budget proposal.

Each program must be reviewed and justified every year. If a program cannot be satisfactorily justified or justified at the existing level of funding, it is supposed to be discontinued or have its budget reduced. This procedure is designed to encourage managers to seek out less expensive alternatives for a program and to create new programs or products for funding. Realistically, however, a proposal that advocates offering new services and discontinuing old ones many not be practical for many public and nonprofit organizations, particularly those that have little flexibility in devising alternatives because salaries constitute the bulk of the budget. Thus, Brueningsen (1976) suggests that ZBB be perceived more as an attitude than a formula.

Rather than reducing every program to a zero budget, some organizations do not use zero but start with a percentage of the current budget (Welsch, Hilton, and Gordon, 1988). For example, all operating units in an organization might be given approval for at least 70 percent of the current budget, with any amount over that requiring justification through the ZBB process. Freeman, Shoulders, and Lynn (1988) suggest that the ZBB process be used on a periodic basis to review the level at which services should be offered. Either of these two approaches may be useful for organizations faced with a declining demand for their services and a need to make program and budget adjustments.

In conclusion, the focus for PPBS and ZBB is on the cost-benefit analysis of programs and activities. Although quantitative data are used as much as possible, the final comparison of benefits and costs is subjective and sensitive to interpretations. Both methods are time-consuming and require personnel with special expertise. Guthrie, Garms, and Pierce (1988) point out that while both PPBS and ZBB are centralized systems, the important difference is that PPBS sets goals at the top, with a downward budget-development process, while ZBB builds from the bottom.

Budgeting Subsystem 2: Adoption

In the second budgeting subsystem, the input is the approved budget that is the output from subsystem 1, which must be presented to an outside body or official for adoption (see Figure 7). The processing of the input varies from one organization to the next. In some cases, the amounts approved and the plan for their use may have to be defended in a public hearing, before a panel, or at a

Figure 7. Budgeting Subsystem 2.

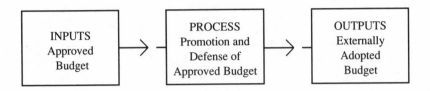

meeting with a public official. Regardless of the process, the desired output for this subsystem is adoption of the budget by an elected body, a government agency, a public vote, a vote of the membership, and so on. When this occurs, the organization will receive a revenue award.

The strategies and activities used to promote and defend an approved budget for adoption vary not only from one organization to another but also from one year to another and from one budget to another within an organization. As anyone who has had to defend a budget knows, it is not typically a pleasant task for either the person defending the budget or the reviewers evaluating the proposal. One suggestion, therefore, is that both parties try to relieve the tension as much as possible and to maintain a positive atmosphere. A threatening, aggressive posture by either party at a budget defense not only is unpleasant but also sets the stage for a negative working relationship between the parties after the budget has been adopted and implemented.

If managers hope to receive a fair and unbiased reaction to a budget proposal, they must present the budget request as clearly and accurately as possible. If errors are to be made, the time for them to appear is not when a budget is being considered for adoption. One strategy in presenting a budget is to pad, or increase, the amounts requested in anticipation of a budget cut. In some cases, the reviewers of a budget, both for approval and for adoption, assume that it has been padded. The amount by which a budget is padded is sometimes called the "fudge factor"; the amount by which a budget is "fudged" across the board is sometimes as much as 5 to 10 percent.

In a discussion about the realities behind budget strategies,

McCaffery (1989) reports that some administrators push for increments for a variety of reasons, some take a textbook approach, some
pad their budget requests, and others project themselves into the
role of the superior reacting to budget proposals. However, as
McCaffery points out, budgeting is an ongoing process and should
not be considered a one-time event. This ongoing process involves
human relations that cannot be developed and maintained on a
once-a-year schedule. The discovery of the use of the fudge factor
can bring harm to these relationships, can turn the adoption process
into a game, and can discredit a manager.

Managing the Approval and Adoption Process

In managing the approval and adoption process, an organization
must establish a management plan with deadlines. In most cases,
this is accomplished through the use of a budget calendar, which
sets deadlines to ensure that the budgets are prepared, presented,
and acted on in time. This plan begins when each unit is to start
to prepare its proposed budget for internal approval and continues
until it is adopted. In other words, the plan spans both subsystems
1 and 2.

The organization prepares first a master calendar plan and
then several budget calendars, or plans, such as one for the operating units, one for supervisors, one for the board, one for staff offices,
and so on. Through the use of the individual calendars, greater
detail can be provided to guide the people who are working on the
budgets at the different stages of preparation, review, approval, and
adoption, and they do not have to study a master calendar to determine where they fit into the process. An example of a master budget
calendar used by a municipality is provided in Exhibit 1. Such a
budget calendar can be developed for any type of organization. The
calendar simply sets forth the deadlines for internal approval and
for external adoption and includes notations on the deadlines set
according to law or policy.

In the calendar shown in Exhibit 1, internal budget approval
begins with the distribution of budget forms and corresponding
instructions by the business office. From October 15 to November
10, the budget units submit their budget expenditure estimates, and

Exhibit 1. Municipal Master Budget Calendar.

Event	Earliest Optional Date	Latest Statutory Date
Distribution of budget forms and instructions	July–Sept.	
Submission of departmental requests and estimation of preliminary revenue	Oct. 15–Nov. 10	
Administrative budget hearings	Nov.	Nov.
Presentation of budget by CEO		Jan. 15
Introduction and approval of budget	Jan. 1	Feb. 10
Filing of three certified copies	3 days after approval	
Publication (minimum of 10 days before hearing)	Jan. 1	Mar. 10
Filing of annual financial statement	Jan. 2	Feb. 10
Budget hearing (28 days after approval)	Jan. 29	Mar. 20
Adoption of budget	Jan. 29	Mar. 20
Filing of two certified copies	3 days after adoption	
Filing of one certified copy with county board of taxation	Jan. 29	Mar. 31

the appropriate official in the organization submits the revenue estimates. The business manager then reviews the proposals, prepares a report of the expenditure and receipt estimates, prepares the materials for internal budget hearings, and schedules the reviews, which in this example may begin by November 1 and, as set by law, must be concluded by the end of November. The CEO then presents the proposed budget to the town council no later than January 15 for approval no later than February 10.

The budget then moves forward for adoption. The adoption process begins when three certified copies are filed with the appropriate state and local officials within three days of approval, which means no later than February 13. The annual financial statements must also be filed by February 10. The approved budget must be published by March 10 for the public hearing to be completed twenty-eight days after the budget approval but no later than March

20, the last date by which the budget may be adopted by public vote. Upon adoption, a copy is filed with the county tax board.

When there are no legal guidelines to follow, a budget plan may be developed by conducting the process in reverse—that is, establishing a set of calendar dates by starting at the time the budget must be submitted for adoption and working back through the approval and review process to the lowest budget unit in the hierarchy preparing a budget. The schedule must provide for opportunities for meetings and time for the budget materials to be prepared and distributed.

After the master calendar is created, the organization should establish budget calendars for the various operations, presenting beginning dates, deadlines, review periods, hearing dates, and so on. Each of these calendars should be accompanied by a set of budgeting forms and supporting data, which may include budget expenditures for prior years, the current budget, expenditures to date, number of people served or programs delivered, and possibly the amount expected to be allocated next year. This information should be as quantitative as possible and prepared with the assumption that the unit or office does not have such information readily available. This can be critical for new managers in the organization.

When an organization is large and has several hierarchical levels, a budget request by the lowest operating unit in the organization is typically presented to the next level in the hierarchy for review. The budgets from the lower units are then combined by the higher level and presented for review by the next level in the hierarchy. This budget preparation and review process is continued through the approval level.

In some cases, the preparation of the budget is used by managers as a way to obtain a public reaction to the budget and perhaps a psychological commitment to it on the part of employees who depend on it for their salaries and support, such as hospital employees; people from whom the revenue will be received, such as dues-paying members of the organization or taxpayers; or people who receive the services provided by the organization, such as students or parents of students.

When a budget plan involves the public, a calendar must allow time for them to receive the information, read and study it, and then have an opportunity for genuine input. A budget hearing should not be a superficial gesture. In one nonprofit organization, the budget materials were passed out to the members at the meeting in which the budget was to be adopted by a formal vote. When the members were given an opportunity to ask questions, some of the questions demonstrated lack of understanding of the budget (causing noticeable frustration to the board); others were not even related to it. A better approach would have been for the board to have the budget distributed in advance in order to give the members an opportunity to study it and to voice private criticisms to a board member before the open hearing. A formal presentation should have been given at the beginning of the budget meeting to set the content for the meeting and possibly answer a lot of questions, particularly questions asked of board members in advance of the meeting when the budget was distributed. This approach would have saved a lot of time and frustration.

Summary

The budgeting system as described in this text is divided into three subsystems; this chapter discussed the first two subsystems, approval and adoption of the budget. The input for the first subsystem is the estimated revenue or income to be received and the estimated expenditures submitted by each budget unit in the organization. The output is the approved budget, which is the input to the second subsystem. After the approved budget is presented and defended, the output of this system is an adopted budget, which means that the organization is promised that it will receive a revenue award.

In preparing a budget proposal for approval in the first subsystem, an organization must have its budget units prepare cost estimates. To accomplish this, it may utilize one or a combination of the basic budgeting methods: line-item budgeting, performance budgeting, and program budgeting. In the category of program budgeting are the popular procedures called planning, programming, budgeting system (PPBS) and zero-based budgeting (ZBB).

While a line-item budget provides only the expenditure information, the performance budgeting method includes a description of what will be accomplished with the money, presented in measurable terms. Program budgeting adds to these two elements the "why" of the budget: it shows the line-item information, explains the objectives of the expenditures, and describes how they will be achieved.

The PPBS method requires that the budget proposal set forth the short-term and long-term objectives, alternative approaches to achieving the objectives, costs of the program alternatives, and a structure with procedures to review the plans, programs, and budgets. With ZBB, on the other hand, every budget in an organization starts at zero each year, and all existing and proposed programs must be approved for the coming year. Each budget proposal is processed up through the organizational hierarchy, ranked at each level, and then given to the CEO for the preparation of the organization's budget proposal.

After the proposed budgets are processed by the management of the organization, they are presented to the CEO or governing board for approval. Upon approval, the output of the first budgeting subsystem has been obtained. This output then serves as the input for the second subsystem. The objective of subsystem 2 is the adoption of the approved budget by an external body that will provide the budget award.

Because the two budget subsystems complement each other, a management plan should be developed to span both operations. In most cases, this is best accomplished through the use of a budget calendar, which is a budget plan that sets deadlines to ensure that the budgets are prepared, presented, and acted on in time for approval and adoption.

4

The
Third A
of Budgeting

Allocation

The third *A* of the budgeting subsystem is the allocation of the budgets to the units, presented graphically in Figure 8. The input for this subsystem is the approved and adopted budgets. Subsystem 3 then concerns the budget allocations to the units within the organization, control over the receipt of revenue, and control of expenditures. Assuming that the subsystem processes are performed correctly, the output will be an acceptable budget report at the end of the year.

Figure 8. Budgeting Subsystem 3.

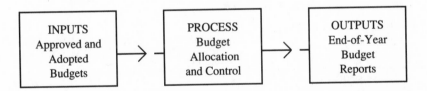

This chapter focuses on the allocation of the budgets to the units in the organization; revenue and expenditure control is the subject of Chapter Five. The two major components of budget allocation are the amount being allocated and the budget numbering framework used in the allocation.

The Amount of the Allocation

Before discussing how the budgets are allocated, managers must be clear as to what is allocated, when, and why. While the approved budget determines the amount to be distributed, the author has found that managers and students often have difficulty accepting it.

Possibly this is because the text describes budgeting in terms of administrative subsystems that are related to business activities, rather than other purposes of budgeting, such as planning, programming, or political relationships. While these latter perspectives on budgeting are also important to managers, this book concentrates on the topic from a business science viewpoint.

The reason that both the approved and the adopted budgets are needed for input to this subsystem is that (1) the estimated revenue and expenditure amounts in the approved budget are the reference for the allocations that are made to the budget units, and (2) the adopted budget represents the amount of revenue to be received by the organization. The two amounts may not be the same. In reality, the actual chronology of events is usually as follows: (1) the budget is approved, (2) the budget allocations are made as per the amount of the approved budget, and (3) the budget is adopted. If the amount of the adopted budget is *greater* than the approved budget, and therefore the amount allocated, the traditional practice in many organizations has been to make no changes in the budget allocations; if the adopted budget is *less* than the approved budget, the allocations are often reduced.

Appropriation Accounting. Appropriation accounting is so named because the amount allocated to the budget units is called an "appropriation." Bailey (1989) explains that an organization's appropriation represents the amount of money authorized to be spent. The accounting system uses the account called "appropriation" to record this amount. This entry is typically made after the budget has been approved internally, before the allocations are made, and before the budget is adopted.

Appropriation accounting has both a major advantage and a disadvantage. The advantage is that the appropriation, or budget allocation, is based on the estimate of future revenue to be received—the amount that is expected to be collected and awarded to the organization by the revenue source through taxes, pledges, income receipts, and so on. The allocations are usually less than the estimate of the revenue that will be received, because future collections may be less than promised if the economy weakens, people do not pay what they promised in pledges, or a self-supporting operation does not generate the business income expected.

The disadvantage with this practice is that an organization may be too conservative in determining the appropriated amount to be allocated to the budget units. If the amount of revenue awarded by the adopted budget is somewhat greater than the amount allocated for expenditure, it creates what this text calls "the gap." In some cases, this gap is allowed to exist until it is allocated during the last quarter of the fiscal year or is added to the residual balance in the fund at the end of the year. An organization that allows the gap to become too large and to last too long into the year may not be maximizing the use of the revenue and income received. How relevant are the proposed spending plans of the budget units if there is a large gap and then money is allocated for equipment in the last operating quarter of the year?

When an organization is not sure whether the amount in the adopted budget will be received, then, of course, the managers should follow a conservative approach; for example, a nonprofit public TV station probably would not wish to allocate all of the pledge money promised in a campaign but rather would base its allocations on the amount that management estimates will be received. On the other hand, a less conservative approach would be called for when a college or university is promised money by the state or federal government.

The allocation of money to the budget units may be further complicated by the accounting practice, discussed in Chapter Seven, of recognizing uncollectibles: When the adopted budget is entered into the accounting system, an estimate is made of the amount that will not be received or collected. This amount is recorded in an uncollectible account in the accounting system and thus reduces the amount of revenue recorded. It is important that managers understand the full implications of these practices. For instance, if management follows a conservative approach in making the allocations to the budget units and the accounting system sets aside an estimated amount of the revenue award as uncollectible, the gap may be much larger than realized. This may also result in the estimated revenue in the approved budget, the amount allocated to budget units, and the estimated amount of revenue to actually be received all being different. In such a case, management of the financial resources becomes quite complex (although there is less risk of overexpenditure). When managers do not see the total picture, they may not understand where the residual at the end of the year came from. Thus, the objective of management in this regard is to study the total picture in order to seek a balance that will best serve the organization—a balance that is neither too risky nor too conservative.

The best practice is for managers to monitor the size of the gap and make corresponding adjustments. In some cases, organizations adjust their budget allocations on the receipt of the adopted budget so that the difference between the amount of revenue promised (after subtracting the uncollectible estimate) and the amount allocated to the budget units are the same (or as similar as possible).

In discussing what is referred to here as the gap, Scheps and Davidson (1970, p. 90) state that colleges and universities have two budgets: "the legislative budget and the internal or operating budget." They recommend that the operating budget, which is the amount shown in the appropriations account and is used to set up the budget allocations, be adjusted as recommended above if the legislature fails to award the amount of money requested. They also note that a budget award may be in a lump sum or may detail how the money is to be spent. When the budget award is accompanied by a detailed expenditure plan, the college or university must follow this plan. This means that the appropriations account and the allocated budgets may have to be revised accordingly. Of course, the points made by Scheps and Davidson can be applied to any public or nonprofit organization using the appropriation accounting method to enter budgets into the accounting system.

While the gap can be explained in much greater detail in terms of the logic of accounting (see, for example, Bailey, 1989; Freeman, Shoulders, and Lynn, 1988; Henke, 1977; Meisinger and Dubeck, 1984: Scheps and Davidson, 1970), the purpose here is not to discuss accounting logic but to emphasize the interactions between the accounting and budgeting systems. The following example illustrates these interactions in terms of the gap.

Assume that the total in an approved budget is $600,000 and the accounting entry to the appropriation account is $560,000 (that is, the amounts allocated to be spent total $560,000). If the awarded revenue in the adopted budget is $600,000, that amount is recorded in the revenue account, but the amounts allocated to the budget units are not changed. There is thus a gap of $40,000 between the revenue to be received and the total amount allocated. However, the accounting department estimates that of the $600,000 award, $30,000 may not be collected. Thus, there is now a $10,000 gap.

On the other hand, assume that the adopted budget awards $550,000 in revenue, and the amount estimated to be uncollectible is still $30,000. In this case, the allocations should be decreased immediately by at least $40,000 ($560,000 originally allocated less $550,000 awarded less $30,000 uncollectible, or $520,000) unless the organization uses some of the residual remaining in the fund balance from previous years to cover the $40,000.

Cuts and Supplements. After a budget award is made, an organization may receive a budget cut or additional revenue, called a budget supplement. Typically, the budget allocations need to be adjusted in response to cuts or supplements. McCaffery (1989) describes one situation in which the manager explained that if a budget award was not what was requested, she could make up the difference in a request for a supplement. This is a situation many managers have experienced more often in recent years, and it could mean that a third dimension to the budget process is evolving. Supplements can be a concern for some organizations if the award of a supplement bypasses regular procedures and personnel that are routinely involved in approval and adoption of budgets.

If budget supplements become more common, they may need to become a formal part of the planning process. This would mean that budget proposals would not be an output for action but would be a part of a larger process, which would have ramifications for budget planning, budget programming, outputs, and the political process; for example, supplements might be used as a means for an agency to establish stronger control over an organization's operations. As a result, managers would have to set up contingency plans for cuts and supplements at the time budget proposals are prepared and then to closely monitor the changes in the amounts of the revenue awards, the amount estimated to be uncollectible, and the

budget allocations. This could be accomplished only through regular adjustments to the appropriations account, the budget
allocations, and the revenue account.

One of the methods designed to keep organizations from
abusing budget supplements (though the definition of *abuse* may
be quite subjective) is the use of what are called "funding formulas." Recently, the use of these formulas has been extended to operations within organizations. Guthrie, Garms, and Pierce (1988)
describe such an application in the form of school-site budgeting,
the allocation of revenue to district schools according to a formula
designed to ensure that money is divided properly. This form of
budgeting, which is growing in popularity, requires considerable
coordination with various bodies, including the collective bargaining agent.

The Nonprofit Dilemma. Controversy and confusion currently accompany the accounting and budgeting practices to be
followed by nonprofit organizations when recognizing revenue.
Those organizations that come under some degree of oversight by
a governmental body are to follow the standards set forth by the
GASB, while those that do not fall under any oversight are subject
to the standards of the FASB. Regardless of precedent or tradition,
nonprofit organizations must abide by some standards.

Many nonprofit organizations formally recognize revenue
when cash is received, not when it is promised (the cash-basis method of accounting, discussed briefly in Chapter Six). According to the
practices set forth by the FASB, budgets are not entered into the
accounting system, and revenue is to be recorded when pledges are
received. As a result, nonprofit organizations (not under governmental oversight) may appear to have a lot of revenue when they
actually have only a lot of pledges, some of which will not be paid.
This appearance may affect an organization's ability to attract contributions as well as the nonprofit status of some organizations
(Millar, 1990). To reconcile this situation, these organizations must
calculate and record the amount of pledges estimated to be
uncollectible.

On the other hand, nonprofit organizations that are subject
to the standards of the GASB enter their budgets into their account-

ing systems. Thus, the estimates for the approved budget, not the amount of the pledges, are the reference for the allocation of money to the budget units in the organization. Pledges represent the estimated amount of revenue to be received (the equivalent of the award from an adopted budget), and the estimate of the uncollectible pledges lowers the amount of revenue determined to be received by the organization. The amount allocated, which is based on the approved budget, could then be less than the amount of the pledges. The amount shown in the revenue account would be decreased by the pledge amount that is estimated to be uncollectible. Through this process, managers in the organization have considerable control over the amounts shown on their books in the different accounts as well as the amount allocated to be spent by their budget units. If, at any time, the organization feels that the amount in the uncollectible account is too great or too small, the revenue account and the allocations can be adjusted.

Another complaint (Millar, 1990) is that nonprofit organizations following the FASB standards must count donations, including volunteer time and works of art, as revenue and assets in the year received. The important difference between the GASB and the FASB in this case is the use of funds. The FASB does not use funds, and so the donations are not placed under a separate set of accounts. Thus, valuable paintings donated to a museum would be shown as revenue received during the year instead of being placed in a separate restricted fund. A cash donation for a trust would appear as revenue and not be recorded in the restricted fund, as it would under the GAAP. The use of one set of accounts and corresponding financial statements may make an organization appear to be quite wealthy when, in fact, the value of the assets and the donated cash would not be intended to pay general operating expenses. Consequently, the difference between nonprofit organizations that are subject to some oversight by a governmental body and those that are not is quite significant and has considerable implications, some good and some unfortunate.

Setting Up the Budget Numbers

Budgets, according to Knezevich (1973, p. 111), are to serve as "instruments of fiscal responsibility and control" and are to provide "a disciplined way to manage expenditures.' Budgets should be monitored through a preplanned and orderly process to ensure that (1) revenue is received, (2) the amount of money spent does not exceed the amount of revenue awarded, and (3) the allocations are spent according to the budget plans. In order for managers to monitor receipts and expenditures, the organization sets up a budget-numbering format. The numbers used in this format are called budget numbers. While budget numbers are sometimes confused with accounting numbers, these are two different sets of numbers. A major point in this book is that the two sets of numbers must be designed so that two systems are integrated. This can be accomplished through an arrangement whereby the budget numbers and accounting numbers are merged into a common set of numbers at some point in their numbering schemes. Thus, the budget-numbering framework described below is set up so that it can be merged with the accounting numbers to ensure the integration of the two systems. (The merging of these two sets of numbers is described in Chapters Six, Seven, and Eight.)

The merging of the two sets of numbers is one way to respond to the concern expressed by Charles A. Bowsher, comptroller of the United States, who states that "good financial information underscores the need for well-designed, integrated budgeting and accounting systems" (1988, pp. 58–59). He continues that "because current systems are not integrated, budgets are frequently developed without reliable information on what has occurred." Bowsher argues that systems should be consistent across all agencies so that any differences in financial data are due to "differences in fact rather than differences in the accounting treatment of the same facts."

Principle 10, part b, of the GAAP provides that funds, sources of revenue, programs, organizational units, activities, characters, and classes of objects are to be classified through the use of budget numbers. This text recommends a numbering format that identifies each fund and, within each fund, each revenue source, each budget unit, and the different expenditure categories used by the organization. One very elaborate numbering scheme being implemented by a large national operation even has a number for every possible supply item that could be purchased. Needless to say, the maintenance of this budget-numbering system will be expensive, which could be a problem, since the cost of the maintenance of the system should not be greater than the savings in labor and control provided by the structure. The numbering arrangement described below should be viewed as a suggestion, since the format used by an organization should be designed to fit the operation of that organization.

There are several popular misunderstandings regarding budget numbers. First, there is no universal, standardized budget-numbering framework for public and nonprofit organizations. Some authors (Hartman, 1988; Kehoe, 1986; Matkin, 1985) discuss the budget framework and details of the budget structure in reference to the method used to prepare the budget, such as line-item versus program budgeting or centralized versus decentralized, or a method that relates to the activities of the organization. Although there may be some standardization within a particular group of organizations (such as universities), their budget numbers will not be the same because of the differences from one end of the spectrum (a small private college) to the other (a large land-grant state university). Another point of confusion between accounting numbers and budget numbers is found in some organizations that operate with a single-entry accounting method and incorrectly refer to their numbers as "accounting numbers." This causes confusion when an accounting auditor looks for the accounting numbers and instead finds a budget-numbering scheme.

Because budget numbers are not accounting numbers, the description of the budget-numbering structure for an organization is most likely to be found in the description of the organization's financial procedures (for example, how to process a purchase order) or in a computer operations guide rather than in its accounting manuals. The budget-numbering system is often an arrangement worked out by the business manager or accountant or between the business manager and a computer programmer.

In some large organizations with a central computerized budget system, a complaint is heard that the budget numbers and reports are established for the benefit of the computer and not the manager. For example, because a computer has a limited number of columns, the budget reports use symbols (such as > or *) and subtotals important to the computer, but there is usually no index to the symbols and totals on the printouts. In one organization, when the auditors requested a manual describing the format for a printout, none could be found (and it is doubtful that one ever existed). In another case, a state investigator assigned to audit several budget awards made to an institution became extremely frustrated with the customized monthly computer printouts, because a manual was not available and footnotes describing the symbols and subtotals were not provided on the printouts. The bookkeepers used a manual method instead of the printouts to reconcile the budgets, and they could not adequately communicate the meaning behind the symbols, subtotals, and differences in column totals. The auditor was sure that there was a plot to cover up improper expenditures. Eventually, he found a unit manager who explained the computer printouts, which then permitted a comparison of the printout information with the manual reports prepared by the bookkeepers. The auditor left in an angry state of mind and with a considerable loss of respect for the people in the organization. This example illustrates how important it is for managers buying a commercial computer software package or a central computer system to be sure that it is integrated and user friendly.

The budget-numbering framework should be an outline that identifies each source of revenue, the fund receiving the revenue, the units to which the money was allocated, and how the revenue was spent. This framework may use any number of digits. An example of a budget-numbering format using ten digits is as follows:

Digits	Designation
First and second	Fund (operational, self-support, restricted, and so on)
Third and fourth	Revenue source (local, state, federal, earned income, donations, and so on)
Fifth and sixth	Unit or activity, sometimes called function, assigned a budget (division, department, and so on)
Seventh through tenth	Expense category, sometimes called the object of expenditure

or object code (salaries, supplies, travel, and so on)

With this format, the funds could be given numbers from 01 to 99 (not 00, as this may cause problems with some computer programs). Each fund could have ninety-nine revenue sources with numbers from 01 to 99, and there could be from one to ninety-nine units assigned a budget in the organization. In cases where budget units are located at different geographical sites, the first digit could represent the location, or a three-digit number could be used, with the first number representing the site. The numbers for expense categories would be the same for all budgets in the organization. With the format above, these categories may use numbers from 0001 to 9999. Thus, using an X to represent each digit, a budget number would appear as XX-XX-XX-XXXX, with the first two X's representing the fund, the next two representing the revenue source, the next two representing the budget unit, and the last four representing the expense category.

This number format could be used by most organizations. Although in some cases more numbers are needed, some organizations may feel the need to add numbers "just in case." In one organization, a twenty-four digit number was used when only six digits were needed. This created extra zeros and made the budget reports difficult to read, which increased the probability of error.

With the above format, a specific budget chart for an organization could be organized as follows:

Fund Numbers

01	Operations
02	Self-support
03	Restricted
04	Fixed-asset
05	Debt
06	Physical plant

Revenue Source Numbers

01–09	Local government
10–19	State government

20–39	Federal government
40–59	Private donations
60–79	Income operations
90–99	Internal resources

Budget Unit Numbers

01	Central management
02	Business office
03	Personnel
04	Physical plant
05	Director of programs
06	Department A
07	Department B
08	Office of public service

Expenditure Category Numbers

1200	Salaries—regular employees
1210	Salaries—part-time employees
1230	Hourly wages
1290	Extra compensation
2100	Supplies
3010	Telephone installation
3020	Telephone
3050	Travel
3060	Subscriptions
3100	Services—other
3110	Services—professional
3120	Services—educational and honoraria
3160	Computer services
3170	Textbooks and other publications
3210	Postage
3450	Rentals
4100	Equipment repairs
6100	Renovations
7100	Equipment
8440	Student awards

The following example illustrates how this budget chart would be used. The city of Intolerance was founded in the seventeenth century with the assumption that any deviation from the beliefs of the founders would not be tolerated. Because these beliefs were adhered to rather strictly by some people in the city, a Public Institute for Kindness (PIK) was established to promote tolerance.

PIK has two departments, shown in the above budget chart as Department A (budget unit 06) and Department B (budget unit 07), which are responsible for promoting kindness and handling complaints about intolerant behavior. Department A is assigned the east side of the city, and Department B is responsible for the west side. PIK has a fifteen-member board (five appointed by the mayor, five chosen from business and industry by the Chamber of Commerce, and five elected by the city residents), a chief executive officer (budget unit 01), a business office (budget unit 02), a personnel office (budget unit 03), a program director (budget unit 05) and a physical plant (budget unit 04).

In addition to receiving revenue from city, state, and federal sources, the organization may earn income through its office of public service (budget unit 08) by offering special-interest workshops and seminars and by providing personal counseling. The money received from the workshops and seminars is placed in the self-support fund (fund 02) and is used primarily for the salaries of the coordinator and secretary and for catered coffee, doughnuts, lunches, snacks, and so on for the people attending the workshops and seminars. It is important that PIK keep this money in a separate fund under a separate revenue account, because public tax revenue and grant money cannot be used to pay for food.

After all of the budgets are approved by the CEO and the board, the business manager allocates money to each budget unit (numbers 01 through 08). The disbursement of the revenue for PIK is shown in the chart in Exhibit 2. This chart reveals the following information:

1. The operating fund (fund 01) has combined the revenue received from the local government (revenue account 01), state government (revenue account 10), a federal program grant (revenue account 20), and private donations (revenue account 40)

Exhibit 2. Revenue Disbursement Chart.

Fund	Revenue Accounts	Budget Units
01—Operation	01, 10, 20, 40	01, 02, 03, 05, 06, 07
02—Self-Support	60	08
03—Restricted	41	06
	42	08
	11	06
04—Fixed-Asset	10	02
05—Debt		
06—Physical Plant	90	04

for budget allocations to central management (budget unit 01), the business office (budget unit 02), the personnel office (budget unit 03), the program director (budget unit 05), Department A (budget unit 06), and Department B (budget unit 07). Organizations often call this budget the operating, or general, budget, because it represents money from the operating, or general, fund for daily or general operations.

2. The self-support fund (fund 02) has one source of revenue, income earned (revenue account 60), which is distributed to the office of public services (budget unit 08).

3. The restricted fund (fund 03) shows three sources of revenue: two donations and a grant. One donation (revenue account 41) has been restricted for the east side (Department A, budget unit 06) for special workshops for an especially intolerant section of the city. The second donation (revenue account 42) was made to the public services office (budget unit 08) for the purchase of new furniture. The third revenue source (revenue account 11) is a state grant provided to Department A (budget unit 06) to gather data for analysis in reference to the special workshops to be offered in the intolerant section.

4. The fixed-asset fund (fund 04) has one revenue source, provided through the state budget (revenue account 10) and designated for the business office (budget unit 02) to buy computer equip-

ment in order to install a new double-entry accounting processing system.

5.   The loan in the debt fund (fund 05) has been paid off, and the
     fund is not in active use.

6.   The physical plant fund (fund 06) has the use of revenue ac-
     count 90 for the internal transfer of money from other budget
     units to the physical plant budget (budget unit 04) for services
     provided by the physical plant.

   A master list of the revenue accounts and budget units would
be a useful reference for those reviewing such a chart, as well as
preparing budget forms, reviewing budget reports in relation to the
cash flow, making allocations, and modifying the allocations after
the budget award is made.

   When a budget unit in PIK makes an expenditure, a number
is used to identify the fund, budget unit, and expenditure category
on the appropriate form (such as a purchase order, requisition,
wage payroll, and so on). For example, when Department A (budget
unit 06) makes an expenditure of $2,300 for salaries (expense cate-
gory 1200) against the general operations budget (fund 01), the
budget number on the salary payroll form is 01-06-1200. In some
cases, the business manager may have to record charges against a
specific revenue source budget used for the general budget allocation in order to show specific line-item charges against a line-item
budget award. Because the operating fund has several revenue
sources being used for the allotment to Department A, the business
office would then have to charge the $2,300 against the budget of
one or more of the revenue sources (such as local tax revenue 10)
used in the allocation.

   If a budget unit receives an allocation from more than one
revenue source in the same fund, it may have to identify which
revenue source should be charged when an expenditure is made. For
example, Department A (budget unit 06) has two allocations (revenue sources 41 and 11) in the restricted fund (fund 03). When
Department A makes an expenditure from one of the budgets, the
form must identify which revenue source should be charged. Thus,
a purchase of supplies charged to 3-11-06-2100 indicates that the
state grant (revenue account 11) is being charged. In order to be

consistent, an organization may have the budget units indicate which revenue source should be charged and use a 00 or 99 digit if the general operating budget in the operating fund is to be charged. Thus, if supplies were purchased by Department A from the general operating budget, the number for the supplies charge would be 01-00-06-2100 or 01-99-06-2100. If required, the business office would then apply this charge to one of the four revenue source budgets.

Budget Reports

Budget reports are internal working documents for managers and board members, in contrast to financial statements, which are prepared by the accounting system for public and governmental distribution. There are two basic types of budget reports needed by an organization: one for revenues and one for expenditures. The revenue report is a greater concern for the business officer, the managers in central administration, and the governing body than for the managers of the budget units. On the other hand, reports on expenditures are important to the managers of the budget units, the business manager, the administrative managers, and the board.

Although the variations in budget formats are interpreted by some people as indicating that incorrect forms are being used, the information contained in budget reports is dependent on the budget method (such as line-item, program, PPBS, and so on), the format of the budget structure, the funds in the organization, the hierarchical arrangement of the management structure, personal preferences with respect to the innumerable renditions that may be created, and so on. Revenue and expenditure reports may be shown on separate pages or on the same page; they may show expenditures in relation to revenues; they may show year-to-year comparisons; and they may show percentages in terms of revenue received or expenditures made for each account in relation to the budgeted amount, to the budget total, to prior years, to prior months, and so on. For example, a transportation system in one large city produces each month a complex, three-part, thirty-one-page revenue and expenditure budget report that is extremely comprehensive and complicated.

As Hartman (1988) points out, an organization's budget report must be designed to meet the specific needs of management.

Regardless of the design, the budget reports must inform managers (1) how much revenue has been received, (2) how much of the revenue has been spent, and (3) whether the money is being spent according to the awarded budget plan. This information should then help managers to ensure that the organization's expenditures are in line with its revenue; as Matkin (1985, p. 259) puts it, to overexpend is a "cardinal sin," and to underspend "often carries sanctions."

Revenue Reports. Revenue budget reports show how much revenue has been promised to an organization and how much of this expected revenue has been received. The information for the revenue reports is provided by the accounting system. There should be a budget revenue report for each fund showing all of its sources of revenue, as well as a report on all of the funds in the organization. An example of a budget report for the revenue in the operations fund (01) in PIK is provided in Exhibit 3. This revenue report shows that of the $468,000 awarded to the operations fund, there is an outstanding balance of $20,850. A look at reports from previous years will enable a comparison with the receipts in those years. More importantly, managers must compare this report with the expenditures report discussed below to determine the relationship between the amount of revenue received and the expenditures.

Exhibit 3. Sample Revenue Report.

Public Institute for Kindness
Operations Fund (#01)
BUDGET REPORT—REVENUES
May 31, 1991

Revenue Account #	Revenue Source	Budget Award	Received to Date	Balance
01	Local tax	$295,000	$289,000	$ 6,000
10	State tax	153,500	141,150	12,350
20	Federal tax	14,500	12,000	2,500
40	Optimist club	5,000	5,000	---
	Totals	$468,000	$447,150	$20,850

Expenditure Reports. What information should be provided in an expenditure report depends on the management level receiving the report. For example, a budget unit needs an expenditure report that provides the balance for each expenditure category in its budget allocation. A composite of two or more budget unit expenditure reports is needed for managers who are responsible for two or more budget units, such as the director of programs in PIK, who would receive a budget report showing the expenditures of Departments A and B. By looking at these reports as well as the budget report for the director's office, the director can work with a larger budget picture and perhaps make revisions in the allocations, if necessary. Finally, a summary budget report on the expenditures in a fund provides a breakdown for each budget unit in the fund; another summary report may be generated for all of the funds in the organization. These summary budget reports are important to the managers in central administration, the business manager, and the governing body.

The information reported in the budget expenditure reports comes from the accounting system. This information must include the amount of money allocated, encumbered, and expended and a balance for each expenditure category or budget unit. (Some budget reports may also present comparisons in dollar amounts and percentages for the amount of money spent to date, spent in previous years, projected to be spent by the end of the year, and so on.) Encumbrances represent money that is committed but not actually spent. For example, if an organization sends out a purchase order, the accounting system immediately encumbers, or sets aside, the amount of money that it will need to pay for the order when it arrives. (This category is labeled "committed," on some budget computer printouts; the proper term, however, is *encumbered.*) At one time, orders were typically not encumbered unless the amount exceeded a specified level, such as $1,000, because of the extra work involved with encumbrances. In recent years, however, the computer has allowed organizations to automatically encumber every purchase and salary contracted for the year, regardless of the amount.

Two examples of expenditure budget reports for PIK are provided in Exhibits 4 and 5. Exhibit 4 shows a summary report for the operations fund. This summary shows that the operations fund

Exhibit 4. Sample Expenditure Summary.

Public Institute for Kindness
Operations Fund (#01)
EXPENDITURE SUMMARY
May 31, 1991

Budget Number	Budget Unit	Amount Budgeted	Encum- brances	Actual Expenditures	Balance
01	Central management	$100,449	$ 9,777	$ 88,407	$ 2,265
02	Business office	41,970	4,256	36,343	1,371
03	Personnel	34,672	3,819	26,934	3,919
05	Program director	56,519	3,492	50,653	2,374
06	Department A	115,690	12,203	101,412	2,075
07	Department B	118,700	11,704	102,412	4,584
	Totals	$468,000	$45,251	$406,161	$16,588

and all of the budget units in the fund are in a good financial position as they enter the last month of the fiscal year. Most of the encumbrances are for salaries, and the balances are not too large, except possibly that for the personnel department. A follow-up check with the personnel officer might be useful in order to ensure that the $3,919 will be spent. The report also indicates that to date there has been a cash expenditure of $406,161 and that $45,251 is encumbered.

A comparison of these figures with those in the revenue report for the operations fund (Exhibit 3), which shows $447,150 received to date, reveals that the cash expenditures as of May 31 are covered. However, when the encumbrances ($45,251) are added to the cash expenditure ($406,161) and subtracted from the revenue received to date, there is a negative balance of $4,262. The cash flow—that is, the cash received minus the expenditures—must be followed closely in the month of June. If PIK is not required to spend all of the money in the operations fund by the end of the year but is permitted to retain a residual balance of 10 percent, or approximately $45,000 in the operation fund from one year to the next, a late receipt of revenue will not be a problem in June.

It must be noted here that cash payments for grants and special projects supported by state and federal governments as well as foundations are often made on a predetermined schedule, which may cause cash-flow complications. These payment schedules differ from institution to institution, but the following example is illustrative: On a $20,000 project, a payment schedule is established whereby the organization will receive 25 percent ($5,000) of the award within the first thirty days of the project, 50 percent ($10,000) after a midyear project report is received and approved, and a final payment of 25 percent ($5,000) after the final project and expenditure reports are received and approved. If the final expenditure report for the $20,000 grant shows that $18,000 was spent, the final cash payment will be $3,000 rather than $5,000 (a popular misconception is that the organization would receive the total amount and then return $2,000 to the granting agency). Because the final report cannot be submitted until after the project has been completed, the organization would have to have $3,000 to cover the project expenditures until the final expenditure report had been prepared, submitted, and approved and the final payment made.

Exhibit 5 shows a unit budget expenditure report for Department A as of May 31, 1991. The critical components, or bottom line, in this report are the balances for each budget category. The encumbrances column shows that the total amount allotted for salaries for the year has been set aside or expended, $760 worth of supplies are on order, the monthly telephone rental or $75 for the last month of the fiscal year (June) remains encumbered, $86 in travel has been committed, there is a printing job in process for $150, and a mailing for $35 has been committed. An encumbered equipment repair order is scheduled for an annual maintenance service visit due on June 15 if the money is available. In the balance column, the first concern should be with equipment repair, where there is an overexpenditure of $15, which must be corrected by taking $15 from another category or canceling the annual maintenance service. In addition, the balance in the printing category is quite low, and more money should possibly be transferred into this category if there are plans to have more documents printed for the beginning of the new fiscal year.

Exhibit 5. Sample Budget Expenditure Report.

Public Institute for Kindness
General Operations Budget
BUDGET REPORT—EXPENDITURES
Department A (#06)
May 31, 1991

Account Number	Account Name	Amount Budgeted	Encum- brances	Actual Expenditures	Balance
1200	Salaries	$ 96,000	$11,000	$ 85,000	$ --
1230	Wages	12,000		10,400	1,600
2100	Supplies	2,500	760	1,660	80
3020	Telephone	1,500	75	1,390	35
3050	Travel	1,440	86	1,076	278
3170	Printing	900	150	741	9
3210	Postage	1,100	35	977	88
4100	Equipment repair	250	97	168	(15)
	Totals	$115,690	$12,203	$101,412	$2,075

As may be noted in both the revenue and expenditure budget reports, additional information on these reports could be helpful to the manager. For example, did equipment repairs exceed the budgeted amount at the same time last year? If this is an annual problem, the new budget proposal should reflect it. What was the printing allocation as compared to last year? If the printing allocation is inadequate, the budget proposal should be revised or there is a need for better planning. Such questions are always asked in a board meeting but are difficult to answer without the proper data on hand.

Managing the Budget Modifications

As discussed previously, modifications to a budget may take place at any time during the fiscal year. Three types of modifications may be made after a budget award is made: budget amendment, which is a change in the allocation of money from one expenditure category to another or from one budget unit to another; a budget supplement, which is made when additional money is added to an existing budget award; and a budget cut, which takes place after a budget award has been made and allocated because some of the revenue either will not be received or must be given back.

Budget modifications must appear in the allocated budget reports, and the operating plans should be revised accordingly. These changes should follow a formal process that corresponds to the procedures and method used to prepare the original budget for approval (such as line-item, PPBS, ZBB, and so on). When an amendment is made to a budget and an allocation is transferred from one budget category to another, it may simply require the manager to make the change in the computer. In some organizations, however, an amendment cannot be made without the permission of the governing board or organization providing the money, such as a government office awarding a grant.

Budget Amendments. Amendments may create stress when it is uncertain whether approval will be received for a transfer, but the most frustrating factor related to a budget amendment involves the imaginary budget line discussed earlier. In many organizations, managers may make a budget transfer either between categories below the line (such as from supplies to travel) or between categories above the line (such as from salaries to wages) but not from a category below the line to one above the line (such as from wages to supplies) or vice versa. The ostensible reason for restricting transfers over the budget line is to ensure that a specified amount will be spent to hire personnel and not be used for exotic trips or plush furnishings.

If this restriction were instituted in the case of PIK, the large balance shown for wages in the expenditure report for Department A (Exhibit 5) could not be transferred to any of the categories below the line; the unspent money in wages could be transferred only into the salaries category or possibly from Department A to Department B. One way around this problem, which is not technically appropriate but is not unethical or illegal, would be for Department A to work out a trade with Department B; for example, Department

B might pay the equipment contract in exchange for wage payroll money. This option may not please some administrators but is often used by managers to the benefit of their organizations.

A governing board may require that it approve all amendments before they are made, may prefer simply to be informed of amendments after the fact, or may require that it act on all amendments above a specified dollar amount and simply be informed about amendments under that amount before they are made. Some governing bodies permit budgets to be amended at any board meetings, while others permit them to be made only at set times of the year, such as quarterly. Restricting the times when amendments may be made helps to make board meetings shorter and more efficient, as budget discussions can eat up hours of a board meeting, but this also means that a budget deficit will continue on the report until the board meeting when amendments can be approved.

In an organization that requires all expenditures to be frozen, or remain unprocessed, in a budget category with a deficit, the need to wait for a board meeting for an amendment approval causes considerable complications; in the real world of some organizations, managers use procedures to get around the problem, such as using other budget categories to process an expenditure and then transferring the charge back after the amendment is made. These actions simply create more work and often cause problems in a budget system because improper budget category numbers are used to "trick" the computer. In one case, a clerk who learned how to trick the computer embezzled nearly $20,000 before being caught.

If amendments are delayed but purchases can still be processed against an overdrawn budget category, another set of problems can be created. When an expenditure is made in a category with a negative balance, the negative amount is increased and must be mentally subtracted from another budget category or several categories with positive balances. Then, when other expenditures are processed against the categories with positive balances, the future effect of the budget amendment may be forgotten. Thus, the deficit is compounded. As a result, budget amendments should be made as soon as possible, and following approval, the budget records should be immediately adjusted, and the amendment should be noted formally on all future budget reports.

Budget Supplements. When a budget supplement is awarded to cover an overexpenditure or to expand programs, it must be immediately entered into the accounting system and shown in the budget records. More importantly, all budget supplements, as well as amendments, should be carefully processed through the managers, CEO, and governing board in the organization in the same manner that the original budget proposal was processed. When a budget proposal is processed, managers should sign a form indicating their formal approval of the program and budget. The same managers who approved the original proposed budget should formally provide signature approval for all amendments and supplements to that budget and the corresponding program changes.

Budget supplements and amendments are a serious concern, because they may mean that an organization is agreeing to modify the way the revenue will be spent to support its activities. If supplements and amendments are not properly approved, the result can be a program or department run by people outside the organization. This is a method that allows one organization to set up a conduit in another organization, which means that one organization uses another to spend money.

In a recent tragic scandal where budget amendments and supplements were used to set up a conduit, money was given to an institution ("Institution X") by another organization ("Organization Y") to set up a center to offer services that complemented the mission of Institution X. All program proposals for this center were properly processed by Institution X, and as the center grew in popularity and level of services provided, so did the amount of money awarded to Institution X for the center.

Eventually, officials in Organization Y became more active in the supervision of the operations of the center. As the programs expanded, this supervision became more direct, and frequent budget amendments and supplements were generated. Over time, because the use of the amendments and supplements became common, Organization Y was no longer required by Institution X to follow proper procedures for the approval of budget changes. In time this led to the bypassing of Institution X's manager who was assigned to oversee the center. Next, other procedures were bypassed, including the requirement that formal bids be solicited for contracts because a contractor was specified in the budget supplement provided by Organization Y.

Eventually, money was supplied to the center in Institution X through budget supplements initiated by Organization Y and then spent for contracts that bypassed the bidding process. In turn, the contractors provided kickbacks to the official in Organization Y who authorized the revenue award for the budget supplements to Institution X. Thus, unknown to Institution X, a conduit was set up. As a result of the failure of Institution X to follow proper procedures, the center and the careers of the vendors and the official who received the kickbacks were destroyed, and the reputations and jobs of many innocent employees were lost. Unfortunately, after an investigation was completed, the managers in Institution X did not recognize (or did not choose to recognize) the cause of the problem and did not set up strict procedures for the processing of all amendments and supplements. As a result, history has the opportunity to repeat itself.

Budget Cuts. Budget cuts may be the result of economic change or poor financial forecasting. If strict procedures are followed in appropriation accounting and the allocated budgets are not modified after a budget award, a problem can be created if the allocation was too optimistic. Eventually, the organization will have to face up to the shortfall in revenues and either cut the allocated budgets or freeze expenditures. In some cases, the next step is to find someone or some economic situation to blame for the optimism.

Summary

The approved and adopted budgets are the input to the third budget subsystem. After a budget is approved, allocations are made to the budget units. The amount of revenue to be received is provided by the adopted budget. The expenditures against the allocations and the revenue receipts have to be monitored, or controlled, by the organization.

The organization's accounting and budgeting systems must interact in order for managers to monitor the budget allocations and the revenue receipts. This is accomplished when the budget and accounting systems use a common set of numbers at some point in their numbering schemes. The budget numbers for an organization must identify each fund and then each revenue source, budget unit, and expenditure category in the fund.

Through the accounting system, budget reports are generated that show the status of the revenue received by the organization along with the amount of money that has been expended and committed to be expended by each of the budget units. The ultimate task for managers is to use these reports to ensure that the amount of money spent does not exceed the amount of money allotted to each budget category and that the amount of money spent or encumbered to be spent does not exceed the amount of cash in the organization.

A feature that can complicate the management of a budget is a modification of a budget award after it has been received. A budget modification may be an amendment, which is a change in the distribution of money in a budget; a supplement, which is the receipt of additional money for a budget award; or a budget cut. These budget modifications are important to managers for two reasons. First, they require that the plans and activities of the organization be formally changed to correspond to the budget modification. Second, when these changes occur, they must be acted on by all of the managers who reviewed and acted on the original budget proposal.

5

Making
the
Budget System
Work

This chapter completes the description of the budget system by discussing the process in budget subsystem 3 that is concerned with control over receipts and expenditures. The subsystem output, an accurate budget report at the end of the year, is dependent on proper control. In addition, budget control is extremely important to the general management of an organization; for example, it is necessary if operational decisions are to take into account resource availability and consumption.

Although public finance is beyond the scope of this text, it must be noted that accurate budget information is critical to the larger financial management picture of an organization. A primary factor enabling a public or nonprofit organization to attract public revenue is its ability to demonstrate that its resources are being used efficiently and effectively. The word *efficiency* in the context of public finance means that the benefits produced by an organization justify the costs of producing those benefits (Breneman and Nelson, 1981; Coombs and Hallak, 1987); this is determined through a cost-benefit analysis. This corresponds to the suggestion presented by Principle 9, part c, of the GAAP that budget comparisons be presented in financial statements.

While the criteria used to measure benefits are complex, costs are easily obtained from accounting records and budget reports. However, when an organization presents costs (as unit costs, total costs, average costs, current versus inflationary costs, capital costs, and so on), it must make this information available and be able to guarantee that it is accurate, which is possible only if appropriate accounting and budgeting systems are maintained. For example, a school may wish to demonstrate that its operation is cost-efficient by comparing its instructional-hour costs and administrative overhead with national or state averages. This requires knowing the proportion of its costs attributable to instructional and administrative activities (as opposed to counseling, clerical, coaching, and other costs), as well as how many hours of instruction were delivered. Or a police department might want to break down its costs by patrol hours to provide a better measure of services than a count of arrests.

Current practices in the budget control process may best be understood in the context of the changes in budgeting philosophy that led to the development of the different budgeting methods described in Chapter Three and to the establishment of the use of cost-benefit analysis ratios. As Schick (1988) explains, budget control was at one time the responsibility of the guardians of an organization, such as a governing body, who were external to the organization or government agency. As a result, an organization would have to obtain approval from the external body before it could make arrangements with a vendor, place an order, authorize an employee to take a trip, or make any other type of expenditure, and this approval could take an immeasurable amount of time. Later, control shifted to an internal operation that permitted professional managers to authorize expenditures by the organization by following the rules and policies set forth by the governing board. However, in some cases (such as an expensive foreign trip), a board might reserve the right to make approvals on an individual basis. Schick feels that more important than the procedural change was the change in attitude about budget control: the passing of the responsibility for expenditure control from a governing body to the professional managers. He is concerned, however, about how well current control practices are functioning and whether new methods of budget control are needed or the current practices simply need to be managed more effectively. As Bowsher (1988) notes, effective budget control requires modern integrated accounting and budgeting systems; Principle 9, part b, of the GAAP states that the accounting system is to provide the basis for budget control.

The concerns about budget control expressed by Schick, Bowsher, and the GAAP are not atypical. The focus for this control must be on the receipt of money provided in revenue awards in exchange for services or goods, as well as budget expenditures. Each organization should establish a set of procedures that takes into account its unique individual situation: the size and number of its budgets, the number and type of funds it uses, its sources of revenue, its hierarchical structure, legal restrictions on its operations, and so on. Then it must ensure the integration of its accounting and budgeting systems. This means that the budget system feeds budget information into the accounting system, and, in turn, the accounting records are used in the preparation of budget reports, both the reports utilized by the budget system for control purposes and the end-of-year reports. Once this system is operational, the organization can implement new and more sophisticated ideas about control and expansion as well as the creation of larger enterprises.

Overview of the Budget Management Process

Making the budget system work requires a detailed management program to process and control revenue and income receipts and budget expenditures. Attending to the nitty-gritty details of the budget management program is often seen as a dry and boring task. It is true that setting up the management program is not an exciting intellectual exercise for many managers and is not seen to be directly related to the offering of day-to-day services; however, establishing such a program requires an understanding of the mission and structure of the organization as well as a knowledge of accounting and budgeting systems.

Brown (1988) outlines several key internal control elements that should be part of a budget management program, such as adequately trained employees with clear lines of authority, a separation of duties among employees, proper authorization procedures, appropriate documents (such as purchase orders), adequate records for all expenditures, and physical control over assets and records. In addition, Anthony (1988) points out that a budget program must be able to relate current spending to planned spending, to the programs provided by the organization, and to the managers responsible for supervising the expenditures; and Gross and Warshauer (1979) note the importance of cross-checking in the budget control process. These activities must be built into the planned budget management programs of all organizations. Once the basic components have been put together into a program, the organization should tailor its program to meet its own unique needs.

Expenditures. The foundation of a budget management program for expenditure control is a two-way communication process between the budget unit and the business office. This process should include the people who initially reviewed and approved the budget proposal, who were involved in the allocation of the budget award to the budget unit, and who are responsible for the supervision of the budget unit.

When a manager of a budget unit wishes to make a budget expenditure, the information related to the expenditure (such as fund, cost, unit budget number, expenditure category, vendor, date, and so on) is entered on a form, signed by the unit manager, and then processed through the appropriate offices in the organization to the central business office. The managers in each office review the request and indicate their approval by signing the form. When the form reaches the business office, the budget is checked for sufficient funds and, if the funds are adequate, the business manager approves the expenditure. When the order is placed, an entry is made in the accounting system. After the order is received and payment is made, another entry is made in the accounting system. Using the accounting entries, the business office prepares a budget report to be used for the monitoring and control of the budget by the unit managers. The budget report thus is the instrument used to communicate information from the business office to the manager of the budget unit. In addition, each person who previously reviewed and approved the forms containing the expenditure requests should receive a copy of the budget report.

Each office that participates in the processing of the expenditure form should maintain records of the requests. When the periodic budget reports are received, the budget unit and each of these offices should reconcile the budget report with its budget records. This reconciliation, which is described in detail below for a manual and a computer operation, is a cross-check between the entries in the accounting system that prepared the budget reports and the records in the budget system.

Receipts. The basic objective of a management process for receipts and earned income is to have total control over all revenue and income at the time it is received by an employee in the organization (Gross and Warshauer, 1979). As with the process followed for budget expenditures, the process for handling revenue and income receipts must establish a two-way communication process.

When money is received by mail in a central office, a record is made by the employee who opens the mail, the money is transmitted for deposit via an exchange of receipts between employees, and then, upon deposit, a record is made in the accounting system. When money is received by an employee directly, a receipt must be issued, and then the same process is followed as for money received by mail.

Periodically, a revenue budget report is prepared with the information from the accounting records. Each party receiving or processing money must receive a copy of the budget report in order to reconcile the report with receipt records and make a cross-check between the two systems. When the bank statements are received, they must be reconciled with the deposit records and accounting entries (discussed further in Chapter Seven). In addition, at unannounced times, a manager's or internal audit (discussed in Chapter Eleven) of the receipt records must be conducted for each employee receiving or processing money for deposit. Thus, as noted in the chapters on funds and the budget numbering format, the accounting and budgeting systems must ensure that each revenue and income source can be identified to make possible the reconciliation of budget reports and bank statements as well as the conducting of internal audits.

In sum, the management plan requires a strict set of basic rules that ensure that

1. Budget receipts and expenditures are processed through the proper offices.
2. Records are maintained by each office that processes expenditures or receipts.
3. Budget reports are distributed to the appropriate offices.
4. The offices receiving the budget reports compare them to their office records.

It is an old rule in accounting that if proper policies and procedures are established and followed at all times, a misappropriation will require a violation of procedures and thus will be easily detected. If too much flexibility is permitted in the system, the financial temptation will eventually become too great and the improper use of money by usually honest people will become inevitable; in other words, the risk becomes worth it. Gross and Warshauer (1979) propose that a moral responsibility of an employer is to set up a proper program with internal controls that will remove as much temptation as possible. When money, goods, or assets are pilfered, an extremely difficult question that managers have to ask themselves is whether the act was the result of employing a dishonest person or the result of placing too much temptation before an otherwise honest employee.

Revenue and Income Control

Upon the receipt of money by an organization, a manager has three immediate tasks. The first is to determine whether the money can be accepted and, if so, the terms of the agreement under which it is accepted. The receipt of money by an organization is part of a business transaction in which either goods or services have been or will be provided in exchange for that money. Such an agreement cannot be made without proper authorization. When a governing board approves a budget for the receipt of money from taxpayers, a government agency, or a self-support operation, it is authorizing the organization to offer services or goods and to accept the money that will be used to deliver these services or goods. In a case illustrating the necessity of such authorization, an employee of an institution entered into an agreement, on his own, to provide professional services to another organization. The other organization was prohibited by state regulations from paying the employee directly and so sent a check made out to the institution. However, the institution could not accept the check, even though the services provided were within the scope of the mission of the organization, because the agreement to provide them had not been authorized. The institution's managers refused to seek post hoc approval from the board, and so the check was returned and the employee was not reimbursed for either his time or his expenses. Proper prior authorization for such arrangements is important to the authority of the board and involves numerous legal issues, such as protection against claims that the services or goods were not acceptable, appropriate, or ethical.

After ensuring that the money may be accepted, the second task for the manager is to determine where in the organization the money will be received. Procedures will vary depending on whether the money is sent to an office or is collected by an employee from a client or customer. But regardless of the program for which the money is intended, the form in which it is received (such as a check, cash, purchase order, or credit arrangement), or who it comes from (such as taxpayers, a private party, another organization, or a collection agency), the procedures must be clearly described to ensure that there is control over the money at the time it is received.

The third task of the manager is ensuring the proper processing of the money through the organization and into the bank account. Again, the procedures will differ according to whether the money is received through the mail or directly from a customer. Although the two procedures are quite similar, the slight differences are significant. In both cases, an organization should

1. Establish a routine for handling all cash transactions (deviations are typically a clue that something is wrong).
2. Make sure that the money is received and the bank deposit made by two different people (*never* the same person).
3. Be sure that receipts of cash and disbursements (payments) are two separate activities and involve two different offices or at least two different people.
4. Make deposits and the corresponding entries in the accounting system daily for all receipts.
5. Have all receipts preprinted and prenumbered, with separate sets of receipts (possibly color-coded) given to each office receiving money.

Although these basic guidelines may seem to be elementary, they are not always followed, and their violation can be disastrous. In one situation, a bookkeeper took advantage of her institution over an extended period of time to the tune of more than a million dollars. She was able to do this because she was solely responsible for the receipt of all money, making the deposits, making the accounting entries, processing all expenditures, and writing the checks to pay for all goods and salaries. The governing board thought that it was saving money by having one person do the work of three, but in the end it created an enormous burden for the local taxpayers.

When a payment is received by a clerk at a counter or a secretary at a desk, either a cash register with a tape or a receipt book should be used. The list below provides a basic outline of procedures for handling receipts. These procedures require a minimum of three people: a clerk to receive the money, a bookkeeper or project director to whom the money is given by the clerk, and a business manager or member of the board (treasurer) who makes the deposit and the entry in the accounting system.

1.   When an employee receives a direct payment in the form of cash, check, purchase order, or credit card payment from a customer, the employee gives the customer either a prenumbered receipt from a receipt book or the receipt tape from a cash register. If a prenumbered receipt is used, the employee records on it the amount received, the name of the customer, a description of the service, and the date and then signs it.

2.   If a cash register is used, it provides a copy of the receipt given to the customer, indicating the form of payment. If a receipt book is used, the employee records on the receipt stub the date, the amount received, a description of the service, and the method of payment (cash, check number, purchase order number, or credit card). The employee then initials the stub if the receipt book is used by more than one employee.

3.   All checks are immediately endorsed with a hand stamp with the wording "Pay to (organization)." (This immediate endorsement provides one of the best means to protect a receipt.)

4.   All receipts are transmitted to the bookkeeper or project director at the end of the day with a cash register tape or cash transmittal form including the date, activity, budget unit, budget revenue or income name and number, and amount of cash collected, a list of checks and the amount of each, copies of credit card slips and purchase orders, and the total amount collected.

5. The cash transmittal form is signed by the employee who collected the payments and the bookkeeper or project director. A copy of the transmittal form is given to the employee delivering the money to the bookkeeper or project director, a copy is retained by the bookkeeper or project director, and a copy is enclosed with the receipts for forwarding to the person making the deposit.

6. The bookkeeper or project director submits the receipts with a copy of the transmittal form or cash register tape to the business manager or board treasurer for deposit into the bank account.

7. The business manager or board treasurer makes the bank deposit (using a deposit slip provided by the bank) and then makes the entry in the appropriate revenue or income account in the accounting records.

8. All deposits are reconciled with the bank statement and appear on monthly budget reports.

9. Copies of the budget reports are given to the person making the deposits, the bookkeeper, and the employee who collected the payment. Each person verifies the amounts on the budget reports with his or her records.

10. Internal audits are conducted frequently (and are unannounced) to compare the amounts on the receipt stubs or cash register tapes, cash transmittal forms, deposit forms, bank statements, and budget reports of the employee collecting the payments, the bookkeeper or project director, and the business manager or treasurer.

11. An audit is conducted by outside accountants at the end of the fiscal year.

In this process, the money received is recorded at the point of collection, the amount is transmitted to a second party, who verifies it, and then a third party makes the deposit and enters it into the accounting records. Thus, any embezzlement will require the cooperation of three parties who do not work together on a daily basis. Gross and Warshauer (1979) recommend a very similar set of procedures, except that they feel that cash collection should involve two people, such as the person taking the money and the person directing the program. These steps are not foolproof, but they do provide some protection, possibly the best that can be offered, to the receipts of the organization.

An example of what can happen when these procedures are violated involved a simple deviation from the recommended routine. In this case, the bookkeeper made out the transmittal forms herself and did not give copies to the employee collecting the money (violating steps 4 and 5). When the bookkeeper received the budget report for several income operations, she then prepared her own budget report for each of the activities (violating step 9). No internal audit was conducted (in violation of step 10). By chance, a chronic overexpenditure in one of the operations was noted; a review showed that the receipt records for this activity did not match the balance in the budget report. When an internal audit was finally conducted, it revealed that the bookkeeper had been depositing only the checks and pocketing the cash. The total amount from all of the activities in the income account was so great that the bookkeeper had been able to manipulate the expenditures to maintain a positive balance. As the bookkeeper explained to her supervisor, just before the police took her away, the temptation had been just too great. The money was first taken as a "loan," and then the "loan" became too large to repay. The embezzlement continued for more than two years, until eventually the "loaned" amount became so great that even the total amount collected by check for all activities in the account could not cover it. She knew that an overexpenditure was inevitable and that she would be caught.

When money is received by mail, the procedures are very similar to those outlined above except for the first two steps. The revised steps are these:

1. The employee who opens the mail counts the payments and lists them on a form or enters them into a cash register or computer.
2. At end of the day, that same person totals and records the amounts received.

Steps 3 through 11 are the same as above except that the employee gives the money to the bookkeeper for processing, along with the copy of the receipts record tape plus a cash transmittal form. In some cases, the person opening the mail may have to group the payments by revenue or income source and then make a separate record and transmittal form for each source.

There are two other ways to handle steps 1 and 2 above. First, for cash received by mail, a receipt may be filled out and returned by mail (some organizations refuse to accept cash payments). Second, Gross and Warshauer (1979) feel that two people should be present when the mail is opened and the money counted. If a second person (such as a program director but *not* the bookkeeper) is available, this would be very desirable.

Fidelity Bonds. One method used to offer protection for the money received by an organization is allowing only bonded or insured employees to handle it. Such employees are protected through fidelity bonds—which are insurance contracts that cover any fraud or embezzlement by a bonded employee up to a predetermined amount. This insurance does not cover thefts by employees who are not bonded or not employed by the organization and does not apply to business losses resulting from poor management practices or carelessness.

Fidelity bonds are considered to be effective because, while a public or nonprofit organization often will not press charges against an employee who has been dishonest, an insurance company will. Fidelity bonds are not expensive given the potential cost of embezzlement. When an organization files a claim under a fidelity bond, it must demonstrate to the insurance company that the illegal act has taken place; in other words, the internal records must be able to prove that an employee was dishonest. In some cases, a bonding company may wish to review the internal controls of the operation before providing any insurance or setting a fee. Thus, as Meigs and Meigs (1984) point out, a fidelity bond is not a substitute for internal control.

Expenditure Control

A business transaction is an economic exchange in which one party agrees to pay cash to another party in exchange for goods or services. These business transactions must follow a set of procedures that will protect both parties, much like those outlined above for the receipt of money. The procedures must be clear and precise to ensure that the exchange will be properly executed, the transaction will be recorded in the accounting system and reported in the budgeting system, and the payment will be made as agreed upon by both parties.

As with receipt of revenue, the authorization function is an important part of the budget expenditure process. With the change in the philosophy of budget execution, professional managers in public and nonprofit organizations now have the authority to make expenditures themselves rather than the governing board having to act on each transaction. Thus, after a budget has been awarded, the authorization to make an expenditure against that budget is given to the manager of the budget, except under exceptional circumstances as defined by the board. When the budget is allocated to the units in the organization, the managers of these units are then provided with the authority to make expenditures against their budget allotments; however, their superiors may reserve the right to review their expenditure requests. When a budget is not allocated throughout the organization but is centralized, the authority to make expenditures is retained by the manager of the central office.

The authorization of an expenditure and the approval of that expenditure are two different acts and should involve two different people. Authorization of an expenditure means that the expenditure is considered to be appropriate under the terms of the budget award. Approval, however, indicates that budget balances have been checked and the money is available. The person who approves the expenditure is usually in the business office. This person may make the transaction, or purchase, or it may be made by a third party. In a large organization, an expenditure may require the signatures of additional people, such as a supervisor of the manager of the budget unit, the purchasing agent, and a buyer who works directly with the vendors. In some cases, if the amount is over a specified number of dollars, an executive in the organization may also have to authorize the expenditure. In small organizations in which only one professional manager is employed, the manager may authorize the expenditure, a board member then approves it, and the manager then makes the purchase.

Forms. When initiating an expenditure, an organization should use a set of forms that creates copies when prepared to provide a written record of the transaction along with the authorization and approval signatures on all copies. These forms, which have the organization's name and address on all copies, may be extremely elaborate or quite simple, depending on the size of the organization. Following are descriptions of some of the basic types of forms that may be used by an organization. Note that the information to be entered on the form is not all provided by the initiating department but is added to the form as it is processed.

A *purchase order* is a form used to enter into a purchase transaction between the organization and an outside vendor. Purchase orders are prenumbered for record-keeping purposes and come in a set with carbon copies for the office that initiated the expenditure, the purchasing office, the buyer, the vendor, the business manager, the accounting department, equipment inventory (if appropriate), a cross reference for an alphabetical file, and the receiving department. The form provides spaces for information needed for the transaction, such as a description of the item to be purchased, the quantity, the unit price, the total amount, the address of the vendor, where the items are to be shipped, the authorization signature, budget numbers, accounting numbers, the date of the order, a phone number, a purchasing approval signature, a buyer's signature, the terms, the shipping agreement, the date needed, and any other information that may be relevant to the organization (contract numbers, sole-source agreements, and so on). In addition, on the back of the vendor's copy may appear a legal statement regarding the terms and conditions of the purchase, such as rights to cancel an order, inspection and acceptance of a shipment, protection against the sale of patents not authorized by a vendor, insurance on shipments, nondiscrimination, bankruptcy of the vendor, extra charges, taxes, buyer number, vendor number, a special section for equipment purchases, and so on.

A *quick order* is a form used to make a purchase for less than a specified dollar amount, such as $50 or $100 or $250, depending on the size of the organization. Quick orders are like regular purchase orders except that they go directly from the manager who authorizes the expenditure to a vendor, with copies to the accounting or business office and an extra copy to the vendor. An approval signature is not required before the form is released. After the vendor fills the order, the extra copy given to the vendor is returned with the invoice to the unit that initiated the order or to the accounting or business office that processes the payment. The information on the quick order is usually not as complete as that on a regular purchase order; it includes such data as a description of the item, quantity, unit price, total cost, budget numbers, accounting number, name of the vendor, name of the organization for shipment, date, and authorization signature. The legal terms and conditions of the purchase may appear on the back of the vendor's copy.

A *requisition,* or requisition for check, is used when a vendor requires a payment in advance or a check to be given to the initiating unit to be sent or given directly to a vendor on the delivery of goods or services, such as for an honorarium paid at the time a presentation is given, monthly bills with fixed amounts to be paid on a regular basis (telephone bill, rental payments), an employee who needs a cash advance for a trip, receipt of supplies for which the vendor requires a payment upon delivery, and so on. A requisition for a check may be drawn without any receipts or even a purchase agreement; however, a receipt for payments should be filed later and attached to the copy of the requisition. The information to be recorded on a requisition form includes the person or company to which the check is to be made payable, the address of that person or company, the date or dates when the check or checks are to be delivered, along with a detailed explanation for the request, special instructions with respect to the mailing of the check, the date of the request, the date the organization is to receive delivery, an authorization signature, an approval signature, budget numbers, accounting number, amount, and check number. In some cases, the requisition is accompanied by a purchase order (which is preferable, even though arrangements by a purchasing agent are not usually necessary), and the purchase order number must be noted on the requisition form. Copies of the requisition request are provided to the originating unit, business officer, accounting department, and any other department involved in the transaction, such as equipment inventory.

An *internal purchase order* is used when one department or fund requests goods or services from another department or fund within the organization. An internal purchase order should be prenumbered and provide such information as a description of goods or services, unit price, quantity, total amount, name of the requesting unit, name of the unit providing the goods or services, fund and budget numbers and accounting number to be charged, fund and budget numbers and accounting number of the unit to receive the payment, authorization signature, approval signature, and date of request. In some cases, a special approval is required if the transfer exceeds a specified amount, such as $50 or $125 depending on the size of the organization. Copies of the internal purchase order are provided to the unit making the request, the unit supplying the goods or services, the business officer, and the accounting department. Some organizations allow the use of "blanket orders" by which one department may transfer money to another department in advance in order to establish credit; for example, a department might transfer $100 to a supply store in order to pick up supplies as needed rather than having to prepare an internal purchase order each time.

Travel forms are used when employees are reimbursed for travel expenses. A travel form requires such information as the name and address of the person requesting reimbursement, date of the request, date of the travel, a list of expenses and their amounts, expense items, total amount requested, amount of any advance for travel via a requisition, total reimbursement, purpose of the travel, requestor's signature, authorization signature, approval signature, budget numbers, and accounting number. Copies of the form should be provided to the person making the request (to be used for income tax claims if the employer does not cover 100 percent of the expenses), the originating unit, the business officer, and the accounting department. The policy regarding travel reimbursement should be readily available to those filing for travel reimbursement, especially people who are not employees of the organization.

A *wage payroll form* is used to record information regarding hourly wages, which, unlike salaries, may vary from week to week.

This form indicates the name of the worker to be paid, Social Security number, dates and hours worked, hourly wage, total amount earned, budget numbers, accounting number, authorization signature, and approval signature. For regular hourly employees, a preprinted form may be used on which only the hours, total amount, and signatures must be entered. The office initiating the payment should have on record a form used by the hourly employee that provides the name and Social Security number of the employee, the date and hours worked, and the signature of the employee.

Because the authorization and approval signatures are critical records for expenditures, signature cards may be filled out by employees who authorize and approve expenditures. The information on a signature card includes the name of the employee, the budget number and name of the account for which the employee is authorized to make expenditures, the effective date, and the employee's signature. These cards are used by clerks to check signatures when processing forms. They come in handy when a new manager is hired and the clerks are not familiar with his or her signature (and also when a signature bears no resemblance to the name it represents). In addition, in some large organizations, an administrator may wish for a subordinate to sign his or her name. In such cases, the subordinate should sign a signature card with the superior's name and the subordinate's initials; for example, "James T. Smith/cwg." This signature then is used by the subordinate when signing all forms. A signature stamp is not recommended, because it could get into the wrong hands and be used improperly.

Disbursements. The actual disbursement of funds or payment by check is a separate act related to a transaction and is conducted by the accounting system. These payments, meaning the preparation and mailing of checks, should not be a part of or involve the same people providing the authorization and approval for an expenditure via the budgeting system. Although the procedures for making disbursements are discussed in detail in the description of the accounting system in this book, the important point here is the interaction between the budgeting system and the accounting system for the payment of goods and services.

A payment for goods or services is made after the budget unit informs the accounting or business office that a shipment has arrived or services have been rendered. Possibly the invoice will be forwarded by the budget unit to the business office and the payment will be made; however, the invoice may be sent directly to the business office. If it is sent directly to the business office, a payment should not be processed unless receipt of the goods or services is verified. A chronic problem in many large organizations is that verifications of receipt of goods or services are not forwarded to the business office or the budget unit does not forward the invoices for payment, and payments thus do not get processed. At the end of the fiscal year, this causes extreme problems in closing the books, not to mention the problems experienced by a vendor who is waiting for a check. However, it is even worse when an organization makes payments without any verifications. In some large organizations, a verification is required only for purchases above a specified amount, such as $1,000; this may save employee time but cannot honestly be defended, and such neglect is a management failure.

An important consideration in the purchase and payment of merchandise is the terms and conditions of the purchase. When a purchase order is processed, as explained in the last chapter, the money for the purchase is encumbered against the expenditure category in the budget. When the ownership of the goods purchased passes from the seller to the buyer, an accounting entry must be made (changing the status of the purchase from an encumbrance to an accounts payable in the accounting records and from an encumbrance to an expenditure on the budget reports). This transfer of ownership from the seller to the buyer is determined by the shipping agreement. This agreement also determines how much of the shipping is paid by each party.

A shipping agreement uses the term F.O.B., which means "Free On Board." If the shipping agreement is "F.O.B. Shipping Point," the seller places the goods on a carrier (such as a truck at the plant or a nearby freight train), and the buyer pays for the transportation from that point. In this case, the goods change ownership when they are placed on the carrier. If they are damaged after being placed on board, it is the buyer's problem. If the shipping agreement is "F.O.B. Destination," the seller pays for the transportation of the goods to the buyer and is responsible for any damage that may occur en route. For example, if the buyer is located in Philadelphia, a shipping agreement "F.O.B. Destination" means that the seller pays for the transportation of the goods to the buyer's location of business. If the seller agreed to pay the costs to the Philadelphia Airport, the terms would be "F.O.B. Philadelphia Airport." In this case, the buyer assumes responsibility for the goods at the airport and pays for any storage costs and possible damages while they are at the airport and the cost of transportation of the goods from the airport to the business location. Thus, when the buyer assumes the transportation charges, the ownership changes and an accounting entry is made; however, a payment is not made until an invoice is received. Usually, the transportation costs for the buyer are added to the cost of the goods purchased, whereas the transportation costs for the seller are considered to be a selling expense. This differentiation is important in determining the charges made against a budget category and in preparing financial statements.

Another important facet of the terms and conditions of a purchase is a discount. Most for-profit companies make a considerable effort to negotiate discounts when purchases are made, in order to lower costs. A typical discount agreement is noted as "2/10,n/30," which means that a 2 percent discount will be awarded if the bill is paid within ten days of the invoice date and otherwise the full amount (net) is expected within thirty days. Too often, such discounts are ignored or not negotiated by public and nonprofit organizations. With a little effort, a manager can get a discount at the time a transaction is made and then ensure that the payment is made on time. In one case, for example, a seller was more than pleased to give a discount on purchases of animal food in large quantities if the payment for the purchase was made within ten days of the date of the invoice. The more difficult task in this case was getting the organization to process an invoice within ten days.

Using Budget Reports and Office Records

A serious problem for many organizations is that the budget reports prepared by a central business office are not up to date. For example, assume that the PIK business office in the city of Intolerance sends each budget unit a report on the last day of each month. If the budget unit office maintains no records of expenditures, the managers of the unit will have no knowledge of changes in budget categories from one budget report to the next. Therefore, as time progresses, the budget report becomes more obsolete. This problem is compounded by the time required to generate budget reports. For example, if the PIK business office has to allow two working days for the staff to type the information or enter it into the computer, print out the reports, and then distribute them, the budget report will not include any of the expenditures processed over the last two or three days of the budget period. In addition, if the business manager must allow the office staff time to collect the latest information being processed, place it in the proper categories and columns, add the columns, and reconcile the balances, this will add another two to five working days to the time by which the budget is out of date. Thus, the information in the budget reports will be as current as four or more working days prior to the end of the month, rather than the last day of the month. In addition, when a manager receives a budget report on the first or second day of the month, the information will not include anything that is being processed from the budget unit to the business office over the previous four- or five-day period. Because of this four- to five-day period, the budget reports may now be eight to ten working days out of date when received. Consequently, the last budget report for a unit may not be of much use during the last half of the month because it will in reality be more than a month old. In at least one organization, budget reports are not even prepared during the summer months, which allows too much flexibility, requires managers to fly by the seat of their pants during the summer, and discredits the importance of the manager who has been authorized by the board to execute a budget.

To ensure that its budget reporting system provides up-to-date information every working day of the fiscal year, an organization may either institute a budget computer system with computer terminals for each office that has a budget or establish a manual filing system to complement the budget reports. Either of these will allow the bookkeeper or manager to check a balance in any budget category before authorizing an expenditure. This type of a check is called a *preaudit*. Budget computer systems that allow for instant preaudits are available in a variety of software formats for small as well as extremely large public and nonprofit organizations. These systems are the ideal solution to the problem.

With a computer system, each office with a budget can enter an expenditure request into the computer, the computer will check the balance in the budget category, and if there is an adequate balance in the budget category, the computer will forward the request to the next office, which, in turn, can verify the budget balance, approve the request, and transmit it to the next office via the computer. When the request reaches the business office, the computer can print out the expenditure request in the proper form. In addition, through the use of the computer, an office can determine the status of an expenditure request in the organization's system at any time and receive an up-to-the-minute budget report. In some cases, the computer is programmed to flag or refuse to process an expenditure that would overexpend a budget category or appear to the computer to be improper. For example, if Department A of PIK wanted to buy $200 of supplies from the general budget, the budget number 01-99-06-2100 would be entered into the computer. If the $200 was available, a purchase order could be prepared upon entry of the name of the vendor and the vendor's address. If the $200 charge would overexpend the balance in supplies, the computer could be set up to refuse to prepare the purchase order.

A printed computer-generated budget report usually uses a different budget report format than that presented in Chapter Four. These reports often provide a list of all the expenditures for each budget category for the budget period. Minimally, a computer printout should have the following columns for each budget category:

1. The beginning budget balance.
2. Encumbrances with a form number, such as a purchase order number.
3. Expenditures for the budget period with the form number, invoice number, check number, and date of payment.
4. The balance for the category.

Because a computer system with communication capabilities to each budget unit requires a considerable investment, an organization may choose instead to use a manual filing procedure so that each unit with a budget can maintain its own up-to-date budget. This budget process must complement the manual or computer format used to process the budget reports in the central business office. In one process, four file folders or filing sections (encumbrances, received, paid, and reconciled) were used and copies were simply moved from one folder to another, sometimes with notations. With the information in the folders, an up-to-date budget balance or budget report can be quickly prepared at any time. This process is outlined below.

Section 1: Encumbrances. When an expenditure request is authorized and forwarded to the next level for approval, a copy of the form used to process the expenditure (a purchase order form, wage payroll form, and so on) is placed in a file folder marked "encumbrances." Usually, there is one encumbrances folder for the entire budget; however, a different encumbrances folder could be used for each category in a budget. When the office budget report is updated from the files and the new encumbrances are added to the amount on the budget, a note that it has been entered is added to the copy of the form, which is then returned to the same file. When a computer printout is reconciled with these records, the encumbrances should be checked off on the budget printout, and those not appearing should be noted. If encumbrances appear on the printout and not in the folder, then the printout is in error.

An example of this process is as follows: Department A of PIK uses one encumbrances file folder for wages and another for nonwages. On June 5 a purchase order for $50 worth of supplies is sent to the director's office for processing, and a copy of the purchase order is placed in Department A's encumbrances file. When an up-to-date budget report is prepared by the clerk in Department A, the encumbrance for supplies is increased by $50, and the balance remaining to be spent in the category is reduced from $80 to $30.

Section 2: Received. When a delivery is received or service provided, the copy of the request form in the encumbrances file is marked "received" and moved to the "received" file. When the up-to-date budget report is prepared, the encumbrances for supplies do not change. In many organizations, the unit receiving the delivery informs the business office of the delivery (through a memo or an internal voucher) so that the business office can process the payment when the invoice is received. In some cases, the delivery may include the invoice, which is then forwarded to the business office. By using the received file, the clerk and manager can easily check to find out what has and has not been delivered. When deliveries have not been received after a specified period (30 days for example), a tracer (follow-up letter sent through the organization and to the vendor) should be processed.

For example, Department A of PIK has received $40 worth of the $50 supply order. The clerk makes two copies of the purchase order in the encumbrances file. A notation is made on the original and the two copies of the amount received ($40) and the amount not received ($10). The original is placed in the encumbrances file to show that $10 worth of supplies was not yet received, one copy goes into the received file to show the $40 of supplies received, and one copy (possibly with the invoice if it was included with the delivery) goes to the business office to show that $40 worth of the supplies has been received. The up-to-date budget is not changed, as the $50 is still encumbered and not paid.

Section 3: Paid. When the invoice is received and a payment made, the copy of the order form is moved from the received file to the paid file. If the department does not receive the invoice, it may be informed that the payment has been made through the computer budget report, or a copy of the invoice marked "paid" may be sent to the department after the check has been mailed. The department then changes the up-to-date budget by decreasing the amount in the encumbrance column and increasing the amount in the paid column. If there is a difference between the amount on the purchase order and the amount paid, the up-to-date budget should be modified accordingly.

For example, PIK has received an invoice for the $40 supply delivery, but the amount shown on the invoice is $44. The invoice is forwarded to the business office, and a check is prepared and mailed to the company. A copy of the invoice marked "paid" is sent to Department A. The clerk in Department A notes the change in the amount ($40 to $44) on the copy of the purchase order in the received file. The copy in the received file is moved to the paid file, and the up-to-date budget is modified by decreasing the encumbrances by $40, increasing the expenditures by $44, and changing the balance for supplies from $30 to $26.

Section 4: Reconciled. When the computer budget report from the central business office is received, the amount of the encumbrances in the up-to-date budget is checked against the amount shown in the encumbrances column of the office budget report. Because the office budget report is more up to date, the amounts in the computer report will have to be reconciled to include any orders in process in the organization and not included in the computer budget report. In addition, the amount shown in the paid column of the up-to-date budget should be checked against the paid amounts in the budget report. When the two amounts are reconciled, the copies in the paid file are moved to the last section, or "reconciled" file.

For example: PIK distributes a budget report on June 15, two weeks before the end of the fiscal year. The report for Department A shows the payment for the $44 worth of supplies. The clerk reconciles the supply balance on the report, which should have a balance of $26 in supplies, against the supply balance shown in the office records, which should be $26 on the up-to-date budget report maintained by the clerk. After the balances in the budget report and office records are reconciled, the clerk in Department A moves the copy of the supply order (showing $44) from the paid file to the reconciled file.

To extend our example one step further, assume that PIK requires that Departments A and B and the Office of Public Service forward all budget proposals and expenditures to the office of the director of programs for the director's approval. In other words, the director must review and approve all budget expenditures. As a result, a clerk in the director's office should maintain a budget file identical to the one described above for each budget assigned to Departments A and B and the Office of Public Service. This allows

for improved budget control and thus reduced chance of embezzlement by adding a third party to the process.

Budget Projections: Red Light/Green Light

At the beginning of a budget period, the manager should formulate
a plan for the execution of the budget, meaning how the budget
money will be expended over the budget period. One method that
is both helpful and easy to set up is to have the manager project
what percentage of the budget will be expended each month for
each budget category. For example, the money in a budget category
may be projected to be spent in equal increments over a twelve-
month period, in which case the budget report each month should
show that 8.33 percent of the money has been spent in that category.
On the other hand, the manager might know that in the first two
months the amount spent in a category may be small (say 5 percent),
then the next four months may be greater (say 10 percent), then the
next two months smaller (say 5 percent), then the last four months
greater (say 10 percent). In either case, these projected percentages
can be used as a guide and then parameters can be established.

As a result, if the budget report shows that the expenditures
to date are within 2 percent of the projected expended amount, plus
or minus, the amount spent would be considered acceptable and in
the green-light zone. If the expenditures are between 2 and 4 percent
plus or minus, the budget would be in the orange (or caution) zone
and should be monitored carefully over the next month or two. If
the expenditures are over or under by more than 4 percent, then the
category is in the red zone and either a revised projection is needed
or the budget should be amended. Note that the percentage parameters include both upper and lower limits; this is because underex-
penditures may be as harmful as overexpenditures. If the budgeted
money is not being used until the last sixty days of the budget year,
the program is probably not getting the full benefit of the allotment. Some managers see such a practice as an exercise of caution,
but most professional managers view it as a wasteful and weak
method to manage an allotment.

The red light/green light method can be used by an entire

organization, particularly if a computer is used to prepare the budget reports. Each manager can simply provide the percentage projections for each budget category at the beginning of the year and then, through the use of a set of parameters in the budget report, be informed of the zone for the expenditures in each category. If the unit manager's report indicates a problem, the budget projections can be revised or an amendment made. If a unit's budget is in the red zone and the unit manager does not take action, then the business manager or executive manager should consult the unit manager. Alternatively, the executive manager or business manager may set specific dates, such as the end of every quarter, when budget projections must be reviewed and revised. If some units are not on schedule, then amendments, supplements, or recisions may be in order.

Budget projections should establish budget plans that are related to a program plan, enhance control over budget allotments, and eliminate the need for emergency measures at the end of the fiscal year for overexpended budget units. However, these projections cannot be established and the corresponding controls cannot exist if the budget system is not implemented properly.

Summary

A budget system must have a set of procedures for the receipt of revenue and for expenditures.

The following basic procedures should be used for the collection of money:

1. Before any money can be received by an organization, the governing board must authorize the offering of the program and approve the budget and, if applicable, the rates to be charged.
2. Revenue received by an employee is recorded and given to a bookkeeper or project director for recording and transmittal to a business manager or board treasurer for deposit.
3. Deposits are entered into the accounting system, which is used to prepare the revenue budget reports and to reconcile the budget deposits.
4. The budget reports are distributed to the employees who receive

the money, to bookkeepers, and to project managers, who rec-oncile their records with them.

5.   Unannounced internal audits of the records of all personnel handling money are regularly conducted.

The procedures used to control budget expenditures are as follows:

1.   Unit managers who are allocated a budget prepare budget plans with expenditure projections and parameters for each budget category.

2.   Using proper forms for an expenditure request, unit budget managers authorize all expenditures against their budgets unless this function is formally delegated to a subordinate.

3.   The expenditure forms are processed for review by personnel as directed by the organization and then approved by the business manager and director of purchasing, if applicable.

4.   All expenditures are recorded in the accounting system, which is used to make all payments and to generate monthly budget reports.

5.   Budget reports are provided to each office in which a person acts on or reviews a budget expenditure so that that office can reconcile its office records with the budget report.

6.   Budget unit managers compare their budget reports with their budget projections according to the parameters for each budget category.

6

Understanding the Language of Accounting

The objective of this and the next two chapters is to present the accounting system so that managers can use the system to the best advantage of their organizations. The focus of this presentation is not on bookkeeping details but rather on the basic purpose of an accounting system, which, as Meigs and Meigs (1984) explain, is to record, classify, and summarize business activities. To accomplish this, the language of accounting is set forth in a manner that allows a manager to work with the system, not to make accounting entries.

Figure 9 presents the basic elements of an accounting system: inputs, process, and outputs. When an organization enters into business transactions, such as revenue awards, payments of cash, budget expenditures, budget revisions, payment of invoices, payment of salaries, and so on, records of the transaction are made; these records are the inputs to the accounting system. The process consists of classifying and summarizing the information contained in the records so that it can be used to prepare the organization's budget reports and financial statements—the system's output. Chapter Seven describes the inputs and the processing of the information into the system, and Chapter Eight presents a discussion of

Figure 9. Accounting System.

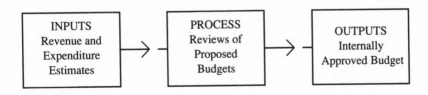

the outputs. But first, this chapter describes the language of accounting in terms that will enable managers to work with the system.

A Tale of Two Systems

As discussed earlier, there are two accounting practices: double-entry and single-entry accounting. Single-entry accounting is often referred to as the checkbook method (Gross and Warshauer, 1979). This text is concerned only with double-entry accounting.

Double-entry accounting is used in both the "cash-basis" and the "accrual" accounting methods (neither method is relevant to single-entry accounting). These two accounting methods use much of the same jargon, forms, and statements; however, there are important differences between them which revolve around the recognition of revenue and income, expenses, inventory, and depreciation. In the cash-basis method, income is recognized and recorded when it is received and expenses are recorded when they are actually paid. On the other hand, the accrual method recognizes income when it is earned, not when it is received, and records expenses when they are actually incurred, regardless of when they are paid.

As an example of how the recognition of revenue and expenses by the two methods differs, assume that an organization is awarded a grant of $100 on May 1, the project takes effect on July 1, and the $100 is received on July 10. With the cash-basis method, the $100 is recorded as revenue in the accounting system on July 10 (date received). Under the accrual method, it is recorded on July 1 (the date the award is effective or earned) and the cash recognized on July 10. With respect to expenses, assume further that the organization receives an invoice of $50 for supplies delivered on December 28 and writes a check to pay it on January 5. Under the cash-basis method, the expense is recorded when it is paid, which is January 5; in the accrual method, however, it is recorded on December 28.

The accrual method is most likely to be used by for-profit companies because of tax regulations. The government would prefer to have income declared when earned rather than when received and expenses declared when incurred rather than when paid; otherwise, for-profit companies might be able to manipulate their income statements to their advantage and to the government's disadvantage. However, in contrast to for-profit companies, which can spend money as it is earned, a public or nonprofit organization should not spend money awarded to it until the notification of a budget award is received. In addition, budget awards usually set dates by which the money awarded must be spent (although some types of awards, such as revenue awards for buildings, equipment, or debt retirement, as well as donations, do not usually set deadlines).

To further explain the difference between the two methods by continuing the example regarding the $100 project, the organization would definitely not want to record the $100 until the budget award is received. When the organization follows the cash-basis method and does not record the $100 as revenue until the check is actually received, the double-entry method prevents any money from being spent on the project until July 10. With the accrual method, the revenue would be recorded on July 1, when the award takes effect and the project may begin, although an organization may balk at spending any money until the first cash payment is received. This may seem to be a trivial difference, but managers should be sensitive to its implications, especially when the organization awarding the revenue operates on a different fiscal year from that used by the receiving organization and may not make any cash payments on the award for three months.

With respect to expenses, however, the situation may be different. For example, if the supplies received on December 28 and paid for on January 5 are to be used for a project that ends on December 31, the organization would want to record the payment as of December 28, since the project money must be spent by the ending date of the grant period (although many organizations are provided with a grace period for making payments on outstanding invoices). The purpose of setting such deadlines is to ensure that the money awarded to an organization is spent as intended and not intentionally retained as part of a strategy to build up a "war chest" by setting aside encumbrances that are greater than the eventual payments. The temptation to create and misuse a large war chest is also why, for many organizations, limitations are imposed on the amount of money that may be held as a reserve in a general operations fund.

Because the two accounting methods are basically on opposite ends of a continuum, a modified cash-accrual method is often used; indeed, such arrangements are recommended by the GAAP. With such a method, an organization may use the accrual method in one fund and the cash-basis method in another (such as the cash-basis method to record interest earned on investments and the accrual method to record tuition received in advance) or to record expenses on an accrual basis in one fund and the cash basis in another (such as using the accrual basis method in a self-support fund through which goods are purchased and resold and the cash method for projects with revenue awards that cannot be carried beyond a specific date).

Real Accounts

Accounting systems are made up of accounts that have dollar amounts assigned to them and represent economic entities, such as accounts for buildings, notes payable, supplies, and so on, that exist within an organization. Accounts are classified under one of five account groups. Three of the account groups are called assets, liabilities, and equity or fund balance. These groups are called "real accounts" because they are permanent—that is, their balances are carried over from year to year. Revenue and expenses are the other two account classifications. They are called "nominal accounts" because they are used for one year, or budget period, after which they are closed to a zero balance and then opened as new accounts in the new year or operating period.

Assets. A definition of assets can be broken down into two parts. The first part is that they represent what an organization owns or is owed. Examples of such accounts are cash, accounts receivable, notes receivable, equipment, buildings, inventory, bonds and other investments, and so on.

In some cases, assets may be divided into subgroups. One subgroup may be called "current assets," meaning the cash account, accounts receivable, inventory, and any other asset account that can be converted into cash within a short period of time (such as one year or operating period) without disrupting normal operations. At the same time an organization could create a subgroup called "long-term assets" or "fixed assets" to represent such items as stocks and bonds as well as buildings and equipment plus intangible assets. Intangible assets are entities that have value but do not represent a physical substance (examples are patents and copyrights). In some cases, an organization may prefer to show its land, building, and equipment holdings separately from its other fixed assets and, therefore, create a long-term asset subgroup labeled "buildings and equipment." With the arrangement set forth by Principle 5 of the GAAP, the fixed assets of the governmental funds appear in the general fixed-assets account group, and those of the proprietary and trust funds are also to appear in those funds. However, with the arrangement recommended in this text, the fixed-asset fund shows all long-term fixed assets, such as buildings, equipment, and land. Investments and other long-term assets are to be shown in the funds in which they were established (such as the investment fund, restricted fund, debt fund, or self-support fund), with the exception of the general fund.

The second part of the definition for assets is that they are needed to conduct the daily operations of the organization and are expected to provide future economic benefit to it. For example, a building is necessary to the daily operation of an organization, and it will also provide future economic benefit. However, a point to be noted here is that the value shown for a building may represent not what it is worth on the market but rather what it cost at the time of its purchase. This book value technically represents the asset's economic value to the organization—what it gave up economically to own the asset. In some cases, the value of such an asset may be misleading and need to be reassessed, with a new book value assigned. For example, an old building whose value has been shown on the books at $50,000 for the past twenty-five years may now, because it is in the middle of the city's financial district, be considered to be worth $500,000. For the organization's financial statements to have more credibility, the value of this asset may need to be revised.

In addition, there may be occasions when an organization

chooses to present its accounts in both "cost" or "book" value and "current" or "market" value terms. Such a presentation would be helpful when comparing the financial worth of one organization in relation to another, or the current values to other time periods.

A final note must be made about the depreciation of assets, which is discussed further in Chapter Ten. The depreciation of an asset is a way of allocating the cost of an asset over a period of time, such as a building or equipment. Thus, the amount shown for an asset minus depreciation does not represent the market value of the asset but the book value, meaning the original cost minus charges (depreciation) against that cost for use over time. After an asset has been completely depreciated, the remaining amount is considered the salvage value. If an asset will continue to be used to the economic benefit of the organization after it has been completely depreciated, it may be given a new value and then depreciated further. Depreciation is advocated by the GAAP in Principle 7.

Liabilities. Liability accounts represent the debts of the organization, or what is owed. When merchandise, a loan, or a service is received and not paid, an organization has a debt to pay. This debt is called a liability. Debts are not the same as expenses. When an expense is incurred but not paid, a liability is created. When an expense is incurred but the invoice is paid immediately upon receipt of the goods or services, a liability is not created. When a liability is paid, the amount is deleted from the books via the double-entry method. The amount in the expense account remains on record until the accounting books are closed at the end of the fiscal year or budget period.

Liabilities may be grouped into two categories: current liabilities and long-term liabilities. Current liabilities are debts that will be paid within the fiscal year, such as merchandise bought on a thirty-day credit agreement. Long-term liabilities are those that extend beyond the current fiscal year, such as a twenty-year mortgage or five-year bonds. Principle 5 of the GAAP maintains that long-term liabilities of the proprietary and trust funds should appear in those funds, and that long-term liabilities of the other funds should appear in the general long-term debt account group. This agrees conceptually with the practice described by this text, which shows the long-term liabilities in the fund in which they are incurred, such as the self-support fund and the restricted fund, but not the general fund. Since the debt fund is created for the long-term debts of the organization, the general fund would not have any long-term debts.

The management of liabilities is a problem for organizations whose managers do not enforce a strict payment policy, such as meeting an expected thirty-day payment agreement or adding a service charge to a payment when a thirty-day due date is not met (sometimes because the processing time is longer than thirty days). Failure to recognize service charges or taking an inordinately long time to process a payment is irritating to many businesses. In some cases, private businesses have been known to refuse to deal with certain institutions because of their payment practices.

The liabilities of an organization are important to the budget expenditures discussed in Chapter Five. As explained earlier, when a purchase order is authorized, approved, and released, it is reported as an encumbrance. When the goods are received, the encumbrance becomes a liability until it is paid. If carrying charges or interest charges are added to the purchase price, these amounts are considered to be an expense to the budget and are not added to the value of the merchandise purchased. If the purchase price of the merchandise has increased or if expenses are incurred, the manager of the business office should have the unit budget manager authorize payment of the additional amount. The importance of this is illustrated by the case of an audit of a city's accounting records. The audit revealed that the money paid to vendors was consistently greater than the amount authorized in the original purchase orders. The additional amounts had never been authorized by the unit budget manager (the mayor of the city) but had simply been added to the amount to be paid by the business manager, who was acting as the purchasing agent. In response to this audit, the business manager was fired and more than $100,000 of state aid was withheld from the city until it could demonstrate fiscal responsibility.

Equity and Fund Balances. In a set of self-balancing accounts, equity and fund balance accounts fulfill the same function but have different rationales behind them. To illuminate the difference between these two accounts, a description of equity is provided first.

Equity, sometimes called owner's equity, represents the amount of an owner's investment in a business plus the profits that have been added to the investment (Meigs and Meigs, 1984). For instance, when a person starts a business with $10,000 in cash, the $10,000 is recorded as an asset under the cash account and also as the equity of the business (an example of a double entry). If at the end of the first month of business, the owner has a net profit of $1,000 (meaning income exceeds expenses by $1,000) and adds it to the investment, the owner's equity in the business is increased to $11,000.

To the contrary, when a budget award is made to a public or nonprofit organization, the award is not considered an investment. The purpose of the fund balance is to show the fund's financial position and changes in it (Freeman, Shoulders, and Lynn, 1988). If there is a residual balance left over from the revenue award at the end of the year and the organization may retain it, this residual is not called a profit but is simply considered an increase in the fund balance.

One controversy that surrounds the use of these accounts occurs because some accountants object to the use of an equity account in any form by a public or nonprofit organization. This is because the term *equity* implies ownership, and public and nonprofit organizations cannot be owned, bought, or sold by private individuals (Henke, 1970). In addition, equity also implies a profit motive. When a public or nonprofit organization receives a budget award, the money is not considered an investment and a surplus at the end of the year is not a profit. However, on the other side of the argument, some organizations have operations that do not receive a budget award but do earn income that results in profits or losses (for example, a retail store in a hospital or university or invested capital). In these cases, the use of a fund balance, which implies that a budget award was made, would not be proper, and so an equity account showing profits or losses is used.

In some rare cases the term *net worth* is used by organizations in places of *equity* or *fund balance*. Finney and Miller (1957) point out that the use of this term should be discouraged because of the misunderstanding that might arise if a person interpreted *net worth* to mean what a company or organization is actually worth. Because assets and liabilities are recorded at cost (not current value) and because depreciation is a way of distributing the cost of an asset over the expected life of the asset (not a way of adjusting the market value of the asset), *net worth* is not an accurate term to use in accounting. For this reason, Finney and Miller and the current textbooks on accounting use the term *equity*.

Consequently, for justified reasons, there is a difference of opinion about the use of words *equity* and *profit* versus *fund balance* by public and nonprofit organizations. In NCGA Statement 7, the Governmental Accounting Standards Board (1987) indicates that when a governmental agency retains an ongoing financial interest in an operation, it has an equity interest. There terms are discussed further in Chapter Eight; for now, the term *fund balance* will be used to represent the difference between assets and liabilities in a public or nonprofit organization, with the assumption that income-generating funds may show a profit and subsequently an increase in the fund balance. In any event, it is important that managers recognize that the terms have different meanings and their use in financial statements should be carefully considered. It is hoped that some clear standardization will emerge in the future.

The Double-Entry Accounting Formula

The accounting formula of the double-entry method is the key to its success. This algebraic formula is:

$$\text{Assets} = \text{Liabilities} + \text{Fund Balance}$$

This is abbreviated as : $A = L + FB$. It means that what an organization owns (its assets) is equal to what it owes (liabilities) plus the amount in the fund balance. Another way of expressing the formula is:

$$\text{Assets} - \text{Liabilities} = \text{Fund Balance}$$

This means that if the liabilities are subtracted from the assets, the difference is the amount in the fund balance. The first version of

the formula (Assets = Liabilities + Fund Balance) is considered to
be the standard version because of how the real accounts are presented on the balance sheet.

A balance sheet (described in detail in Chapter Eight) is one
of the major financial statements prepared by both for-profit and
public and nonprofit organizations. It presents an overall financial
picture of each fund in an organization as of a specific date. There
are two different formats used for balance sheets. In one format,
called the report form, the assets are shown in the upper section of
the report, and the liabilities appear with the fund balance in the
lower section. An example of this format is provided in Exhibit 6.

Exhibit 6. Balance Sheet—Report Form.

Public Institute for Kindness
Balance Sheet
June 30, 1991

Assets		
Cash		$ 3,540
Taxes receivable	$3,500	
Less allowances for uncollectible taxes—delinquent	1,000	2,500
Accounts receivable	350	
Less allowance for uncollectible accounts receivable	150	200
Building		20,000
Equipment		2,250
Supplies inventory		530
Total assets		$29,020

Liabilities and Fund Balance	
Liabilities:	
Accounts payable	$ 1,800
Bonds payable	15,000
Total liabilities	$16,000
Fund balance:	
Reserve for encumbrances	$ 4,400
Fund balance	8,620
Total fund balance	$13,020
Total liabilities and fund balance	$29,020

Note: Assets ($29,020) = Liabilities + Fund Balance ($29,020)

In the other format, called the account form, the assets are shown on the left side of the sheet and the liabilities and fund balance on the right, forming a *T* shape, as illustrated in Exhibit 7.

Exhibit 7. Balance Sheet—Account Form.

Public Institute for Kindness
Balance Sheet
June 30, 1991

Assets	*Liabilities and Fund Balance*

In other words, assets appear on the left side of the balance sheet *T* and liabilities and the fund balance appear on the right side. This *T* format is used quite extensively in accounting to demonstrate the effects of a transaction; the popular name for the figure is a "*T* account."

Debits and Credits. The next step in understanding the accounting formula and the double-entry system is the means by which the accounts in the formula are changed. This is accomplished through the use of bookkeeping entries. In this text the entries themselves are not described; rather, the way they affect the input and processing of information in the accounting system is explained.

When a transaction occurs in an organization, a bookkeeping entry is made in an accounting journal, as discussed in Chapter Seven. The additions or subtractions to a balance in an account are made by recording debits or credits in a journal. Debits cause an increase to assets (the left side of the *T*), while credits cause an increase in liabilities and fund balance accounts (the right side of the *T*). Conversely, a credit decreases an asset account, and a debit decreases a liability and fund balance account. Debits and credits may also be presented in the form of a *T* account, with the debit balance on the left (same side as the asset side) and the credit balance on the right (same side as the liability and fund balance side).

Debit Balance Side	Credit Balance Side
Debits (+ assets)	Debits (– liabilities and fund balances)
Credits (– assets)	Credits (+ liabilities and fund balances)

In each journal entry, the amount of the debits must equal the amount of the credits in order for the accounting formula to balance. The relationship of assets, liabilities, and fund balance accounts to debits or credits is shown below:

Assets		Liabilities and Fund Balance	
Debit Side	Credit Side	Debit Side	Credit Side
Balance side			Balance side
Increases	Decreases	Decreases	Increases

In other words, assets have a debit balance, and liabilities and the fund balance have a credit balance. Therefore, a debit entry will increase an asset, and a credit entry will decrease an asset. At the same time, a debit entry will decrease liabilities and fund balance, and a credit entry will increase liabilities and fund balance. The effects of debits and credits on the real accounts can be summarized as follows:

Debits   Increase an asset account
          Decrease a liability account
          Decrease a fund account

Credits   Increase a liability account
           Increase a fund account
           Decrease an asset account

Nominal Accounts

Because assets, liabilities, and fund balance are always discussed in an accounting text first, the error typically made is to try to relate expenses and revenues to assets or all three real accounts. This is not the case. Rather, expenses and revenues should be perceived in relation to the fund balance, or owner's equity. This rationale, which can be followed easier by thinking of a for-profit operation, is as follows. Equity represents the owner's investment and the profits earned by a company. As a result:

1. Expenses decrease the profits and the owner's equity.
2. Income increases the profits and the owner's equity.
3. Therefore, because equity is shown on the right side of the balance sheet, and a credit balance shows a positive balance, income accounts must have a credit balance in order to add to the equity account (and appear on the right side of a T account), and expense accounts must have a debit balance to subtract from the equity account (and appear on the left side of a T account).

The same is true for the fund balance, which has a credit balance: expenses lower the fund balance, and revenues increase it. Because of this relationship to the fund balance, revenues have a credit balance like the fund balance accounts, and expenses have a debit balance as they detract from the fund balance.

Consequently, when an expense is incurred and recorded in a journal, the expense account is debited, and when revenue is received, the revenue account is credited. The formula $A = L + FB$ is now modified as follows:

Assets + Expenses = Liabilities + Fund Balance + Revenue

or

Assets = Liabilities + FB + Revenue/Income − Expenses

The following T accounts exhibit the application of debits and credits to expense and revenue accounts:

	Expenses		Revenues	
Debit Side	Credit Side	Debit Side	Credit Side
Balance side			Balance side
Increases balance	Decreases balance	Decreases balance	Increases balance

Therefore, the actions of debits and credits on accounts is extended as follows:

Debits Increase an asset account
   Increase an expense account
   Decrease a liability account
   Decrease a fund account
   Decrease a revenue account

Credits Increase a liability account
   Increase a fund account
   Increase a revenue account
   Decrease an asset account
   Decrease an expense account

At the end of the year or operating period, the books are closed, and the balances for the revenues and expenses are changed to zero. The balances in these accounts are transferred via journal entries into the equity or fund balance account. If the revenue account balances are greater than the total of the expense accounts, there is a positive impact on the equity or fund balance. If the reverse is true, then the effect is negative.

Encumbrances. As noted earlier, when an organization processes an order to make a purchase, money will be committed, or encumbered, by the accounting system. At one time, encumbrances were made only for large purchases, but with the advent of the computer, encumbrances can be made for every purchase. Encumbrances are convenient, as they ensure that the money needed for an expenditure is formally set aside by the accounting system and subtracted from the allocation in the budget reports.

An encumbrance account is neither a real account nor a nominal account; that is, it is neither a liability nor an expense. It should not appear on the annual balance sheet statement, as it could give the impression that money is being retained to pay an outstanding order. Essentially, an encumbrance account is a temporary working account.

Because an encumbrance is a future expense and must be deducted from the revenue allotment, these accounts have a debit balance as do expense accounts. For the double-entry method to balance, another account must be used when an entry is made for an encumbrance account. This second account is the "reserve for encumbrances" account, which is credited when an encumbrance account is debited. Like the encumbrance account, it is a temporary working account to be used for internal control.

If an encumbrance remains at the end of the year and the order cannot be canceled, the money must come out of either the fund reserve or the revenue awarded for the coming year. If permitted, the money to pay for an encumbrance can be legitimately transferred to the next year through a series of entries. Regardless of whether an encumbered amount can be carried over from one fiscal year to another, the encumbrance account is to be closed to a zero balance at the end of the year. If an encumbered amount is carried into a new year, the revenue to pay for the encumbrance is transferred temporarily into an account in the fund balance called the "unreserved fund balance" or "unappropriated fund balance" (Freeman, Shoulders, and Lynn, 1988; Gross and Warshauer, 1979). At the beginning of the new period, an entry is made to return the amount to the encumbrance account. The money to pay the invoice would come from the revenue placed in the "unreserved fund balance."

Contras. Contras are accounts that have a negative effect on an asset account. For example, when an organization receives a revenue award based on the collection of taxes, it knows that some of the money will not be collected. This uncollectable amount must be estimated and recorded in the accounting records at the same time as it is recorded in the revenue account as per a budget award. The account used to record the estimated uncollectible taxes is called the "allowance for uncollectible taxes" (discussed in more detail in Chapter Nine). The amount estimated to be uncollected is subtracted from the amount entered into the revenue account.

Contra accounts are not assets or any of the type of accounts discussed above, but are "contra asset accounts" because they are subtracted from an asset account balance. In the balance sheet shown above, there were two contra accounts for two different receivable accounts. A section of the balance sheet is presented again to show the accounts:

Cash		$3,540
Taxes receivable	$3,500	
Less allowance for uncollectible taxes—delinquent	1,000	2,500
Accounts receivable	350	
Less allowance for uncollectible accounts	150	200

Note that the contra accounts appear directly under the asset they refer to and are indented to indicate that they are not an asset account. The amounts for the asset and the contra account are listed in a separate column to the left and the amount of the balance is shown in the column to the right, along with the amounts of the other assets, such as the cash account.

Another contra account is "allowance for depreciation." Rather than at the beginning of the year, depreciation adjustments are made at intervals throughout the year after the cost for the use of the asset can be justified. The accumulated depreciation remains on the books as long as the asset is on the books and is revised if the value of the asset is revised.

Chart of Accounts

The chart of accounts is a list of numbers that are assigned to each account in the accounting system and are used in the processing of information through the system. A range of numbers is established for the assets, liabilities, fund accounts, revenues, and expenses. Each account is assigned a number and as new accounts are created, unused numbers are assigned to them. The chart of accounts may vary from organization to organization, but it should be the same for all funds in an organization. For example, asset accounts may be assigned the numbers 1 through 29, 100 through 299, or 1000 through 2999, so that if the first digit of an account number is 1 or 2, the account is an asset (or account numbers beginning with the digit 1 could be used for current assets and numbers beginning with 2 for fixed assets). Accounts are always ranked in the same order, with assets first, liabilities second, fund balance third, revenues fourth, and expenses fifth. The first asset account number is always given to cash. Asset numbers are then assigned according to the accounts' liquidity, or ease of being converted into cash. An example of a chart of accounts is as follows:

> Assets: numbers 100 to 299
> Liabilities: numbers 300 to 499
> Fund accounts: numbers 500 to 599
> Revenues: numbers 600 to 699
> Expenses: numbers 700 to 999

Of course, other numbering systems could be used, such as 100–199 for assets, 200–299 for liabilities, 300–399 for equity or fund balance, and so on.

An asset contra account is given a number in the asset series immediately following the asset account number that it contradicts. Encumbrances are given numbers in the expense series, while the reserve for encumbrances and fund transfer accounts appear in the fund balance series. The numbers assigned to accounts should allow for new accounts to be added.

Finally, two important points should be noted. First, these accounting numbers have no relationship to budget numbers. Second, each fund should have its own set of self-balancing accounts, chart of accounts, and set of accounting numbers. Thus, an organization with three funds would have three sets of accounts, and each set of accounts would have a cash account with account number 100.

Summary

An accounting system in a fund in an organization may use one or two accounting methods: the cash-basis method and the accrual method. The difference between the two methods lies in how they recognize revenue and income, expenses, inventory, and depreciation. With the cash-basis method, income is recognized and recorded when it is received, and expenses are recorded when they are actually paid. With the accrual method, income is recognized when it is earned (not when it is received), and expenses are recorded when they are actually incurred (regardless of when they are paid). In some cases, an organization or a fund in an organization may follow a modified accrual method in which the cash-basis method is used for revenue and income and the accrual method is used for expenses, or vice versa.

The accounts in an accounting system are classified according to five account types. Assets, liabilities, and equity or fund balance are called "real accounts" because they are carried over from year to year. Revenue or income and expense accounts are called "nominal accounts" because they are used for one year or budget period.

Double-entry accounting uses an algebraic formula in which assets equal liabilities plus fund balance. A simple interpretation of this formula is that what an organization owns (assets) is equal to what it owes (liabilities) plus the fund balance. Extended to encompass the effect of revenue, income, and expense accounts on the fund balance, the formula becomes "assets equal liabilities plus fund balance plus revenue and income minus expenses."

The accounts in the formula are changed through the use of debit and credits, which are entered into the system through bookkeeping entries. An entry that causes the balances in the accounts to be either decreased or increased must change the amounts in at least two accounts so that the accounting formula remains equal.

There are two special accounts that are neither real nor nominal: encumbrances and contra accounts. Encumbrances are used to set aside money in the accounting system when a purchase is ordered. Contra accounts are used to decrease the balance shown for an asset account. An uncollectible contra amount is recorded in the accounting records at the time the amount of revenue to be received is entered.

The accounting system is given a strict sense of order through the use of a set of account numbers, called the chart of accounts. This list contains accounting numbers that are assigned to each account in the accounting system. These numbers are important in the processing of information in the accounting system.

7

Tracking Financial Information

Core Accounting Processes

As noted earlier, the input into an accounting system is the information recorded when business transactions are made. This information is processed through the system to provide the output—a set of financial statements.

For the double-entry method to ensure the accuracy for which it has been noted for the past 600 years, specific procedures must be used to record entries and process the information. There is no room for creativity; the emphasis is on conformity. This is true whether the cash-basis or the accrual method is used.

The description in this chapter about how the input is entered into and processed through the system uses accounting forms and entries to demonstrate how the information is processed but does delve into the bookkeeping details. Those details may be found in any basic bookkeeping and accounting text. A preview of the basic forms used to record and then process the accounting information follows.

1. The *journal* is a form used to record the initial record of a business transaction through debit and credit entries to accounts.
2. A *ledger* is a set of forms, such as cards, that are created for each individual account in the system. The ledger forms show all of the debit and credit entries made in the journal for the accounts. Thus, the individual ledger form is used to maintain a balance (debit, credit, or zero balance) for each account.
3. A *trial balance* lists the debit and credit balances for each account in the ledger. The totals of the debit and credit balances on the trial balance must always be equal; if they are not, an

error has been made. The trial balance is prepared monthly along with the budget reports.

These accounting forms and a set of self-balancing accounts must be used for each fund in the organization.

When an organization enters into a business transaction, a manager has several concerns, the first being that the transaction is entered into the system properly. This requires that a record of the transaction (such as a purchase order, salary contract, memo for a budget amendment) be made available for the entry into the system and that this record then be kept on file. This record is called the source document, and will be referred to throughout the next several chapters.

Another concern is that, once the the transaction is accurately entered into the accounting system, future information related to the transaction will be entered into the records, such as the record of the receipt of the goods ordered on a purchase order and then the payment of the invoice. This means that the system must be designed so that a manager can be kept up-to-date on the status of the transaction, such as through periodic budget reports. A good accounting system will provide this for each budget unit in each fund. This is where the interaction between the accounting and budgeting systems comes into play.

Recording the Input into the System

An organization may use one or several journals to record business transactions. Each entry for a business transaction must be backed up by a source document, which may be a purchase order, invoice, memo, contract, delivery receipt, organizational policy (for closing and adjusting entries), and so on. This source document is important and should provide the data needed to enter the information into the accounting system. In addition, each transaction must be backed up by an authorization signature from the manager of the budget being charged.

In some cases, additional entries are required for milestones related to a transaction. Some of the entries may be automatically recorded by a bookkeeper, while others may need to be authorized before an entry can be recorded. For example, when a purchase order is submitted to purchase supplies, an entry is made to encumber the purchase. The purchase order with the authorization signature is the source document to back up the entry. When the ownership of the supplies changes hands as provided by the shipping agreement, the encumbrance must be removed from the records and the amount entered into the appropriate expense and liability accounts. The source document for these entries is the shipping agreement or delivery receipt, and no authorization for the entries is needed. The next milestone is the payment of the invoice. An authorization signature is needed on a payment voucher before a check can be drawn. The purchase order, delivery receipt, invoice, and payment voucher are the backup source documents for the entries and the check. A check can then be signed and an entry made in the journal. As discussed later in Chapter Eleven, the source documents are also the keys to an audit.

Thus, accounting journals serve as the business diary of an organization, and, as with any good diary, entries should be made in it every day. Figure 10 presents the first part of a flow diagram that illustrates the steps in processing information through the accounting system. As the figure shows, the first step represents the transaction being recorded in the journal.

Figure 10. The Accounting Process: Initial Entries.

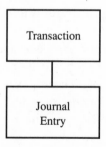

Making Entries. When amounts that appear on a source document are entered in a journal, the entry must include one or more debits and one or more credits. In each entry, the amount of the debits and credits must be equal. This equality ensures that the accounting equation ($A = L + FB$) will balance. The entries for a fund in an organization may be made in either a general journal or a special journal, according to the needs of the fund. Special journals, which can save clerical time and improve control, are described later in this chapter; the description of the accounting process here assumes the use of a general journal. The basic format of a general journal entry is as follows:

1. The first set of columns is used to record the date of the transaction.
2. In the description column, the first account in an entry is the debit, which begins next to the date column.
3. The credits entry goes immediately under the debit or debits and is indented three or more spaces.
4. A brief description of the entry follows, beginning next to the date column.
5. After the description column is the posting reference column, in which the number of the account is entered when the amount is posted to the account's ledger.
6. The last two columns are used to record the amounts of the debit and credit. The debits and credits are not totaled in a general journal, as the only check is whether the amounts of the debits and credits are equal for each entry.

Examples of three transactions are given here; the corresponding entries are illustrated in Exhibit 8.

Transaction 1: An organization releases purchase order #686 for a $300 typewriter. Using the purchase order as the source document, a journal entry is made to encumber $300 in the general journal (shown in the first entry with

Exhibit 8. General Journal Entries.

General Journal

Date		Description	Posting Reference	Debit	Credit
1991 Jan.	2	Encumbrances Reserve for encumbrances To purchase typewriter from Smith Co. (PO#686)		300	300
	20	Reserve for encumbrances Encumbrances To remove encumbrance for the purchase of typewriter from Smith Co. (PO#686)		300	300
	20	Office equipment Accounts payable Received typewriter bought from Smith Co. (PO#686)		300	300
	30	Accounts payable Cash Pmt. on typewriter bought on credit— Smith Co. (PO#686)		100	100

a debit to encumbrances and a credit to reserve for encumbrances).

Transaction 2: The organization takes ownership of the type-writer upon delivery. The typewriter is delivered on January 20. One entry (entry two) is made to remove the encumbrance and another entry (entry three) is made (debit) to the asset account "office equipment" for $300 and (credit) to the liability account, "accounts payable," for $300.

Transaction 3: The organization makes a payment of $100 on the typewriter on January 30. This entry (entry four) consists of a debit to accounts payable (to reduce the liability) and a credit to the asset account "cash" (to reduce the asset).

For auditing purposes, it is critical that general journal entries ensure the following:

1. The entries are in chronological order.
2. The correct name of the account is debited.
3. The correct name of the account is credited.
4. An explanation for the entry is included.
5. If appropriate, a source document number is included with the explanation.

Processing the Input

The next step in the accounting process is to post, or transfer, the journal entries into the ledger. To ensure accuracy in this sorting process, a specific set of bookkeeping procedures must be followed. A ledger may be a loose-leaf notebook, a set of cards, or entries in a computer. Each account in a ledger has a separate page, card, or computer code. For example, the asset account "cash" would have a separate page, card, or code. In some computer programs, the posting to the ledger is done automatically when the journal entry is made. Regardless of the method used to post the accounts, the flow diagram for the accounting system is now extended as shown in Figure 11.

Figure 11. The Accounting Process: Posting Entries.

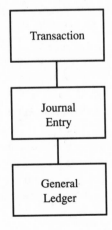

In the posting process, each debit or credit in a journal is transferred to the page or card for that account in the ledger. *T* accounts (described in Chapter Six) are typically used as working documents to represent ledger cards in which the left side of the *T* is the debit side and the right side is the credit side. If an account is debited in the journal, then the amount is entered on the left side of the *T* account. The opposite is true for credit entries; they go on the right side of the *T*. As a result, the *T* account below represents a cash account, which is an asset and has a debit balance. This account has a beginning balance ($1,500 on May 1) and three journal entries ($300 debit on May 9, $400 credit on May 15, $200 credit on May 25). After the entries are posted, it would appear as follows:

Cash

| 5/1 Beg. bal. | 1,500 | 5/15 | 400 |
| 5/9 | 300 | 5/25 | 200 |

Because *T* accounts are used only as working forms, to demonstrate ledger postings, there is no formal means followed to present a balance in a *T* account. Rather, the amounts on the debit and credit sides are totaled, the totals are written down in pencil (in accounting, these are called "footings"), and then the balance in the account is written in pencil on the side where the balance exists. In the example above with totals of $1,800 on the debit side and $600 on the credit side, the balance of $1,200 would be written on the debit side (somewhere between the dates and the amounts above the total).

Most ledgers used by bookkeepers are not *T* accounts but forms that provide for a running balance. Exhibit 9 provides examples of such ledger forms for the five accounts, which were the accounts used in the general journal entries shown in Exhibit 8, and shows that the journal entries have been posted to the appropriate ledger accounts. Note that the account numbers are in the upper-right-hand corner of the ledger and that the cards are arranged in numerical order. As the journal entries are transferred, or "posted," to the ledger, an updated balance is computed for each account as of the day of the entry into the journal. When the accounts are

Exhibit 9. General Ledger Forms.

CASH | | | | | | Account No. 100

Date		Explanation	Ref.	Debit	Credit	Balance
Jan.	1	Forward balance	x	3,000		3,000
	30		1		100	2,900

OFFICE EQUIPMENT | | | | | | Account No. 220

Date		Explanation	Ref.	Debit	Credit	Balance
Jan.	20		1	300		300

ACCOUNTS PAYABLE | | | | | | Account No. 301

Date		Explanation	Ref.	Debit	Credit	Balance
Jan.	20		1		300	300
	30		1	100		200

RESERVE FOR ENCUMBRANCES | | | | | | Account No. 650

Date		Explanation	Ref.	Debit	Credit	Balance
Jan.	2		1		300	300
	20			300		---

ENCUMBRANCES | | | | | | Account No. 801

Date		Explanation	Ref.	Debit	Credit	Balance
Jan.	2	office equip.	1	300		300
	20				300	---

posted, the account number is written into the "posting reference" column in the general journal and the journal page number (in this case, 1) is written into the "reference" column of the ledger card. When a fund has several journals, the reference number should indicate which one the reference refers to (for example, G1 for page 1 of the general journal). This is quite important for tracing an entry or looking for an error.

If entries are posted manually, the manager should not allow the person doing the posting to be interrupted. In an introductory accounting course, the beginning student is required to make entries and then post them to demonstrate how the bookkeeping steps must be followed. Later in the course, when several special journals, a general journal, and numerous accounts are involved in a posting exercise, the student soon learns that the posting process cannot be accurately accomplished while one is watching TV in the dorm. The same is true for the clerical person who is trying to answer the phone, obtain supplies for other people, and so on.

The Subsidiary Ledger: The Key to Integration

A subsidiary ledger is a second ledger, which will be described here first for a self-support fund. When an account, such as an accounts receivable account, has a number of credit transactions entered into it, the operation needs a mechanism to keep track of balances for the amount owed by each individual customer. This mechanism is a subsidiary ledger, which is like the general ledger described above except that it provides a ledger card on each customer. (Figure 12 shows the flow diagram for the accounting system extended to include the subsidiary ledger.) The process works as follows: When a customer makes a credit purchase, the amount is entered into the accounts receivable account. Upon being posted to the accounts receivable ledger account, the amount is also posted to the customer's subsidiary ledger card. The subsidiary posting brings that customer's credit record up to date. When the customer makes a payment, an entry is made and the amount is deducted from both the accounts receivable ledger and the customer's subsidiary ledger account. Thus, by using the subsidiary ledger, a manager can look up the current balance in any customer's account.

The same process is used for an accounts payable subsidiary ledger, which maintains a record for each business that is owed money. The alternative to a subsidiary ledger would be a separate accounts receivable account for each customer and a separate accounts payable account for each business that has extended credit to the organization. Obviously, these separate accounts can cause complications and extra work (and errors) if there are numerous customers and creditors.

In the above case, the accounts receivable and accounts payable accounts are called "control accounts." Control accounts can be used in a variety of situations. For example, if a fund in an organization has one revenue source and a budget with seven expense accounts, the organization can use a subsidiary ledger for each of the seven expense accounts, with one encumbrance control account and one expense control account (not seven encumbrance accounts and seven expense accounts). When a purchase order is processed to buy supplies and an encumbrance is created, the encumbrance is recorded in the subsidiary ledger for supplies expense. When the supplies are received or paid for, the entries to the encumbrance and supply expense accounts are also posted to the subsidiary ledger, which removes the encumbrance and deducts the expenditure.

Subsidiary ledgers can also be used for revenue accounts. If a fund had five revenue accounts, an accounts receivable control account could be set up with a subsidiary ledger for the five revenue sources. An uncollectible contra account could also be set up to be used in reference to the same subsidiary ledger accounts. When a revenue award is received, the amount to be received would be recorded as an accounts receivable in the journal, posted to the accounts receivable control account, and then posted to the subsidiary ledger named for that revenue source. When money is received, the entries and postings would be made to bring the amount in the subsidiary ledgers up to date.

Subsidiary ledgers are so important to public and nonprofit organizations because they are the means by which the budgeting and accounting systems are integrated. They provide the information for the budget reports. The systems should be arranged so that when a journal entry is made to an accounts receivable, appropriation, expense, or encumbrance account, the entry is posted to a

Figure 12. The Accounting Process: Posting to the Subsidiary Ledger.

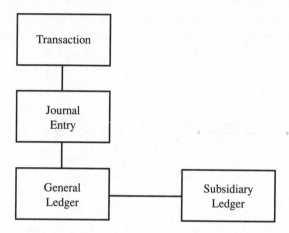

control account and then to the subsidiary ledger, which would have a number that is the same as the budget number for the expenditure category or revenue source.

An example of a subsidiary ledger for supplies expense is provided in Exhibit 10. The form is similar to the one used for the general ledger, but there are two differences. The first is the use of the credit column. In the subsidiary ledger, this column is used when the budget is approved and an entry (credit) is made to the appropriations account. The total appropriation amount is then broken down by expenditure categories according to the allocated budget and posted (credits) to the respective subsidiary ledger accounts. This creates a beginning balance in the subsidiary ledgers and budget reports. In the example in Exhibit 10, there were two postings, of $20,000 and $2,000, to the supplies expense account. As of June 25, the supplies expense account had a beginning balance of $22,000.

The second difference is that the subsidiary ledger has a column for encumbrances. When encumbrances or expenditures are made, the amounts (which are debits) are subtracted from the appropriation credit amount and reduce the balance. Exhibit 10 shows that on July 2, an encumbrance of $500 was recorded and deducted from the account balance of $22,000, to give a new balance of $21,500.

When the expense for a purchase is recorded (as may be noted by the purchase order number in the explanation column), the encumbrance is removed from the record (credit entry in the journal), and the credit is entered in the encumbrance column, with the amount in parentheses to indicate that it is negative. In the example in Exhibit 10, the supplies invoice shows that the cost was $510 rather than $500, which is the amount that was encumbered. This difference is automatically adjusted when the encumbrance is removed (entry with parentheses in the encumbrance column), and the expense is recorded for $510, which adjusts the new balance to $21,490. Thus the budget system's report for supplies expense (budget number 3200) is the total shown in the subsidiary ledger for encumbrances and expenditures and the balance for the account. With the addition of the budget reports, the flow diagram for the accounting system is extended as shown in Figure 13.

When the budget allocation is changed, an entry is made to the appropriations account, which in turn is posted to the control account and then the subsidiary ledger accounts. This then carries through to the budget reports. If an organization decides to set up separate control accounts for each budget unit in a fund, it will have a set of subsidiary ledgers for each budget unit. There may be one accounts receivable control account for all revenues in a fund or different control accounts for different categories of revenue, such as local and state tax revenue. The ledger cards in a subsidiary

Exhibit 10. Sample Subsidiary Ledger for Supplies Expense.

	SUPPLIES				#3200
Date	Revenue Source Explanation	Debit (Credit) Encumbrance	Debit Expenditure	Credit	Balance
May 15	Local Tax			20,000	20,000
June 25	Local Tax			2,000	22,000
July 2	P.O. # 58796	500			21,500
10	Enc. # 58796	(500)			22,000
10	P.O. # 58796		510		21,490

ledger are arranged either alphabetically by customer account or numerically by budget expenditure account numbers, so that the expense and revenue subsidiary ledgers correspond to the budget report format. A note should be made here that the "ledger" is called the "general ledger" to ensure that there is no confusion with the "subsidiary ledger." Subsidiary ledgers are discussed again later, in the presentation of how the accounting and budgeting systems work in harmony.

The Trial Balance: Do the Debits Equal the Credits?

The trial balance is a trial run for the balances of the accounts that appear in the general ledger. First, the subsidiary ledger balances are checked against the balance in the control account in the general ledger to ensure that they agree. The next step is to prepare the trial balance to ensure that the balances in the general ledger are accurate. The trial balance is added to the flow diagram for the accounting process in Figure 14.

Figure 13. The Accounting Process: Generation of Budget Reports.

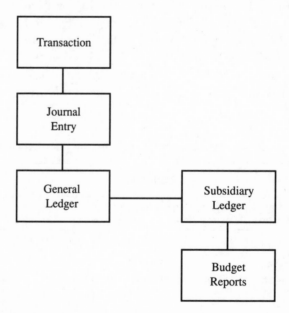

Figure 14. The Accounting Process: The End of a Monthly Cycle.

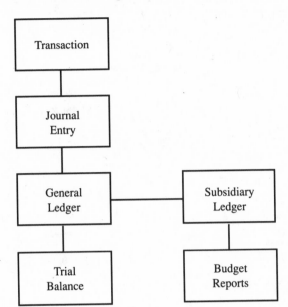

The trial balance is prepared monthly and is considered a working document, not a formal statement. The accounts on the trial balance are arranged as they appear in the general ledger—in other words, by account number: assets (and their contra accounts) first, followed by liabilities, fund accounts, revenues, and expenses and encumbrances. Subsidiary accounts do not appear on the trial balance.

The trial balance has two columns—debits and credits. The amounts of the debit and credit balances from the general ledger are placed in the corresponding trial balance columns. The sum of the debit balances must equal the sum of the credit balances. If it does not, there is an error in an entry; an amount may be incorrect, or the wrong account may have been debited or credited. An example of a trial balance for a self-support fund is provided in Exhibit 11. The double line under the debit and credit totals indicates that the columns are equal. Note that the contra account in the trial balance is listed as a credit balance and not subtracted from the asset account as it was in the balance sheet shown in Chapter Six.

Exhibit 11. Sample Trial Balance.

SMITH SCHOOL
Self-Support Fund
Trial Balance
April 30, 1988

	Debits	Credits
Cash	$4,485.25	
Accounts receivable	1,025.82	
Allowance for uncollectible accounts receivable		50.00
Accounts payable		60.73
Reserve for encumbrances		435.00
Fund balance		500.00
Services income		472.50
Appropriations		7,000.00
Expenses	2,572.16	
Encumbrances	435.00	
	$8,518.23	$8,518.23

The preparation of the trial balance and then the budget reports concludes the cycle for the budget period. The cycle is repeated, usually monthly, until the books are closed and the financial statements are prepared. Financial statements (outputs) are discussed in Chapter Eight; the remainder of this chapter discusses some optional activities associated with the processing stage of the accounting system, such as the use of special journals, vouchers, and so on.

Special Journals

As noted earlier, the use of special journals for a fund can save clerical time and increase control. Special journals are used to record the receipt of cash (cash receipts journal), credit arrangements with clients or customers (accounts receivable journal), payment of cash (cash payments journal), or credit purchases (accounts payable journal). The creation of a special journal is justified only if there is a large number of entries for the accounts in the journal; otherwise, the general journal should be used. For example, special journals would be appropriate for a fund that receives cash and extends credit on a daily basis; however, for a fund that receives revenue four times a year and rarely extends credit, the general journal is appropriate, and special journals should not be used.

Client or Customer Credit and Cash Receipts. Two types of special journals may be used to record the receipt of cash and the granting of customer credit (these may be used with either the double-entry or the single-entry method). The first type, which may be called a sales journal in a for-profit operation or accounts receivable journal for collections, records entries for credit transactions only. An entry in an accounts receivable journal or sales journal is recorded when the invoice (bill) is presented or sent to the client or customer, such as a tax bill. The invoice should describe the details of the transaction. If the credit involves the sale of goods, the invoice is effective when the ownership of the goods is transferred to the buyer, not when the sale agreement is made.

The example of an accounts receivable journal provided in Exhibit 12 illustrates several advantages of this type of journal over a general journal: it uses only one line per transaction, does not require an explanation, can show an invoice number, can be used to keep credit accounts up to date, and requires the amount to be written in the journal only once. In this example, there are six credit transactions recorded. Each line represents a credit and a debit entry. The total is debited to the accounts receivable account (account number 5) in the ledger, and all credits are posted to the corresponding receipt accounts, such as sales (account number 41), taxes,

Exhibit 12. Accounts Receivable Journal.

Date		Account Debited	Invoice No.	Posting Reference	Amount
1988					
March	2	Gerald Garbrick	300	*	100
	5	Phil Gill	301	*	350
	7	Karyl Packer	302	*	225
	10	Helen Harpster	303	*	75
	21	Hugh Fry	304	*	150
	28	Albert Foster	305	*	175
					1,075
					(5)(41)

pledges, and so on. The journal indicates the date, name of the account, invoice number, and amount for each transaction. An asterisk is entered when the account has been posted to the subsidiary ledger for the customer. The double line below the total indicates that it is a final total and considered accurate.

When cash is received on a daily basis, a cash journal may be used to record the entries. As the example in Exhibit 13 demonstrates, the advantages of using the cash journal are that it also requires only one line, can be used to keep all customer accounts in the subsidiary ledger up to date, and does not require an explanation. In this journal, all the debits except discounts are made to cash, and the credits total is posted to sales, accounts receivable, or other. As in the accounts receivable journal, the column totals are posted to the general ledger (number 5 is accounts receivable, number 41 is sales, number 43 is sales discounts, and number 1 is cash). The asterisk or number in the posting reference column indicates that individual amounts have been posted to an account in the subsidiary ledger or general ledger (such as account number 44) so the total under the "other" column is not posted.

Special journals can be modified to fit a variety of situations for control purposes. In the example of a cash receipts journal shown in Exhibit 14, each entry represents a debit to cash for the total of all the column totals at the end of the month, and then a

Exhibit 13. Receipts Journal for Collections and Sales.

CASH RECEIPTS JOURNAL

page 1

Date		Account Credit	Posting Reference	Credits			Debits	
				Other	Accounts Receivable	Sales	Discount	Cash
March	2					68	3	65
	4	Gerald Garbrick	*		50			50
	6	Misc. Sales	44	10				10
				10	50	68	3	125
					(5)	(41)	(43)	(1)

Exhibit 14. Receipts Journal for Contributions.

CASH RECEIPTS JOURNAL

page 1

Date		Account	Posting Reference	Pledges	Donation	Educational Services	Misc.
March	2	Jones Corp.	*	1,000			
	4					40	
	4	Wayne Hoy	*	100			
	6	D. Vroman			25		

credit is posted for the totals to each of the different income accounts. The posting reference column permits a posting to individual accounts in the subsidiary ledger, if applicable.

Credit Purchases and Cash Expenditures. Special journals for credit purchases and the payment of cash operate on the same principle as the accounts receivable and cash receipts journals described above. A journal for credit purchases is called a purchases journal, but a "purchases" account is found only in a self-support operation where credit purchases of goods are made for manufacturing purposes or for resale, not for operational purposes. In the purchases journal, the debit is posted to the purchases account, and the credit is posted to the accounts payable control account, with additional entries to a subsidiary ledger. Because a purchases journal is used only for the purchases account, it could be used for a self-support fund but would not be appropriate for a general fund. For a nonprofit organization, the special journal that represents credit purchases for operations (not for goods to be resold) is called an "accounts payable journal." This journal debits the expense control account with a subsidiary ledger for each expense category (rather than a purchases account) for the debit entry and credits the accounts payable account, which also has a subsidiary ledger.

As with the other special journals, with the accounts payable and purchases journals only one line is needed for an entry, an explanation is not required, an amount is recorded only once, only the totals are posted to the general journal, and individual accounts are posted to the subsidiary ledgers on a daily basis. In addition, these journals may note the invoice date and the terms of sale in order to meet any discounts that are made available. An example of an accounts payable journal is presented in Exhibit 15. In this example, six credit transactions are recorded. Note that the journal indicates the date, the names of the companies and expense accounts for subsidiary postings, the invoice date (which may not be the same date as the entry date), terms, subsidiary postings, and the amount for each transaction. The total ($1,364) is posted to the general ledger as a debit to the expense control account (account number 75) and as a credit to accounts payable (account number 30). The individual amounts are posted to the subsidiary ledgers for accounts payable and expense control accounts on a daily basis, and this posting is indicated by an asterisk (and possibly the expenditure account number) in the posting reference column.

A cash payments journal is used when any cash is disbursed, including cash to pay salaries. This journal may have as many debit and credit columns as necessary. In the example of a cash payments journal in Exhibit 16, the check numbers are in numerical order, a brief explanation may be given, the cash column always has an entry, and there are columns for debits and credits to "other accounts" with space to give account names, as well as columns for accounts payable, for purchases, and for purchase discounts. The totals of the debit and credit columns must be equal. The ledger

Exhibit 15. Sample Accounts Payable Journal.

page 1

Date		Account	Invoice Date		Posting Reference	Amount
1988 Nov	2	MGN Co.—supplies (2/10,n/30)	1988 Nov	2	*	350
	7	J and S—misc. rental (n/30)		5	*	125
	10	Warren Co.—PC equip.		10	*	166
	15	IAG, Inc.—supplies (2/10,n/30)		14	*	435
	21	Harbold's—art supplies		19	*	73
	28	The Book Store—misc. books		27	*	215
						1,364
						(75)(30)

Exhibit 16. Comprehensive Cash Payments Journal.

CASH PAYMENTS JOURNAL

Date	Check No.	Explanation	Credits					Account Debited	Debits				
			Cash	Pur. Disc.	Other Accts. Name	Other Accts. LP	Other Accts. Amt.	Debited	A/Pay. PR	A/Pay. Amt.	Purch.	Expense PR	Expense Amt.
1988 June 3	603	Paid phone bill	710					Misc. exp.				59	710
11	604	Salaries	2300					Sal. exp.				57	2300
15	605	Invoice 5/3 2% discount	980	20					*	1000			
16	607	Purch. goods	150								150		
21	608	Bought equip. on acct. and cash	250		Note Pay	24	250	Office equip.				16	500
			4640	20			250			1000	150		3510
			(1)	(51)			(*)			(21)	(50)		(55)

posting (LP) column for other accounts is used to show that the amount was posted in the general ledger, and an asterisk is placed below the total in the "other account" column to signify that the individual amounts, not the totals, were posted. The totals of the other columns are posted to the accounts named in the heading, and the account numbers are placed under the totals within parentheses. The posting reference (PR) column under accounts payable ("A/ Pay.") and expense shows the posting of entries to the subsidiary ledger.

Like the other special journals, the cash payments journal can be modified to fit the needs of the organization. Another example of a cash payments journal is provided in Exhibit 17. In this example, columns are provided for the debits (rather than a control account with a subsidiary ledger) to the individual expense accounts, with a column for other accounts and the totals can be posted for each account in the general ledger, with the other accounts posted individually. The total for the amount column (the amount of the check) would be posted to the cash account. This journal format could also be used for an accounts payable journal in which the debits would go to the individual expense accounts (rather than a control account) and the total of all account columns would be credited to the accounts payable. (Note: Organizations that do not use the double-entry method should use either cash payment and accounts payable journals or the voucher system described below.)

Vouchers

An alternative to purchases and cash disbursements journals is the use of vouchers. When vouchers are used, a voucher register and a check register are used instead of the purchases and cash disbursements journals. A voucher is a form that is used to provide written authorization for all cash payments and is prepared when an invoice is received or a payroll is due (one voucher is prepared for the total amount to be paid).

When vouchers are processed for approval, they should include all of the supporting documents, such as the purchase order, a receiving report, and the invoice. After a voucher has been approved, an entry is made in the voucher register, and a copy is

Exhibit 17. Modified Cash Payments Journal.

CASH PAYMENTS JOURNAL

page 1

Date	Payee	Check No.	Amt.	Sal. Exp.	Wage Exp.	Supply Exp.	Maint. Exp.	Other Accts.	
								Name	Amt.

placed in a file for unpaid vouchers arranged by due date. The due-date file for unpaid vouchers is important because it helps the business office to take advantage of purchase discounts. On the date the voucher is to be paid, the voucher and supporting documents and an unsigned check are forwarded from the business or accounting office (controller) to the person authorized to sign the check (treasurer). If the check is for a large amount, a second signature (such as the CEO's) may be required. When the check is prepared, an entry is made in the check register, and the check number and the date of payment are entered into the vouchers register.

While voucher forms must fit the individual needs of an organization, they usually indicate the name and address of the payee, date the payment is due, date the payment is made, check number, terms of the sale, date of the invoice, amount, description of the purchase or expense, approval signatures, and account debited or a list of accounts that are typically debited, such as supplies expense.

The voucher register is used to enter credit transactions. Instead of an "accounts payable" account for credit transaction, the account "vouchers payable" (also a liability account) is used. When an invoice is received and attached to the voucher, an entry is made in the voucher register. An example of a voucher register is provided in Exhibit 18. Note that the voucher numbers are in numerical order, there is one credit column for vouchers payable, and there are multiple debit columns (although one column for an expense control account may be used).

Exhibit 18. Vouchers Register.

Date		Voucher Number	Payee	Payment		Credit	Debit				Other Accounts		
				Date	Ck. No.	Voucher Payable	Wage Expense	Supply Expense	Maint. Expense		Name	LP	Amount
May	2	1633	Jones Supply	May 10	593	350		350					
	6	1634	Ace Insurance	14	595	550					Insurance exp.	55	550
	15	1635	Payroll	15	598	1200	1200						
	21	1636	Copper Plumbing			315			315				

The disbursement of money for an organization should involve two people or offices: one to prepare the check and another to sign it. For example, the business manager should prepare the check and then send it with the voucher and supporting documents to the treasurer for signature. After the check is signed, it should be mailed by the treasurer, and the voucher should be marked paid and returned with the supporting documents to accounting. The accounting office should then enter the check number in the voucher register.

When the business office prepares the check, an entry is made in the check register. Like the cash payments journal, the check register is used to record all cash disbursements. When a voucher system is used, the only two accounts entered in the check register are vouchers payable and cash. An example of a check register is shown in Exhibit 19. The payroll is treated as one entry and further detailed in a payroll register (described below). The check numbers are listed in numerical order, but voucher numbers are not. The date and name of the payee are recorded, and the amounts are debited to vouchers payable (21), with credits to cash (1) and purchases discounts (51). The column totals are then posted to the accounts in the general ledger.

A strict set of disbursement procedures is absolutely vital to security, as illustrated by two real-life examples. In one case, someone in an organization was able to obtain several blank checks preprinted with signatures, made them out in exceptionally large

Exhibit 19. Sample Check Register.

Check No.	Date		Payee	Voucher No.	Debits Vouchers Payable	Credits Purchases Disc.	Cash
653	June	24	N.J. Bell	1543	657		657
654		24	Ace Insurance	1532	1,200		1,200
655		27	Ellen's office				
			equipment	1540	1,000	100	900
656		30	Payroll	1545	3,500		3,500
					6,357	100	6,257
					(21)	(51)	(1)

amounts to fictitious people, and then used phony credentials to cash them. The perpetrator was never caught, but the treasurer was fired. In the second case, an organization relied on a computer system for disbursement control. A clerk learned how to override the computer, prepared refund checks made out to former clients, forged the clients names, and used an automatic teller machine to deposit them.

Payroll

One of the major expenditures of most organizations is the payroll. Paying employees involves several unique concerns, such as making sure that the payroll checks are always on time, taking deductions from wages earned, and making the payments for the taxes and benefits on time. How the payroll system is set up affects the accuracy of the cash distribution. The system must ensure that the amount paid accurately reflects the time worked. This may be done through the use of time cards, vacation cards, or verification work sheets to be signed by managers. The verification sheets are often used in relation to the payment of grant funds for auditing purposes.

Usually two standard forms are used in processing the payroll. The first is a payroll record for each employee, showing the employee's name, address, Social Security number, date of birth, exemptions, date of employment, date of termination, position, and so on. On this form, a record is made for the pay period or time worked, salary or hourly rate, gross earnings, deductions, net earnings, check number of the payment, and gross earnings to date. Exhibit 20 shows a typical payroll record form, with columns in which the amounts for each pay period may be entered.

The second payroll form, illustrated in Exhibit 21, is the payroll register, which is used each time a payroll is prepared. This register is used not as a journal but as the source document for a payroll journal entry. This form shows the name of each paid employee with a record of the hours worked, earnings, deductions, and payment. The totals for each category are computed and used for the entry to the journal or voucher register.

The amount of the deductions will vary from state to state

Exhibit 20. Employee Payroll Record.

Name: _____   Position: _____   Pay Rate: _____

Address: _____   Date of Employment: ____   Termination Date:

_____   Exemptions: _____   _____

Social Security No.   Date of Birth:

_____   _____

Date	Hours	Earnings			Deductions			Payment		
		Reg.	Over-time	Gross	FICA	Fed. Tax	State Tax	Net Pay	Ck. No.	Gross to date

Exhibit 21. Payroll Register.

Payroll Period:

Name	Hours	Earnings			Deductions			Payment	
		Reg.	Over-time	Gross	FICA	Fed.	State	Net	Ck.

and organization to organization and from year to year as tax rates change and premiums increase. These forms often note departmental assignments with the appropriate budget numbers related to the payroll charges for each employee.

Petty Cash

In any office, there are times when a small amount of cash is required for minor expenditures; for example, for postal deliveries due, package deliveries with a delivery charge, or special supplies for the office. If there is no petty cash fund, employees must pay such expenses out of pocket. This requires making out a requisition, attaching the receipt to the requisition, processing them through the system for reimbursement, and making entries in the accounting system. The cost of this process may be considerable and, in fact, may exceed the cost of the reimbursement itself. Thus, a petty cash fund may be not only a convenience but also a way to reduce costs.

When a petty cash fund is established, a petty cash asset account is set up, and the amount is deducted from the cash account through a check to be cashed by the petty cash supervisor. When an expenditure is made from petty cash, a petty cash voucher is filled out. The petty cash voucher should be a prenumbered form with spaces for the date, purpose of the payment (for example, postage, special overseas envelope, delivery charge), amount, an approval signature, and the signature of the person receiving the money. A receipt for each purchase should be stapled to a copy of the voucher. In some cases, the voucher may indicate the expense account to which the charge should be made.

When the petty cash fund is replenished, and at the end of the fiscal accounting period, an entry is required to record the expenses and to draw another check to bring the total in the fund back up to the original amount. When the entry is made, the receipts and copies of the vouchers are submitted for reimbursement and the vouchers stamped or punched to ensure that they are not used again.

Reconciling the Bank Statement

Because the bank and the organization keep separate records, the bank statements must be reconciled monthly to see whether they agree with the records of the organization. The process for carrying out this reconciliation is the same as that for a personal checking account except that a written record of the reconciliation is created, and entries are made in a journal.

To make the bank and accounting records agree, the reconciliation must take account of such items as outstanding checks, deposits in transit, service charges, interest earned, checks returned for insufficient funds, and miscellaneous charges. An example of a reconciliation of a bank statement appears in Exhibit 22.

When the bank statement and checking account in the

Exhibit 22. Sample Bank Reconciliation.

Balance in checking account (4/23/89)		3,250
Less:		
Service charge	10	
Collection fee	6	
NSF check (E. Smith)	85	101
Adjusted checking balance		3,149
Bank balance (4/23/89)		3,169
Add:		
Deposit as of 4/22/89 in transit		150
Total		3,319
Less outstanding checks:		
No. 321	75	
No. 327	35	
No. 334	60	170
Adjusted bank balance		3,149

example have been reconciled, journal entries must be made to record the bank charges and the check returned for insufficient funds (NSF). After the reconciliation is complete, a second and possibly a third party should review the reconciliation and the canceled checks. In one instance, an owner of a small private business did not verify the reconciliations made by the accountant. One day the owner acci-dentally came across the company's canceled checks and discovered that his name had been forged on numerous checks for more than a thousand dollars each made payable to the accountant. Further investigation revealed that the accountant had been dipping into the checkbook for several years. Fearing public embarrassment, the owner did not press charges.

Summary

The input and processing of information through the accounting system involve a set of complex accounting principles and bookkeeping practices. This process begins when each transaction is methodically entered into the system. The transaction entries are then transferred in an orderly manner from the book of original entry (the journal) to the general ledger and, in some cases, to the subsidiary ledgers. The information in the general ledger is used to prepare the trial balance, which is a working document that determines whether the accounting entries and transfers are accurate. After the trial balance has been prepared, the information in the subsidiary ledgers is used to prepare the revenue and expenditure budget reports.

In this processing of accounting information, a manager must try to ensure that all transactions are entered properly, that proper authorizations exist for each transaction, and that the source documents have been used for all entries and are on file. In addition, a manager should consider the use of optional special journals and vouchers to save time and improve control over the entry and processing of information.

Associated with the initial entry of a transaction and the transferring of information through the system, the manager must be sensitive to several related features that should exist in the system. These concern a strict set of procedures to be followed in drafting checks, maintaining formal employee records and a payroll register, and the reconciliation of bank statements.

There are two important points noted in this chapter. First, by using the subsidiary ledger to prepare the revenue and expenditure budget reports, the accounting system provides direct feedback to the personnel working with the budget system. The budget reports are not prepared until the trial balance has proved that the debits and credits in the general ledger have equal totals. Second, after the trial balance has been completed, the process leads to the financial statements that are prepared at the end of the fiscal year. These financial statements, which are discussed in Chapter Eight, are critical to the organization and must be understood by managers.

8

Understanding Financial Statements

After the trial balance has been completed and the debits and credits in the general ledger are proved to be equal, the financial statements, which are the output for the accounting system, can be prepared. This does not mean that they are prepared every time the trial balance has been completed; rather, they are generated at the end of the operating year when an organization must report the results of its financial operations for the year and its financial position as of the end of the year.

The financial reports consist of three separate statements prepared at the end of an operating period for each set of accounts. Thus financial statements should be prepared for each fund in an organization and then combined to present an overall financial picture for the organization.

Principle 12 of the GAAP asserts that organizations should prepare financial statements plus reports of their financial position. The information in these statements is used to facilitate management control of financial operations, for legislative oversight, and for external reporting purposes. According to Principle 12, these statements should include comprehensive annual reports covering all funds and account groups. In addition, an organization may then issue separate general-purpose financial statements that provide a fair presentation of its financial position and operations.

In addition to meeting the above needs, financial statements are also considered by some to be relevant to the needs of third parties (Sorter and others, 1974). As simple as this may seem, the "needs" that are to be served by the statements cause the confusion. Chatfield (1974) explains that financial statements were first used to check the ledger balances. As time passed, they were used more for reporting purposes, particularly for investors; eventually this became their primary role over the past one hundred years in for-profit companies. In these reports, a profit company presents the status of its resources and obligations and the results of its operations

(Skousen, Langenderfer, and Albrecht, 1983). The "results of its operations" means profit or loss—the bottom line in terms of performance. Consequently, the financial statements of a for-profit company should be the core of the annual report, for they present both the company's financial status and the results of its performance.

Sorter and others (1974) suggest that the requirements of financial statements in the for-profit sector are equally applicable to the nonprofit sector; however, because cash profit is not the performance objective of public and nonprofit organizations, they propose that such organizations describe the benefits, or results, produced by their operations in nonmonetary terms, leaving the evaluation of the relationship between the nonmonetary benefits and the financial costs to the reader of the annual report. Thus, in the annual reports of many public and nonprofit organizations, financial statements are used as supporting documentation for the nonmonetary results, which in some cases has become unfortunate, as discussed later in the chapter. This supporting documentation may include budget information as well as notes, statistical data, and supplemental accounting information (Berne, 1989); in some cases, formal accounting statements may be entirely replaced by supporting data. Many organizations have concentrated so heavily on nonmonetary benefits that the financial statements have basically become a footnote or a pie chart; unfortunately, if the financial statements do not appear to be important to the organization, the people who read the reports may feel that their tax dollars and contributions are not important or, worse, not respected.

As noted earlier, financial statements are also prepared for use by the managers of an organization (Berne, 1989). In explaining the importance of cost analyses, Coombs and Hallak (1987) state that the past must be used to see into the future: How can the leaders of an organization know where they are going if they do not know where they have been and where they are? For example, assume that the financial statements for a school show that the assets owned by the school include a school building built twenty-five years ago at a cost of $550,000. After being fully depreciated, the current book value is $50,000. Assume also that an average of 2,000 students have used the building each year over the past twenty-five years. The cost per student per year ($550,000 - $50,000/2,000 × 25) is thus $10. Should the school make repairs, undertake major renovations, or build a new building? What would be the reaction of the public to this information?

Many organizations do not show buildings and equipment on their financial statements or, if they do, do not depreciate them. Thus, managers may not be aware of such historical factors as the age of a facility, major renovations that have been undertaken on it, its book value, or its market value; as a result, they may have to base an appeal for money to spend on the facility on an emotional rather than financial point of view (for example, by publishing in the local newspaper a picture of leaky ceilings caused by a forty-year-old roof). This causes the public facilities entrusted by the public to be allowed to deteriorate because of inability or unwillingness to use the past to see into the future.

There are many other complex issues and points of debate related to the content and presentation of financial statements produced by public and nonprofit organizations. This chapter respects those concerns, but focuses on the three basic financial statements and the related processes required to prepare them. Thus, the first concern in the chapter is the time period. Up to this point in the book, time periods have been casually referred to as "budget periods," "operating periods," or "fiscal years." However, a fiscal year is a specific period of time and is directly related to the financial statements. The second concern is the process followed from the trial balance to the financial statements; the third is the financial statements themselves.

The Fiscal Year and the Accounting Cycle

Even though a public or nonprofit organization may be exempt from paying taxes, it still must have an annual operating year on which to base its financial receipts and budgets. This annual business year is called a "fiscal year"; it may be any twelve-month period, such as July 1 to June 30 or October 1 to September 30 (the federal government's fiscal year). A calendar year is the twelve-month period from January 1 to December 31. A calendar year and a fiscal year may or may not be the same period of time. The annual financial statements relate to the fiscal year only.

An *accounting cycle* is not a fixed period of time; rather, the term refers to the interval that begins when the nominal accounts are opened with the first entries through to when they are closed to create a zero balance. After the closing entries are made to the nominal accounts, the financial statements can be prepared. Because financial statements are typically prepared and released only for a fiscal year, the terms *accounting cycle* and *fiscal year* are often used interchangeably. An organization could have more than one accounting cycle within a fiscal year, whereby the nominal accounts could be closed during the year and interim financial statements could be prepared to cover a portion of the fiscal year, although this would not be likely. More likely, however, is the preparation of monthly income statements and periodic balance sheets without the closing entries being made.

An accounting cycle is divided into accounting periods. An accounting period is a time period determined by an organization, usually a month. The trial balance and budget reports are prepared at the end of each accounting period. After a fiscal year has ended, a public or nonprofit organization has a grace period after which it must present the end-of-year financial statements and an end-of-year budget report. This grace period may be as short as thirty days or as long as four and a half months, which is the time allowed by the Internal Revenue Service.

Preparing for the Output: Closing the Books

There is a specific process to be followed through an accounting cycle from the opening of the books to the closing of the books (here again, creativity is not advisable). Some of the steps in this process have been covered in previous chapters, while others are described in this and the following chapter. These steps are as follows:

1. Budget proposals are approved internally.
2. The nominal accounts are opened for estimated revenues and appropriations, budget allocations are made, and the subsidiary ledger accounts are opened.

3.   A budget award is received, the revenue account is opened, and budget allocations may be revised.
4.   Business transactions are recorded in the journal.
5.   Journal entries are posted to the ledger and, if appropriate, to the subsidiary ledger.
6.   The monthly trial balance and budget reports are prepared.
7.   At the end of the fiscal year, the books are closed, and the following sections in a work sheet are prepared:
     a.   An end-of-year trial balance.
     b.   Adjustments (discussed in Chapter Ten).
     c.   An adjusted trial balance.
     d.   Revenues, expenditures, and excess of funds.
     e.   Balance sheet.
8.   The adjusting entries are made.
9.   An adjusted trial balance is prepared.
10. Closing entries are made.
11. The postclosing trial balance is prepared.
12. The financial statements are prepared.

The flow diagram for the accounting system is now complete, as shown in Figure 15.

The Work Sheet. In order that the closing activities will be carried out efficiently, a work sheet is used. The work sheet is a large multicolumn sheet of paper with two columns for each of the five sections enumerated in the list above. An example of a work sheet for the General Institute is presented in Exhibit 23. (This example and the examples of financial statements presented later apply to the forms used for a general fund. Work sheets and financial statements for other types of funds and for the entire organization are discussed later in the chapter.) Note in Exhibit 23 that each section has one column for debit balances and another for credit balances. The first section is an end-of-year trial balance, which lists all the debit and credit balances in the general ledger, including the control accounts for revenue and expenses, encumbrances and reserves for encumbrances, and appropriations and estimated revenue accounts. The next section is for adjusting entries; one adjustment has been made, to close the reserve for encumbrances and to add the amount to the fund reserve. This section is followed by an adjusted trial

Figure 15. Comprehensive Accounting Process.

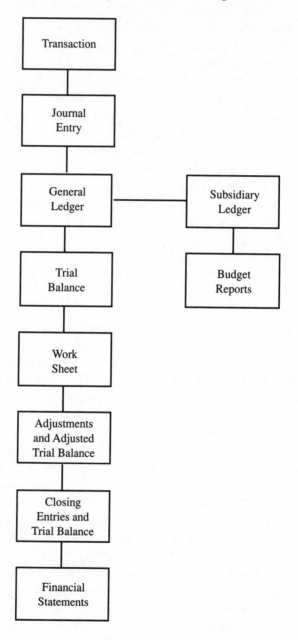

Exhibit 23. Sample Work Sheet.

General Institute
Work Sheet
For the Year Ended December 31, 1990

Account	Trial Balance		Adjustments		Adjusted Trial Balance		Revenue and Expenses		Balance Sheet	
	Debits	Credits	Debits	Credits	Debits	Credits	Debits	Credits	Debits	Credits
Cash	50				50				50	
Accounts receivable	25				25				25	
Expenses	90				90		90			
Estimated revenue	130				130		130			
Encumbrances	15		15		15		15			
Reserve for encumbrances		15								
Vouchers payable		10				10				10
Appropriations		120				120		120		
Revenue		135				135		135		
Fund balance		25				25				20
Fund reserve		5		15		20				20
	310	310	15	15	310	310				
Excess revenues							20			20
							255	255	75	75

balance, which shows that the debits equal the credits after the adjustments have been made.

The next section is for the accounts associated with revenues and expenses. By sorting out the nominal accounts, this section determines whether there is an excess of revenue over expenses, or vice versa. In this example, there is an excess of revenue of $20, which is added to the debit (expense) column to make the two columns equal. This section can be referred to when the closing entries are made. The last section is for the balance sheet, which lists the real accounts (assets, liabilities, and fund balance) and the excess of revenues, which is carried over from the revenue and expense sections. Note: Since the encumbrance was treated as an expense, it was included with the expenses against a revenue claim. This means that the cash to be received or retained to pay the expenses has been increased by $20. At the same time, the fund reserve shows an increased balance of $20, and it can be charged to pay the encumbrance when the invoice is received. This is simply one of several methods that may be used for carrying encumbrances forward.

It is important to note that this worksheet assumes that an excess of revenue can be shown and then, when the books are closed, added to the fund reserve by the set of closing entries. This may not be the case if General Institute is given a final revenue payment equal to the total expenses. In such a case, the expenditures (and hopefully the encumbrances) would be added together, and the revenue already received would be subtracted from the expenses to determine the amount of revenue to be paid to General Institute.

The Closing Entries. As explained above, the work sheet is used as a guide in making the closing entries. In the example illustrated in Exhibit 23, the closing entries would be made for the accounts shown in the revenue and expenses section (the expense control account, estimated revenue, encumbrances, appropriations, and revenue control account). The reserve for encumbrances was closed via an adjustment to the fund reserve. The entries made to the control accounts would have to be posted to the general ledger.

The closing entries involve a number of bookkeeping entries that create a zero balance in all of the nominal accounts and have an effect on the fund balance. These entries also close the budget, and an organization cannot conduct any business until the nominal accounts are reopened again.

Thus, the timing for the closing entries is important. They cannot be made too far in advance, and they cannot be made in the new fiscal year; and it takes a considerable amount of bookkeeping time to ensure that they are accurate. The important points for managers to look for at this time are that all nominal accounts have a zero balance; that the postclosing trial balance shows that the debit balances and credit balances in the ledger are equal; and that, after the closing entries are made, no further expenditures are processed against the budget. These points may seem to be somewhat elementary, but they are not always attended to, and serious muddles can result when they are ignored. One of them took four months to resolve, and another was never cleared up but was buried in a different account in the computer. Predicaments like these may be more common than most people suspect.

Output: The Big Three

Financial statements are prepared for a variety of people: managers, board members, contributors, taxpayers, bankers, government officials, and so on. Managers must be mindful that although the statements are important to them, the general public or the membership of the organization also has a right to be informed. The public or membership should not be considered to be accountants or financial experts, but they do have a stake in the organization. Thus, the financial statements must be clear, easily understood, accurate, and complete.

Financial statements must communicate to the reader the end result, or bottom line (Was there an excess of revenue over expenses?) and the big financial picture of the organization at the end of the year (What is the value of its resources, and what are its outstanding obligations?). Financial statements do not need to be lengthy and complex, though some of them look like student term papers received by professors before a maximum is placed on the number of pages that may be submitted. Unfortunately, there is no such rule regarding financial reports in either the public or the private sector. This is troubling, because sometimes excess verbiage is used to cloud a weakness in content.

Mansfield (1988, p. 137) states that "the financial disclosure and reporting practices of American cities are being challenged in many forums" and that these challenges focus "primarily on the adequacy of financial information." He notes that a publication by Arthur Andersen & Company (1976) points out that government reports are viewed as generally cumbersome, incomplete, and difficult to understand. Berne (1989) points to the New York City crises of 1977 to illustrate how the failure of internal controls can go undetected because of unsound reporting practices. These same criticisms are also leveled at other public and nonprofit organizations, such as public schools, colleges and universities, hospitals, charitable organizations, and churches.

To address these criticisms, Mansfield (1988) calls for greater uniformity as to what should be reported and for compliance of financial statements with accounting guidelines. Bowsher (1988) underscores the necessity for a sound, integrated accounting and budgeting system in order to produce good financial information. This is, of course, impossible for organizations that do not use the double-entry accounting method. Such organizations are able only to issue an end-of-year budget report supported by creative renditions, often very artistic, of the nonmonetary gains produced by them.

The failure to ensure uniformity and appropriate content in financial reports creates numerous problems. One of the effects of such a failure is described by Bowsher (1988, p. 58): When financial statements are unreliable, budgets are often "developed without reliable information on what has occurred," which means that future financial information will be even more unreliable, and on and on in a circular effect.

Financial statements must make three accounting disclosures: (1) the difference between revenue receipts and expenditures and the corresponding effect on the fund balance; (2) the overall financial picture of the organization as of the end of the fiscal year; and (3) the effects of the financial operations on the fund balance for the fiscal year. Thus, three statements should be produced and made public for each set of accounts used by the funds in the organization: the statement of revenues, expenditures, and changes in fund balance; the balance sheet; and the statement of changes in fund balance.

Statement of Revenues, Expenditures, and Changes in Fund Balance. The statement used to disclose the amount of revenue received by an organization and how that revenue was spent is called the statement of revenues, expenditures, and changes in fund balance. Berne (1989) explains that the purpose of this statement is to show the flow of resources through an organization and the corresponding effect on the fund balance. Exhibit 24 provides a simplified example of this statement: the statement of General In-

Exhibit 24. Sample Statement of Revenues, Expenditures, and Changes in Fund Balance.

General Institute
Statement of Revenues, Expenditures, and
Changes in Fund Balance
For the Fiscal Year Ended June 30, 1990

Revenues	
City taxes	$550,000.00
State taxes	6,563.00
Total revenues	556,563.00
Expenses	
Salaries—administration	$130,653.54
Salaries—professional staff	305,421.86
Salaries—clerical	45,960.05
Wages	7,700.00
Supplies	14,986.17
Communications	7,775.20
Travel	12,234.80
Rentals	11,016.05
Equipment repairs	973.00
Equipment	8,140.00
Miscellaneous	6,501.93
Total expenditures	551,362.60
Excess of revenues over (under) expenditures	5,200.40
Fund balances—July 1, 1988	7,575.00
Fund balances—June 30, 1989	$ 12,775.40

stitute, which has one fund and two revenue accounts under one revenue control account; one source of revenue is the local city treasury, and the other is a state office. The bottom line of General Institute's statement shows that the fund balance was increased as a result of excess of revenues over expenses.

Some organizations present additional information in such a statement. Exhibit 25 shows General Institute's statement when it has included its proposed annual budget amounts for comparison

Exhibit 25. Sample Statement of Revenues, Expenditures, and Fund Balance with Comparison to Proposed Budget.

General Institute
Statement of Revenues, Expenditures, and
Changes in Fund Balance
For the Fiscal Year Ended June 30, 1990

	Proposed Budget	Actual
Revenues		
City taxes	$553,000	$550,000
State taxes	7,000	6,563
Total revenues	560,000	556,563
Expenses		
Salaries—administration	$131,000	$130,654
Salaries—professional staff	308,500	305,422
Salaries—clerical	45,000	45,960
Wages	8,000	7,700
Supplies	13,500	14,986
Communications	7,000	7,775
Travel	12,500	12,235
Rentals	11,000	11,016
Equipment repairs	1,000	973
Equipment	8,500	8,140
Miscellaneous	6,000	6,502
Total expenditures	552,000	551,363
Excess of revenues over (under) expenditures	8,000	5,200
Fund balances—July 1, 1989	7,575	7,575
Fund balances—June 30, 1990	$ 15,575	$ 12,775

with what was actually received and spent. This would have different implications for an organization that has to collect the tax revenue (a local government, for example). In this case, under the revenues section, the report would present the adopted budget in the first column and how much of the revenue was actually collected in the second column (the difference being due to uncollectible taxes or a decline in the economy). Under expenses, it would show the amount budgeted to each expense category by the adopted budget in the first column and how much was actually spent in the second column. When an organization has to cut back on services because the amount of taxes collected is less than expected, such a report can be an important public relations document. In some cases, additional columns may be added to show the difference between the budgeted and actual columns in terms of amounts and percentages, the amount spent in the previous year, and so on. However, if too much extraneous information is added to the statement, it can become too complex and confusing for its readers.

A report for an operation in a self-support fund would use a variation of this statement, called an "income statement." Because income is generated by each self-support operation throughout the year, income statements should be produced for each operation throughout the year. These should be prepared in conjunction with the monthly budget reports to show whether the income of an operation is meeting the expenses, as well as how close the revenue and expenses are to the targets proposed in the approved budget. Then, at the end of the year, a final income statement is needed for each income operation. The income statement uses the same basic format as the revenue statement, presenting the income generated by the operation, a list of expenses, and the difference between the income and the expenses. Exhibit 26 shows an income and expense statement for a counseling clinic in a self-support fund within a larger organization. (Note: A discussion of the use of the term *net profit* in an income statement, as seen in Exhibit 26, is presented later.)

Balance Sheet. The financial statement that provides the big picture of the organization as of a specific date is called the balance sheet. The purpose of the balance sheet is to display the resources of the organization (assets and fund balance) and its obligations

Exhibit 26. Sample Income Statement.

The Counseling Center
Self-Support Fund
Income Statement
For the Year Ending June 30, 1990

Revenues

Client fees	$6,563.00

Expenses:

Part-time secretary	$4,564.47
Supplies	631.30
Telephone	98.63
Postage	86.34
Test materials	1,121.19
Total expenses	$6,501.93
Net profit	$ 61.07

(liabilities). This statement gives an overview of the present financial stability of the organization, whereas the statement on revenues, expenditures, and changes in fund balance shows the results of the financial activities over the past fiscal year.

Two types of forms may be used for the balance sheet: the account form, which lists the assets on the left side and the liabilities and fund balance on the right side, and the report form, which lists the assets first and then the liabilities and fund balance below rather than to the right. The sample balance sheet shown in Exhibit 27 uses the report form for one fund with limited assets and liabilities. In an organization with more than one fund, a balance sheet is prepared for each fund, and, as discussed later, a combined balance sheet is prepared for all of the funds in the organization.

Several observations can be made from the information on the balance sheet in Exhibit 27. For example, the ratio between assets and liabilities is large (better than two to one) and there is possibly too much money in the cash account, and some of it should probably be transferred into savings. The fund balance looks strong in relation to the amount of the revenue received (shown as $556,563 in Exhibit 25) but is less than 5 percent of the total annual award This may be important if it is called on in an emergency such

Exhibit 27. Sample Balance Sheet.

General Institute
Balance Sheet
June 30, 1990

Assets

Cash	$12,450
Cash-savings	6,420
Total assets	$18,870

Liabilities, Encumbrances, and Fund Balance

Liabilities:	
Vouchers payable	$ 1,800
Note payable	6,095
Total liabilities	$18,870
Fund balance:	
Fund balance	12,775
Total liabilities and fund balance	$18,870

as major equipment failure) or to cover the payroll if revenue payments are late or if there is an economic shortfall.

Often a balance sheet will have a column for the account balances of the previous year as well as the current year and will present comparisons in the form of ratios and percentages. This permits a reader to note any dramatic changes in the ratio of assets to liabilities, increases or decreases in the fund balance, and so on. Because this information is so important to management, the balance sheet may be prepared as an interim report during the year. In these cases, the books may not be closed, and estimates may have to be made to complete the fund balance section of the statement. Thus, the detailed accuracy of such an interim statement would be questionable, but it still can be a good working document.

Statement of Changes in Fund Balance. The third financial statement focuses on the changes in the fund balance over the past fiscal year. This statement presents the amount of the fund balance at the beginning of the period, the revenues, fund transfers, expenses, and encumbrances for the year, and the amount of the fund balance at the end of the year. Although this may seem to duplicate a section of the statement of revenues, expenditures, and changes in fund balance, it is a recognition of the importance of the fund balance to the financial health of the organization. Henke (1977, p. 37) sees this statement as a "connecting link" in the history of the organization. An example of a statement of changes in fund balance for the one fund in the General Institute is presented in Exhibit 28.

In a self-support fund that generates a profit, this statement may be called a statement of retained earnings. "Retained earnings" is an account in which a private company places its profit to reinvest in the company. Thus, for example, if a company had a net profit of $100,000, distributed $80,000 to its investors, and put the remaining $20,000 back into the company, the $20,000 would be placed in the retained earnings account under the owner's equity section. However, in a public or nonprofit organization with a profit-making operation, the retained earnings account would consist of the total net profit earned by the operation, as there are no investors or owners to whom the profits must be distributed unless some of the profits are transferred to another fund.

The use of the retained earnings account removes some of the concerns described earlier about "equity" being shown by a public or nonprofit organization. In an apparent compromise, some organizations and books use the term *fund equity* rather than *fund balance*. Some others do not use the term *profit* or *loss* but use *excess of income* or *excess of expenses* along with a retained earnings

Exhibit 28. Sample Statement of Changes in Fund Balance.

General Institute
Statement of Changes in Fund Balance
For the Fiscal Year Ended June 30, 1990

Fund balance, July 1, 1989		$ 7,575
Revenues	$556,563	
Expenditures	551,363	
Excess of revenues over expenditures		5,200
Fund balance, June 30, 1990		$12,775

account. In other words, there are numerous renditions. A retained earnings statement for the counseling center described earlier is in Exhibit 29. This statement is simple and to the point. In a brief period of time, the earnings of numerous operations in a self-support fund can be reviewed and decisions can be made with regard to their disposition.

A further comment must be made at this point about the use of the terms *equity, profit,* and *retained earnings* by public and nonprofit organizations. Many organizations actively invest money, particularly money earned by or donated to the organization, and some of these investments are made in a self-support operation within the organization. When they make such investments, which are not peculiar or unethical, organizations must identify the money invested in and earned by the operation. When money is formally transferred into and out of a self-support fund via accounting entries in a journal, *equity* may be the appropriate term used to identify the money invested in the operation along with the words *profits* and *retained earnings.* This may seem to violate the traditional use of the accounting terms as discussed earlier, but traditions are being changed as efforts are made to find ways for the accounting system to formally recognize the profit-making operations that have evolved over recent years. This is evidenced in the financial statements prepared by public and nonprofit organizations and in texts that show a retained earnings account and use the term *fund equity* (Berne, 1989; Freeman, Shoulders, and Lynn, 1988) as compared to the statements and texts of twenty years ago.

Exhibit 29. Sample Retained Earnings Statement.

The Counseling Center
Self-Support Fund
Retained Earnings Statement
For the Year Ending June 30, 1990

Retained earnings July 1, 1989	$540
Net income for the year	61
Retained earnings June 30, 1990	$601

The greatest danger to public and nonprofit organizations in this regard is that profit-making operations may use public money to compete in the free enterprise system. This is more likely if the accounting system does not use the proper rationale for establishing the profit-making operation, use appropriate money, recognize the profits, use the retained earnings in a manner that is consonant with the mission of the organization, and accurately report these activities and results.

Combining the Financial Statements of All Fund Entities

One cause of considerable confusion and complaint about the statements produced by public/nonprofit organizations probably derives from the combined statements. As described throughout this book, public and nonprofit organizations use fund entities (like those described in Chapter Two). Since each fund in an organization has a separate set of accounts, each should have a separate set of financial statements. Because the purposes of the funds are so different, there is considerable variation in the content of these statements. Berne (1989) explains that the balance sheets of different funds are not comparable with each other because each fund has a different focus or purpose. Consequently, an opportunity to review the financial information for all of the funds in reference to each other is needed to give an overall view of the organization. The combined financial statements provide this opportunity by presenting the results of all the funds on one form (Berne, 1989; Freeman, Shoulders, and Lynn, 1988; Henke, 1977). The use of the combined statements, however, does not relieve the organization of the obligation to prepare separate statements showing the details for each fund.

Exhibit 30 shows the form for a combined balance sheet for an operations fund, self-support fund, restricted fund, fixed-asset fund, and debt fund. Another form is used for the combined statement of revenues, expenditures, and changes in fund balance, with a format the same as the combined statement for the balance sheet (Exhibit 30) except the list of accounts in the left-hand column shows only revenue, expenditures, and the fund balance. An organization may also show profit, retained earnings, and fund equity for a self-support fund in this statement, if appropriate.

Exhibit 30. Sample Combined Balance Sheet.

The Hermongous Organization
Combined Balance Sheet
June 30, 1990

	Operations Fund	Self-Support Fund	Restricted Fund	Fixed-Asset Fund	Debt Fund
Assets (list of accounts)					
Liabilities					
Fund Balance/fund Equity					

The combined statements may show amounts for the same accounts, such as cash and supplies expenses; however, many accounts are particular to a specific fund. For example, the operations fund would show an account for receivables, such as taxes or dues receivable, but such receivables would not be found in the fixed-asset fund. At the same time, accounts for land, buildings, and equipment would be found under the fixed-asset fund but not the other funds. In addition, if sets of accounts are used within a fund, they will be listed separately. Thus, the list of accounts presented in the combined statement may be extremely long and, if the print size is reduced to save paper, difficult to read. For example, one organization presented a combined balance sheet that listed more than seventy-five different real accounts for eleven different funds and sets of accounts. A more reasonable approach would be to prepare a statement for each fund or a limited number of similar funds and then condense the information on the combined statement for all funds. This is one reason why there is a need for standardization.

Summary

Financial statements, the output of the accounting system of a public or nonprofit organization, can be prepared after the trial balance has been completed. They present the results of an organization's financial operations over a specified period of time and its financial position as of a specific date. Financial statements are prepared at the end of the fiscal year, although interim statements may be prepared during the year.

At the end of the fiscal year or accounting cycle, entries are made to make adjustments to accounts and then to close the books so that the financial statements can be prepared. These adjustments and closing entries are facilitated by the use of a work sheet, a multicolumn form that lays out on one sheet of paper the trial balance, the adjustments, the adjusted trial balance, the expense and revenue summary, and the balance sheet. The work sheet is a working document used as a guide to make the adjusting and closing entries to the nominal accounts.

The three basic financial statements for public and nonprofit organizations are the statement of revenues, expenditures, and changes in fund balance; the balance sheet; and the statement of changes in fund balance. These statements show (1) the difference between the revenue receipts and expeditures at the end of the fiscal year and the impact of the fund balance, (2) the overall financial picture of the organization as of the end of the fiscal year, and (3) the effects of the fund balance over the fiscal year. In addition, for an income-generating operation within an organization, there may be an income statement to show the profit of an income-generating activity and a statement of retained earnings.

Because public and nonprofit organizations may have numerous funds and special sets of accounts within a fund, the financial disclosures for an organization are presented in reference to each other on combined financial statement forms. These combined statements are used to make the financial disclosures of the organization. In some larger, more complex organizations, the use of these statements must be carefully considered in order to ensure that the detail necessary to meet the stated objectives of the financial statements is provided.

9

Integrating
Accounting
and
Budgeting Systems
for Better
Managerial
Control

A problem in many public and nonprofit organizations is that their accounting and budgeting systems operate as separate entities, or they have only a budget system. The major thrust of this book is that an organization must use both systems, and they must properly interact with each other. This integration is not a simple activity, and it cannot be accomplished by just the accountants or just the managers; it depends on the work and cooperation of both parties. The integration must comply with sound accounting and budgeting principles and be appropriate to the management structure of the organization.

This chapter focuses on the six major points where the accounting and budgeting systems interact. These points of interaction have been noted and discussed as components within each of the systems but now are considered in relation to each other. They can be summarized as follows:

1. The approved budget and the budget allocations (budgeting system) are entered into a fund's set of self-balancing accounts, the ledger and the subsidiary ledger (accounting system).
2. The revenue award of the adopted budget (budgeting system) is entered into a fund's set of accounts, the ledger and subsidiary ledger (accounting system).
3. Budget receipts and expenditures (budgeting system) are recorded in a journal (accounting system).

4. The accounting subsidiary ledger (accounting system) is used to generate budget reports (budgeting system).
5. The closing entries (accounting system) conclude the use of the budget (budgeting system).
6. The financial statements (accounting system) provide an end-of-year report of the budget activities (budgeting system).

Interaction Points 1 and 2: Entering the Budget Approval and Award

When a budget request is approved and the allocations made by the proper authorities in an organization, it is entered into the records of the accounting system. The first entry is made when a budget is approved internally (interaction point 1), and the second entry (interaction point 2) is made when a budget is adopted and an award is made (Freeman, Shoulders, and Lynn, 1988; Henke, 1977; Kuhn, 1970; Skousen, Langenderfer, and Albrecht, 1983). These two sets of entries are referred to as appropriation accounting. Some organizations may feel that they are unnecessary and may not record them. However, these entries are the first step needed to bring the budgeting and accounting systems together and the only way that the two systems can be tied together at the end of the fiscal year. Henke (1977) and Freeman, Shoulders, and Lynn (1988) recommend and discuss in detail the bookkeeping entries associated with appropriation control (Gross and Warshauer [1979, p. 50], however, do not recommend the use of appropriation accounting).

The use of appropriation accounting procedures requires double-entry accounting entries, a set of self-balancing accounts in each fund, an accounting ledger, and a subsidiary ledger. These procedures cannot be used with the single-entry method.

Point 1: Budget Approval. When a proposed budget is approved, an entry is made in a fund's set of accounts to record the approved budget's estimate of the revenue to be awarded and the expenditures expected to be made by the budget units in the organization. As noted previously, all entries must be backed up by source documents; the source document for this entry is the approved budget. An approved budget shows the amount of revenue expected, which is recorded in an estimated revenue account, and the total of the estimated expenses, which is entered into the appropriations account. If the amounts of the estimated revenues and estimated expenditures (appropriations) are not the same, the difference is charged to the fund balance. For example, if an approved budget estimated the tax revenue to be $457,000 and expenditures to be $455,000, the expected surplus of $2,000 would be allocated to an account in the fund balance. Thus, an entry would be made to show (1) a debit to "Estimated Revenue—Taxes" for $457,000, (2) a credit to "Appropriations" for $455,000, and (3) a credit to the "Fund Balance" for $2,000.

An important detail of this procedure is that the estimated revenue account is debited and not treated like a revenue account, which is credited. The same is true for the appropriations account, which is not debited like an expenditures account but is given a credit balance. As noted in Chapter Seven, the amount credited in the appropriations account is posted to the appropriations control account, and then the budget allocations are posted to the subsidiary expense accounts. After these postings are made, the approved budget is on file in the accounting system. The budgets can then be allocated to the operating units. The estimated revenue and appropriations accounts are closed at the end of the year; however, Freeman, Shoulders, and Lynn (1988) describe a procedure in which the appropriations account is not closed to a zero balance. Thus, the purpose of this accounting entry is to formally recognize (1) the amount of money expected to be received, (2) the amount expected to be expended, and (3) the difference between the two amounts.

Point 2: Budget Award. When the budget is adopted through a tax levy, a membership vote, a council or board vote, or some other method, a revenue award is made to the organization. This requires a second entry, for which the source document is the official written notice showing the total amount of the award. For example, if $457,000 was the amount of the award to be received from tax receipts, an entry would be made for the following: (1) a debit to the asset account "Taxes Receivable" for $457,000, meaning that the organization expects to receive cash payments totaling $457,000, and (2) a credit to the revenue account "Tax Revenue" for $457,000.

In this case, note that the budget award is the same as the "estimated revenue" amount and $2,000 greater than the appropriations account. As a result, another entry may be made to (1) increase the amount in the appropriations account by $2,000 and (2) eliminate the $2,000 entry to the account in the fund balance. If the appropriations account is increased, the amount of the appropriation in the general ledger will be increased, which will also require that the amounts in the subsidiary ledger accounts be increased. This, in turn, will mean that the amounts allocated to the budget units will be increased by $2,000.

If the revenue award had been less than the amount in the appropriation account, then the appropriated amount and the estimated revenue account would have to have been decreased. The decrease in the appropriations account would in turn decrease the amounts in the subsidiary ledger and reduce the amounts in the allocated budgets.

If the entry for the budget award cannot be made at or before the beginning of the fiscal year, some organizations have to suspend activities. (Note: An estimate for uncollectible taxes could be made at this time, and a subsidiary ledger could be used with the receivable account; these entries are discussed later in this chapter.) These important entries may be summarized as follows:

1. The budget is approved.
    a. Entries are made to the estimated revenues and appropriations accounts (and fund balance if there is a difference between the amounts of the two accounts).
    b. Entries are posted to the general ledger account for estimated revenue and the control account for appropriations (and possibly to the fund balance account).
    c. Amounts are posted to the subsidiary accounts of the appropriations control account.
    d. The budget allocations are made to the operating units. These allocations are based on the estimated expenditure amounts posted to the above subsidiary ledger accounts.
2. The budget award is received.
    a. Entries are made to revenue receivable and revenue.
    b. Entries are posted to the general ledger accounts for rev-

enue receivable and revenue and possibly to the receivable subsidiary ledger.

3.   If the amounts of the approved budget and the budget award are different, then the difference in the amounts may be entered to the appropriations account and the estimated revenue account (and possibly to the fund balance account).

3.   a.   This amount (the difference between the approved budget and the budget award) is posted in the general ledger to the estimated revenue account and appropriations control account (and possibly to the fund balance account).

     b.   The amount posted to the appropriations control account is used to adjust (increase or decrease) the amounts posted to the subsidiary ledger accounts.

     c.   The allocated budgets are revised (increased or decreased). The revisions are based on changes made in the subsidiary ledger.

Income Budget Approval. With a self-supporting income-generating activity, which does not receive a budget award, a budget should still be proposed for each operation and approved by the organization's CEO, the governing board, or its designate. The approved budget is the source document for the accounting entry. This ties the budget and accounting systems together at the beginning of the process. Unlike a revenue budget request, the income budgets may require only one entry, which is to estimated income and appropriations, as follows: (1) a debit to the account "Estimated Income—(name of activity)" and (2) a credit to the account "Appropriations." This entry would also be posted to the general ledger and subsidiary ledgers, after which an approved budget with amounts assigned to the expense categories would be forwarded to the self-support operation's manager, who could begin business operations.

Instead of the second entry made in the case of a revenue award, entries are made to the income account when money is earned. In addition, expenses are recorded when they are incurred; that is, the accrual accounting system is followed for income and expenses. Therefore, revenue receivable accounts are not needed as they are for revenue awards; however, a receivable account and a subsidiary ledger are used when credit is given to customers or clients. The balances in the income, receivable (for customer credit), and expense accounts must be carefully monitored in reference to each other for cash flow purposes and for comparison with the approved budget estimates for income and expenditures.

When an operation is generating more or less income than originally estimated in the approved budget, a revised budget may be submitted for approval. Upon this approval, a new entry should be made into the accounting system to revise the estimated income and appropriations amounts, which also revises the allocated budgeted amounts. This revision is recommended in order to provide continuing, indirect, strict control over an income operation by the authorities granting the budget approval.

Uncollectibles. Receivable accounts (such as taxes receivable, customer receivable accounts, revenue receivable, and so on) are assets that are used to keep detailed records of the money owed to an organization. In most cases, a subsidiary ledger is kept for each revenue source or customer that is indebted to the organization. When a payment is received, the cash account is increased (debited), and the accounts receivable account is decreased (credited). Unfortunately, managers of organizations, including for-profit companies, know that some of the money owed will not be paid. This requires that an estimate of this amount be made and entered into the books. This estimate is a contra account (introduced in Chapter Six), which means that it reduces the amount in the receivable account.

The estimate of the amount of a revenue award that will not be received is incorporated into the entry for the budget award (interaction point # 2). The amount of this estimate is based on past experience and is approved by the governing body. Some for-profit companies keep elaborate records on overdue accounts and use statistical probabilities to calculate the amounts that will not be collected. In for-profit companies, these estimates are critical, as the uncollected amounts can be written off as a loss for tax purposes. In the public and nonprofit sector, they are just as important, as they have a direct effect on the amount of revenue to be received. Thus, a record of a governing body's approval of the amount estimated to be uncollectible is an important document and serves as the source document for the entry.

If, of a $457,000 revenue award, an estimated $25,000 in taxes is considered to be uncollectible, instead of the above entry made under point 2 the following entry would have been made: (1) a debit to taxes receivable for $457,000, (2) a credit of $432,000 to revenues, and (3) a credit of $25,000 to the contra account "Allowance for Uncollectible Taxes." This produces a more realistic estimate of the amount of revenue that will be received: not $457,000 but $432,000. As described above, the amount recorded in the appropriations account may be adjusted to reflect the amount of money expected. The entry to adjust the appropriations account would be posted to the general ledger and then to the subsidiary ledgers. Thus, the allocations to the budget units would have to be revised. The budgets would now be based on the amount of revenue to be received and not on the amount approved by the governing body or the amount awarded before the uncollectible allowance is deducted. If during the year the amount estimated to be uncollectible is determined to have been too great or too small, the amount in the uncollectible account should be increased or decreased.

At the end of the year or operating period, receivable accounts and their contra accounts are closed to a zero balance. When this is done, the balances in these accounts are transferred into two other accounts, "Taxes Receivable—Delinquent" (an asset) and a corresponding contra account called "Allowance for Uncollectible Taxes—Delinquent." This entry accomplishes two objectives. First, it sets a zero balance in the ledger for the receivable account and its uncollectible contra account for the new year. Second, the end-of-year balance in the receivable account and the related amount that was not collected will remain on the books. This is important, because the managers in an organization cannot write off a receivable or the estimated uncollectible amount; only the governing board may do so. When it does, the "Taxes Receivable—Delinquent" account and the contra account "Allowance for Uncollectible Taxes—Delinquent" are reduced by the amount approved by the governing board. A board should base adjustments on a record of how much of the delinquent amount has been carried from year to year and what the experience has been in collecting these amounts. If a payment is received from an account that has been written off (such as when a piece of property is sold for the amount of delinquent taxes), a specific set of entries is made to record the payment.

Although an uncollectible taxes account may not seem to be necessary in some organizations such as those that use private collection agencies, this is far from the truth. In one situation, a school in a small town using a single-entry method did not make such estimates for the record but relied on the collector's reports. Over a period of years, the collector simply did not report the entire amount that was collected, which was estimated to be near a million dollars, and kept the difference. With a proper records system, estimates based on historical data, and formal board action, this would not have been possible. The collector was finally caught because a close associate turned her in, not because the theft was revealed by financial audits.

The Appropriations Gap. In many public and nonprofit organizations, the double-entry accounting system has been considered the only system needed for the security of and control over all financial matters, while the budgeting system has been used for program planning and the allocation of resources. The integration of the two systems has consisted solely of entries for the approved budget in the accounting system, and any further interactions between the accounting and budgeting systems have been more informal than formal.

In recent years, organizations have become larger (some of them now resemble giant corporations), and budget awards are no longer once-a-year events involving only a few sources but ongoing activities involving numerous sources. With the use of new technology, the budget is being relied on more and more as a working document for management purposes, for control over expenditures, and for reference as greater financial opportunities are provided to organizations. Budgets are ideal for managers, as they are not complex, are directly related to organizational structure and program objectives, and do not require any great accounting expertise in order to be used for budget control purposes. Therefore, they must be accurate and should not allow for exceptions resulting from the appropriations method.

This means that the interactions between the accounting and budgeting systems must be more formal than informal. As CEOs are expected to generate new revenue sources, bring in budget supplements, extend existing resources through more efficient control over the use of revenue, invest money to earn money, borrow money, and, along with their managers, make financial adjustments throughout the year, accurate and up-to-date budget reports are critical. A common weakness, as noted previously, is that because of the traditional use of the appropriations accounting method, the close integration of the two systems is not promoted. A break with tradition is not easy to recommend or to implement.

The major issue of concern in appropriations accounting is the entry of the approved budget to the appropriations account and then the receipt of the budget award. With the traditional application of this method, when the amount in the approved budget does not agree with the amount of revenue to be received in the budget award, the appropriations account and the budgets are not adjusted to reflect the actual amount of revenue to be received. As noted above, the amount entered in the appropriation's account is the total of the authorized expenditures shown in the approved budget and is considered to be appropriate, as it is the amount that the organization has been authorized to spend by a supervising board. This total is then entered into the appropriations control account and is not changed during the year.

Thus, the total of the amounts assigned to the subsidiary ledgers for expenditures may not be in agreement with the amount of money that the organization actually has to spend. Rather, the difference between the appropriated amount (the approval budget) and the amount actually received (the adopted budget) is reflected at the end of the year in the fund balance (Freeman, Shoulders, and Lynn, 1988; Henke, 1977; Kuhn, 1970; Skousen, Langenderfer, and Albrecht, 1983). While adjusting the appropriations account, subsidiary ledgers, and budgets to agree with the amount of revenue to be received may cause accounting complications, these complications cannot be greater than those caused by the failure to allocate all of the money provided to an organization. If a revenue shortfall is feared, an allowance should be recorded in the estimate for un-collectible revenue and not allowed to create a greater budget gap.

Gross and Warshauer (1979) and Gross and Jablonsky (1979) object to appropriations accounting; they believe it causes too much confusion with the fund balance and financial statements. This point is important because, as pointed out earlier, the excesses and deficits created by appropriations accounting in the fund balance may be artificial (Freeman, Shoulders, and Lynn, 1988). If artificial amounts are entered into the appropriations account and the budgets to represent the actual amount of money available to be spent, they must eventually show up in the financial statements.

Artificial amounts are hard to justify in an accounting system that prides itself on accuracy. Essentially, this situation is brought about because of the initial difference in the opening entries between the appropriated amount and the revenue award, which in turn may be exaggerated when appropriated amounts (not revenue awards) are transferred between funds and then when the organization must expand its operations. When this process is extended to other funds, new operations, and subunits (often geographically dispersed), and two different amounts of money in the fund balance are used to represent the revenue allocations and awards, entries are made that are often understood only by the financial experts who created them.

Financial statements are not a public disclosure of anything if the reader cannot understand them. In one organization, the financial statements showed an "unreserved-unappropriated" account in the fund balance. It is likely that a number of people who read financial statements do not have a clear comprehension of what a "reserved" account or an "appropriations" account is and that even those who do probably do not know what an "unreserved-unappropriated" account is. The implication is that it is used to account for money that cannot be legitimately placed in any other account. These problems can be greatly remedied by adjusting the appropriations account to match the amount of the revenue award when the award is made. If accurate amounts are entered into the accounting system, adjustments at the end of the year or the use of general meaningless accounts in the financial statements will not be necessary.

Another reason to avoid the "gap" is that budgets should reflect how much revenue is available for the organization to spend in order to achieve its mission. Thus, the accounting system must respond to changes in the revenue awards or income potential for an operation. Scheps and Davidson (1970) believe that this is necessary for all changes, including supplements, amendments, and transfers. If this is not done, an organization can expect weak interaction between the two systems and possibly an embarrassing set of financial statements at the end of the year. In one case, an organization did not enter several supplements for funded projects into the accounting system but used the original appropriated amounts assigned to the subsidiary ledger. At the same time, the manager and the budget office were working from the revised budgets. At the end of the fiscal year, the subsidiary ledger amounts and the budget records did not agree. The final report for the auditors sent by the funding agent was indeed a "creation."

Splitting a Revenue Receipt. The method used to assign revenue awards to different funds should be carefully considered. As noted earlier, a revenue award may be split and placed in two or more funds; for example, a budget award may be split among the operating fund, the restricted fund, and the fixed asset fund. For a cleaner operation from an accounting point of view, separate budgets should be prepared for each fund that is to receive a portion of the revenue receipt, and the entries to the estimated revenue and appropriations account should be made in the set of accounts in each fund that is to receive a portion of the revenue award. When the award is made, the second set of entries should also be made in the accounts of each fund and the appropriations account revised accordingly.

Another method for handling a split is to record the accounting entries for budget approvals and budget awards in one fund, such as the operating or general fund, and then transfer the money to another fund via accounting entries in both funds. This option may be advantageous in a situation where the board chooses to enter all awards into one fund.

Whatever method is used, the splitting of a revenue award must be done carefully: the source documents that specify the distribution of the award with corresponding approved budgets must clearly indicate the governing board's approval and be on record. In a recent dispute with a bargaining agent, the board and managers of an organization were accused of hiding money in other funds for ulterior motives. In this case, a portion of the revenue award was placed in the general fund and then transferred permanently into other funds without a specified budget to describe how the money was to be spent. If the charge is unfounded, the actions taken by the board (the source documents) to split the revenue should be on record. If the management set aside money without the board's approval, the situation is not healthy for the organization.

Interaction Points 3 and 4: Receipts, Expenditures, and Budget Reports

When money is received after a budget award, an entry is made in the accounting system. The check stub and/or the deposit slip is the source document for the entry. When money is spent against a budget award, entries must be made in the accounting system. The forms used to process the expenditures against a budget (such as purchase orders) are the source documents for the entries. These entries represent the third point of interaction. As with the first two points of interaction, the budget activities require the formal accounting entries to be made to record the transactions. The journal entries are posted to the ledger, and a trial balance is run to ensure that the total of the debit balances is equal to the total of the credit balances. However, before the ledger totals can be used to prepare a trial balance, the control accounts must be checked for accuracy by comparing balances in the subsidiary ledger to the control accounts. The subsidiary ledgers are then used to prepare the budget reports. This represents the fourth point of interaction in which the accounting system is employed to provide feedback into the budget system.

Points 3 and 4 represent the core of the interactions between the two systems. The first two interactions and the last three (4, 5, and 6) typically occur only at either the beginning or the end of the fiscal year. The activities associated with points 3 and 4 may occur every day of every month in the fiscal year. This is where the manager's attention must be focused if a sound financial management program is to exist. This is also where an organization's business personnel and operating managers must work together cooperatively and not as separate units. However, this cannot occur if the previous points of interaction are missing.

Interaction Point 5: Closing the Accounts and the Budget

The closing entries affect the income, revenue, estimated revenue, expenses, appropriations, and encumbrance accounts. They essentially match the revenue against the estimated revenue and the expenditures and outstanding encumbrances against the appropriations. The difference between these entries is either added to or charged against the fund balance. Therefore, after the two entries are made, the fund balance shows their net effect: either positive or negative. With income accounts, the process is the same except that the difference affects the retained earnings account.

While the details of these entries are beyond the scope of this text, they can be summarized as follows: The first entry closes the revenue or income account (debit) and estimated revenue or income account (credit), with the difference entered into the fund balance or equity account (debit or credit). If the estimated revenue account has been revised to match the amount of revenue in the budget award and to reflect all supplements, these amounts should be the same. If not, the differences will appear in this entry. The second entry involves the appropriations account (debit), the expense accounts or expense control account (credit), and encumbrances or encumbrance control account (credit), with the difference entered into the fund balance (debit or credit). If the appropriations account has been revised to reflect the actual amount of revenue awarded, the total amount of the expenses plus encumbrances should be equal to the appropriations. In reality, they are not likely to be equal, because all of the revenue award may not have been spent. Thus, the difference may go into the fund balance, or the final revenue payment to the organization may be adjusted according to the actual expenditures. In the case of an adjustment in the last revenue payment, an entry would be made to reduce the appropriations account and the subsidiary ledger accounts so that the official record will reflect the actual amount of the revenue distribution and expenditures by the operating units in the final report (rather than using footnotes to describe the differences). These two entries bring all of the nominal accounts, including the appropriations account, to a zero balance except in the case of a "reserve for encumbrances," which is transferred to a fund balance account in an adjusting entry. Therefore, the accounting entries have closed down the budget, and no further receipts or expenditures can be processed for it.

Interaction Point 6: Financial Statements

After the closing entries are made, the accounting system is used to prepare the three financial statements for each fund. Each fund may consist of several revenue sources with a corresponding budget for each. The financial statements make two important disclosures that relate to each fund in the budget system. The first is how much revenue or income money was received and how it was spent. Additional data may be added to this disclosure, such as how much revenue was to be awarded as compared to how much was received or how the organization proposed to spend the money as compared to how it was actually spent. This information is important for the managers of the budgets as well as for the people who provide money to the organization. The financial report that discloses this information is the statement of revenues, expenditures, and changes in fund balance.

The second important disclosure is the effect of the financial activities on the balance in the fund, called the fund balance or fund equity. This information is presented in all three financial statements (the statement of revenues, expenditures, and changes in fund balance, the balance sheet, and the statement of changes in fund balance). The balance in each fund is important not only in relation to the budget awards received in the fiscal year just ended but also in terms of the budgets in the new fiscal year. A strong fund balance can provide security for an organization in a year when budget awards are less than desired.

A Multilevel Bureaucracy

Two special options are available to the accounting and budgeting system in a multilevel bureaucracy. These options have strong effects on the interactions between the accounting and budgeting systems as well as deeper implications. This section describes these options through an example of a small bureaucracy.

The township of Blueberry has been granted a revenue award to provide supplemental support for two volunteer fire companies. The township may use a percentage of this award for administrative purposes, such as paying a portion of the salaries for the police radio operator who also monitors the phone on which fire calls are received; however, the balance of the revenue award must be distributed to the two volunteer fire companies, the Smokers and the Sparkies. When the township receives the revenue award, it must be entered into the township's general fund through the entries previously described. The township then has two options as to how it will distribute the money to the volunteer fire companies.

The first option is to enter the revenue award now in the township's general fund into the revenue account, the revenue receivable account, and the general ledger. To receive the money, the two fire companies must present a budget that has been approved by their trustees or officers to the township supervisors. The supervisors will then either adopt the approved budget or revise and adopt it and then make a revenue award.

A lump-sum award may be made, or the notice of the award may be accompanied by a budget outlining how the money must be spent. In either case, after a budget award is made, the transmittal of the money to the two companies is processed by the township via two requisitions, which are entered in the journal as two separate expenditures in the general fund and posted to the general ledger and then to the two subsidiary accounts. If the checks are to be sent to the two fire companies according to a specified schedule, the requisition form specifies when the checks are to be drawn, and the total amount immediately appears as an encumbrance on the subsidiary ledgers of each account. The payment checks are then sent to the Smokers and Sparkies as specified in the requisition. At the end of the year, the township authorities audit each fire company to determine whether the expenditures were made according to the understanding in the budget award.

If all of the award is not spent, the fire company may not be able to receive the unspent balance if it is to be retained by the organization providing the money. (Various proposals have been made regarding the ludicrous practice of spending money to keep it. To encourage the thrifty administration of a budget, one recommendation is that a surplus be shared by the organization providing the money and the one spending it.) If all of the money can be received, it is placed in the fund balance of the fire company to be used as directed in the coming years. In addition, at the end of the year, the township budget report and financial statements show two expenditures: one to the Smokers and one to the Sparkies. The budget reports and audits of the two fire companies are on file in the township office to back up their end-of-year statements and reports.

The second option is for the township to treat the two fire companies as if they were budget units directly under the township's supervision and were receiving budget allocations. When the revenue award is received by the township, the entries are made in the general fund's set of accounts. The township enters the budget allocations into the expense control account and each expenditure category in the township's general fund subsidiary accounts. A budget agreement, or contract, is made between the township and each of the fire companies so that each fire company will spend the money as budgeted by the township.

When the agreement has been signed, the township processes a requisition that encumbers money in each of the subsidiary ledger accounts in the township's general fund in correspondence with the budget outlines given to the fire companies and specifies when the checks will be sent to each fire company. The final payment is included in the requisition but will not be released until the final expenditure reports from the fire companies are received and approved.

If the approved expenditures on the final expenditure report are less than permitted in the contract's budget, the final payment will be less than originally proposed. In this case, the final payment shown on the original requisition will be canceled and a new one processed. The fire companies' budget expenditures will then be entered into the township's subsidiary ledger as shown in its budget expenditure reports. This is accomplished by an entry to the expenditure control account that will eventually be posted to the specific expense categories. Thus, the individual expenditures of the two fire companies are shown in the township's end-of-year budget report and financial statements. These documents may not reveal how much each company received. An audit of the fire companies' records would be required to determine whether their final reports matched the source documents. If the money not spent by the fire companies does not have to be returned to the organization that provided it, the township will place it in its fund balance, possibly in a restricted account for fire protection.

The second option is probably most commonly used, although the specific procedure may vary. It would be naive to think that all of the steps, such as the subsidiary postings, will be carried out. This is unfortunate, since it results in loss of control over revenue during the year.

Both of these options have a number of advantages and disadvantages. With the second option, the greatest advantage to the township (disadvantage to the fire companies) is that, if permitted, it will retain any surplus in the budget award. That is, if some of the revenue awarded to the fire companies is not spent, it will revert (if permitted) to the fund balance in the township's operations fund. This is why this option is the most popular. An advantage for the township (disadvantage to the fire companies) with both options is that they allow it to delay the payments of the revenue award to the fire companies until the last minute, or after the last minute, which means that the township can transfer the money temporarily from the general fund to an investment fund to earn interest. In a huge bureaucracy processing millions of dollars, this can produce sizable earnings in interest, which is money that can be used at the discretion of the board.

In addition, the second option offers the township direct control (and in many cases power) over the amount of revenue provided to the two fire companies. The township could even reduce the award to one of the fire companies by simply changing the contract and the internal requisition at any time. In such instances, the fire companies would want a formal revised contract for a variety of reasons, but mainly to protect themselves. The greatest disadvantage to the second option is that it makes an audit difficult to conduct as the entries in the township's accounting system for the expenditures are not backed up by the proper source documents, but only by the reports from the fire companies. This would require the auditors to visit each fire company if there was any question about the authenticity of the reports or the validity of the expenditures.

A deeper issue regarding the distribution of revenue through a multilevel bureaucracy is the intent of the governing body that makes the money available. For example, how much authority should Blueberry Township have over the amount of the two awards and over how the money is spent by the fire companies? Should the township have the authority to change the intended use of the money by the fire company? Should Blueberry township keep the surplus? Such questions are also relevant to large bureaucracies. For example, federal money distributed to a state government for the use of local governments and agencies is transmitted to the local units by an office in the state's executive branch. How much control does Congress mean to give to the state executive office? How much flexibility does Congress wish to give the local government, school district, hospital, college, labor agency, and so on? Does the accounting and budgeting process provide the flexibility intended by Congress? When the revenue excess can be retained by the state, does Congress intend to allow the state's executive branch to retain any excess of the award in its fund balance, should the money be retained by the local agency, or should it be returned to the federal government for reallocation? If the money is retained by the state government, will it be used in the future by the office in the executive branch to support the local program as originally intended? Is this money used to the benefit of the political party in office? The same set of questions can be raised in reference to a state government making money available to operations through a city or county government.

Summary

This chapter has described six major points where interactions between the accounting and budgeting system should take place. The first two points are when the budget is approved and when a budget award is then made. The journal entries made from the approved budget for the estimated revenue and the estimated expenditures (appropriations account) are used to set up the subsidiary ledgers for the budget allocations. The next interaction is when the budget award is received and entries are made to the revenue account and a receivable account. At this time, adjustments may be made to the appropriations account if the amount of the award is different from the amount in this account. This then requires that the subsidiary ledger and budget allocations be revised.

The next two points where the budgeting and accounting systems interact involve the receipt of revenue payments and the processing of expenditures by the budgeting system. Journal entries are made in the accounting system and posted to the general ledger and then to the subsidiary ledger. A trial balance is prepared to check the accuracy of the debits and credits in the ledger, after which the budget reports are prepared. The activities associated with these two points are ongoing activities that are repeated throughout the year. The budget reports are critical to management and should be monitored closely. When the accounting and budgeting systems are not fully integrated, the budget reports may reflect inconsistencies.

At the end of the year, there are two important interactions between the budgeting and accounting systems. The first pertains to the closing entries for the nominal accounts. These entries indirectly match the revenue receipts against the actual expenditures and outstanding encumbrances. The differences are either charged or added to the fund balance. After these entries are made, the budget is closed. In the second interaction, the financial statements are prepared. These statements provide a full disclosure of the revenue received by an organization, how it was spent, and the effect on the balance in each fund account. Only by understanding the entire process and the interactions between the two systems can managers fully understand and explain the disclosures of the financial activities of their organization.

10

Linking Past, Present, and Future Through Adjustments

Accounting adjustments are made before the financial statements are prepared. The purpose of these entries is to update the amounts in accounts and to allocate income, revenue, and expenses to the proper accounting period—when the income or revenue is earned or when expenses are incurred. The source documents for the adjusting entries are found in an organization's policy manual.

Adjustments are often considered to be the ho-hum part of accounting, the nitty-gritty details that only accountants have to worry about. The sharp manager knows that this is not true. Adjustments are an important activity in accounting, particularly for public and nonprofit organizations. The GAAP advocates the use of adjustments in Principles 7 (depreciation) and 8 (accruals).

Adjustments are discussed at the end of the accounting chapters in this text not because they rank low on a priority scale but because their full impact cannot be appreciated without an understanding of the accounting system. This chapter first provides an overview of how adjustments fit into the accounting system and then describes the four types of revenue and expense adjustments, adjustments made through an inventory procedure, and adjustments made through depreciation.

Adjustments and the Accounting System

The cash-basis method of accounting recognizes revenue (meaning that a journal entry is made) when it is received and expenses when cash is paid. On the other hand, the accrual accounting method makes the journal entry for revenue or income when it is earned and for expenses when they are incurred. For the accrual method to place the revenue, income, and expense accounts in the proper accounting time period, adjusting entries are made to assign the correct portion to each period. In this way, the adjustments link the past, present, and future accounting periods.

The Cash-Basis Method. The rationale behind the use of the cash-basis method, as opposed to the accrual method, by public and nonprofit organizations centers on the practice of making budget awards to provide revenue for the organization to conduct its activities over a one-year period, and not for two or more years. This is reasonable, since such awards are usually made annually, and taxpayers, contributors, or members of an organization would not want to pay an annual assessment that is greater than what is needed to run the organization for a year. With this practice, an annual budget is proposed, approved internally, and then sent forward for adoption. After adoption, revenue is received from tax collections, contributions, or direct payments from another agency. The revenue is recognized when it is received, and expenses are recorded when cash is paid. Theoretically, by the end of the year all of the revenue has been received and has been used to pay off all of the expenses. The nominal accounts are closed at the end of the year, and a new year begins. Any money left over will be either placed in the fund balance or returned to the organization that provided the money, depending on the legal guidelines associated with the revenue award. Thus, the accrual accounting method would not be appropriate for public and nonprofit organizations, as it would spread revenue receipts and expenses over more than one fiscal year.

The logic behind the cash-basis method is unfortunately not realistic. An organization cannot perfectly predict how much money will actually be spent or received in one fiscal year. When preparing a budget proposal, a manager must consider numerous variables that may have a financial effect on the operation and then assign an estimated dollar amount to each variable, such as potential equipment repairs, the possible need for additional personnel to complete a project, extra unexpected costs associated with the offering of a special program, effects of inflation on personnel salaries and benefits, and so on. Managers also must try to keep their organizations' technology up to date (they are often criticized for not doing so), but this requires money to be projected into a budget for new equipment and materials when the potential costs are usually unknown.

Another problem with this logic is that an organization is an ongoing enterprise; it cannot be expected to conclude all business activities on the last hour of the last day of the fiscal year and begin new activities on the first hour of the first day of the new fiscal year. Such an expectation can be costly to an organization; for example, it may mean having to reject a discount to buy materials or a piece of equipment because it is too close to the end of the fiscal year, not having needed work performed over the last three months of the fiscal year for fear that it will not be completed on time, rejecting a short-term project because the revenue may not be received before the end of the year, or not recognizing the cost of the buildings and equipment over their useful life to the organization. An organization must have an ongoing operation, not a series of one-year events.

Thus, for a number of sound reasons, at the end of the fiscal year, there may be revenue or income that has been received for services not yet delivered, income or revenue that is owed to the organization but not yet received, expenses to be paid for which the invoices have not been received, and payments made for goods or services that will be used or received in the next period. Consequently, the logical choice for public and nonprofit organizations is not the cash-basis method but the accrual method, since the adjustments used with this method provide flexibility to a budget and a financial operation.

The Accrual Method. With the accrual method, adjustments are made at the end of an accounting period or fiscal year to bring all accounts up to date before the financial statements are prepared (Meigs and Meigs, 1984; Skousen, Langenderfer, and Albrecht, 1983). Consider the following example: An organization whose fiscal year ends on June 30 rents building to conduct its operations.

The owner of the building, whose fiscal year ends on December 31, offers to allow a 10 percent discount if the rent is paid for one year in advance by January 10. It would be good business sense to pay the rent in advance (assuming that the operation will continue at that location). However, the entire amount of the rent payment should not be charged to the current year, as it would be with the cash-basis method. Instead, half of the rent payment should be charged to the current year and half to the next year. For this to be done, an adjusting entry would have to be made on June 30.

One might believe that it would be appropriate to take the discount and then charge the entire amount of the rent to the current year, as it will all even out when the rent is paid next year for another year in advance. However, this would not be correct. First, the rent will likely increase from one year to the next; second, the source documents for the accounting entry would not stand up to an honest audit; and third, the financial statements would not reflect the actual costs. Thus, the real choice is to either refuse the discount, make the accounting adjustments, or ask for exceptions in the audit (which is undesirable).

Since adjustments involve revenue, income, and expense accounts, they are important to the accurate disclosure of the financial position of an organization (Needles, 1983). The accrual accounting method would make all of the revenue and expense adjustments possible, while the modified accrual accounting method would make selected adjustments. For example, Principle 8 of the GAAP proposes that a modified accrual method be used in governmental funds and, in some cases, in fiduciary funds.

Henke (1977) points out that a weakness of the cash and modified accrual methods is that they do not recognize the cost of all of the goods or services when they are consumed and the revenue when a service is performed or a product is delivered. Ideally, expenses should be charged to the budget that is in effect when the goods are actually used or services are rendered, not charged to the budget of the previous year or deferred to the next year, and revenue payments should be aligned with the delivery of the service or product for which the money was provided. The accrual method attempts to make this match as ideal as possible. As Henke (1977) further points out, the usefulness of the financial statements generated by a cash or modified accrual method is limited, as they do not accurately report the financial position of the organization or the results of the operation. He maintains that the full accrual method provides a more objective and precise measure of the resources made available to an organization and the corresponding use of those resources than does the cash or modified accrual method. Gross and Warshauer (1979) agree that in many instances the financial affairs of an organization are not presented accurately when the cash-basis method is used. Scheps and Davidson (1970) propose that all colleges and universities should use the accrual method.

Adjusting entries should be backed up by stated policies approved by the board, as there must be objective evidence to support them. This is an important point, because adjusting entries that are backed up by objective evidence guarantee greater consistency in the annual financial statements. If there are variations in either the type of adjusting entries made from year to year or the method used to make calculations to arrive at the amount of the adjustments, the financial statements will not be reliable. In addition, the statements are not valid if adjustments are manipulated in an effort to improve the financial picture of the organization (Henke, 1977).

Many public and nonprofit organizations do not make adjustments not because they do not see the need to make these entries but because they use a single-entry, or checkbook, budget method of accounting. Adjustments of entries can be made only with the double-entry method.

The Gap. As noted previously, the appropriations gap is the difference between the total amount of the allocated budgets provided to the operating units and the actual (not estimated) amount of revenue received or to be received. Hyatt and Santiago (1986, p. 87) define an appropriation as "an expenditure authorization with specific limitations as to amount, purpose, and time; a formal advance approval of an expenditure from designated resources available or estimated to be available." When the expenditure authorizations, or appropriations, do not equal the resources that will be made available, the amount authorized to be spent by the allocated budgets may be revised.

In the traditional practice in many organizations, the amounts authorized in the allocated budgets are not changed when the amount authorized to be spent is less than the revenue award. However, when the appropriation amount is greater than the amount of revenue received, the allocations are typically decreased at some time to avoid overexpenditure. The logical practice has been for boards to ensure that the amount of the appropriation (and therefore the allocated budgets) is always less than the actual amount of revenue that will be received; thus, allocations will not have to be decreased. If money is left over at the end of the year, either equipment may be purchased or the books will balance out the difference, and the surplus (or deficit) created by the gap will go into the fund balance. However, this defeats the purpose of using the uncollectible contra accounts. A planned or unplanned surplus should not be used to avoid making an estimate of uncollectible accounts.

The gap is not the same as the planned end-of-year surplus, which is typically included in the approved budget for the fund balance. The plan to have an end-of-year surplus is usually noted and justified in the approved budget, but the gap is not (Freeman, Shoulders, and Lynn, 1988). The purpose of a budget plan is to recognize all revenue in order to ensure that it will be utilized to the maximum benefit of the organization. Thus, the gap has the potential to create an annual slush fund or to provide relief to program managers.

Adjusting entries are made to provide a more precise accounting record of the receipt and the expenditure of the revenue made available to an organization. This, in turn, allows the organization to present a more accurate and objective set of financial statements. To fail to formally adjust for the revenue provided by the gap at the beginning of the year and then to make adjustments at the end of the year is a contradictory set of practices. In addition, if the gap and the adjustments are not recognized or realized, the financial records of the organization are not accurate or valid. This, of course, is not a concern when revenue is plentiful and there are a planned budget surplus, an unplanned surplus created by the gap, and an uncollectible revenue account. When an organization has more money at the end of the year than originally planned, accuracy is not critical, and the financial management of the organization is quite a simple chore. Depending on the unadjusted expense and revenue accounts, sometimes the surpluses may increase and sometimes they may decrease, but there is always enough fat to cover the overexpenditures, which means that the budgeting process is inflationary.

However, a dilemma can be created when there is a decline in economic growth (not a recession) compounded by creeping inflation and an organization's revenue increase is less than that received in previous years. At first the effects will not be felt, possibly not even observed, unless appropriate accounting adjustments are made and a proper set of financial statements exists. The reason is that reserves in the fund, the planned surplus in the budget, and the unplanned surplus create a cushion for a while. When the economic influences and relatively lower budget increase continue into a third and fourth year, the cushion no longer can soften their effects and the budget seems to crash. The impact of the budget declines is now increased by a power of two or three. This will be further magnified if the organization attempts to improve its financial position by expanding services, going into debt, or deferring financial actions to future budgets. This is not to suggest that the organization is lax in monitoring its financial records; however, without appropriate accounting adjustments the financial records will not provide the information managers and boards need at the outset because the financial statements will not reflect reality.

This type of situation, or a similar set of circumstances, could explain why some organizations move from a stable financial position to a crisis within a short period, even though there has been no decrease in the amount of revenue received. For example, some small private nonprofit colleges have had to close their doors in recent years. Some were experiencing a decline in enrollments, although the declines cannot totally explain their crash. No accurate financial analysis of past events, and no vision into the future, can exist if the financial statements do not formally recognize the gap, expense and revenue adjustments, value of the inventory, and book values of buildings and equipment.

In the presentation below, the adjustments are divided into three groups. The first group concerns the four types of expense and revenue adjustments made at the end of a period:

1. Expenses paid and to be charged to the current as well as to one or more future fiscal years.
2. Revenue or income collected in the current period for goods or services to be provided in the current and one or more future fiscal years.
3. Expenses to be charged to the current period but not paid.
4. Revenue or income earned in the current period but not received.

The description of the revenue and expense adjustment is followed by the other two adjustment groups: those for fixed assets through depreciation and for assets through an inventory procedure.

Adjustments for Revenues and Expenses

The objective of revenue and expense adjustments is to place revenue receipts and expenditures in the proper accounting period. There are two types of revenue adjustments and two types of expenditure adjustments. Revenue account adjustments are made (1) when money is received but will not be earned until the next fiscal year and (2) when money is earned but will not be received until the next fiscal year. Expense adjustments are made (1) when money is paid for goods or services that will not be used or provided until the next fiscal year and (2) when goods and services are received but will not be paid for until the next fiscal year.

Encumbrances, which are used only by public and nonprofit organizations, are typically not recognized when adjusting entries are discussed because they are adjusted by the closing entries. As explained earlier, encumbrances can be used to carry unpaid expenses over to a new fiscal year. In this process, the reserve for encumbrances is closed to a fund balance account that will carry the money forward, and the invoice is then paid in the next fiscal year. As a result, the costs of goods and services that are contracted in one fiscal year but will not be paid for until the next can be made through encumbrances.

Expenses Paid for Current and Future Accounting Periods. When an invoice is paid for services or goods (excluding buildings and equipment) that will be of benefit during both the current and future accounting periods, the expense should be charged against the revenue received in the current as well as the future accounting periods. The amount of the charge to each period should reflect the proportion of services or goods used during that period. Thus, the expenditure actually represents two business transactions: a payment for an expense for the current period and a payment for an expense in a future accounting period.

For example, if a police department that owns a gasoline storage tank receives a 5,000-gallon delivery of gas one month before the end of the fiscal year, it should not charge all of the delivery to the current year but should charge part of it to the current year and part to the next year. How much should be charged to the current year and how much to the next year should be calculated in several ways: by estimating daily use, by consulting records of previous gas use, or by actually measuring how much gasoline is left as of the last day of the fiscal year. Similar adjustments would also be needed if the police department prepared quarterly financial reports and wanted to determine how efficiently the new patrol cars used gasoline and whether that had a significant impact on the budget. Other types of expenses that might span two fiscal years include service contracts, insurance, heating oil bills, electric bills, rent, and supplies purchases. If adjustments are not made for such expenses, the charges will be made against the current budgets by default and paid from the current revenue award. This would mean that the current and future financial statements would not accurately reflect the operating expenses for the current period, the excess or deficit to the fund balance, or the assets held for the benefit of future operations.

There are two procedures that may be used to adjust for these expenses: the asset approach and the expense approach. Which approach is preferable depends on the nature of the expense item. With the asset approach, the prepaid item is recorded as an asset and is subsequently reduced each time a payment is charged. For example, if an organization made a rent payment of $6,000 for six months in advance, the payment would be entered in an asset account called "Prepaid Rent" (debit). Each month, that account would be charged (credited) $1,000 for the monthly payment, and the rent expense account would be increased (debited) for the $1,000 payment. At the end of the accounting period, the amount remaining in the asset account "Prepaid Rent" would be carried over to the new year as an asset, and the asset account would continue to be charged each month. The total rent expense for the year would be shown in the rent expense subsidiary ledger. The same arrangement could be used for supplies by entering (debiting) the amount of supplies bought into the asset account "Supplies." As supplies were used, the amount would be subtracted from the asset account "Supplies" (credit) and added to the supplies expense account (debit). If a record of the supplies being used could not be kept, a monthly inventory could be taken and an entry made to the supplies expense account and the asset account for the amount used.

The expense approach is the most common method used. With this approach, when the payment is made, the entire amount is entered (debited) into an expense account, such as a rent expense or supplies expense account, rather than an asset account. At the end of the fiscal year, any unspent amount in an expense account is transferred to an asset account, such as prepaid rent or supplies, and carried over into the next year. For example, the monthly rent and the value of the remaining supplies would be calculated at the end of the year, and then an adjusting entry would reduce the amount in each of the expense accounts (credit) by the amount remaining to be spent or used, and that amount would be recorded in an asset account (debit). The assets would then be carried over to the new year. After the beginning of the year, the amounts in the asset accounts would be transferred back to the expense accounts.

With the asset approach, the organization essentially supplies itself by entering amounts into the expense accounts as the asset is used. With this procedure, the subsidiary ledgers can be used for budget control if the expense entries are made as the asset is used. With the expense approach, the use of the expense accounts eliminate the need to make entries as resources are used.

In many organizations, the allocations made for supplies and materials represent a considerable sum of money. Failing to recognize the consumption and inventory of consumable supplies at the end of a fiscal year or operating period is irresponsible, for several reasons: it affects the reliability of financial statements, it decreases accountability for and protection of the organization's resources, and it gives employees a message that these resources are not important and that, therefore, employees will not be held accountable for their use. Many people who have worked in large public and nonprofit organizations can testify that the control over consumable supplies is often callously disregarded, in some cases with contempt, and the result is quite costly.

Scheps and Davidson (1970) believe that supplies and materials should be regarded in the same manner as is cash. They recommend the use not only of an inventory procedure but also of a subsidiary stores ledger. This would be an advantage in cases where the supplies account is used as a "dumping account" at the end of the year for any unspent money below the line.

Henke (1977) believes that the failure to disclose the supplies on hand is a problem that should not exist. Rather than using the account name "Inventory," which may be misleading, he recommends that the cost of the supplies on hand be shown in an asset account called "Supplies on Hand," which is created along with a fund balance account called "Reserves for Supplies on Hand." At the end of the year, the amount of the supplies left over would be recorded in the "Supplies on Hand" account (debit) and the "Reserve for Supplies on Hand" account (credit). Then, in the new year, as the leftover supplies are consumed, the amounts in the "Supplies on Hand" and "Reserves for Supplies on Hand" accounts will be reduced.

Another procedure is to use the asset account "Supplies on Hand" (debit) to represent the value of the inventory at the end of the year. Then, instead of using a fund balance account (credit), as discussed above, the expense account "Supplies Expense" would be reduced (credit). This would reduce the balance in the expense account at the end of the year by the amount of the inventory on hand. At the beginning of the new year, the amount of inventory shown in the "Supplies on Hand" account would be transferred (credit) to the supplies expense account (debit). This would create a zero balance in the asset account "Supplies on Hand," and the supplies expense account would be charged for the forwarded amount of supplies against the new year's budget. This procedure is similar to a method recommended by Freeman, Shoulders, and Lynn (1988,

p. 216) for recording the use of consumable supplies, except that they use the account name "Inventory of Supplies."

Income Received for Current and Future Accounting Periods. These adjustments are made when cash is received for goods or services in one accounting period but the goods or services are not delivered until the next accounting period. In these cases, the money received is placed (credited) in an account called "Unearned Revenue" or "Deferred Revenue," which is a liability account because the organization has received money and owes some service or product to be delivered in a future accounting period.

A simple example of unearned revenue is as follows: A college collects tuition in May and June for the fall semester, and its fiscal year ends on June 30. When the cash is received, it should be placed in a liability account, which could be called "Deferred Tuition Income" because it owes service to the people who paid their tuition. This means that the money will not get mixed in with current income money but is set aside until an adjusting entry is made after the beginning of the new year on July 1. At the beginning of the next accounting period, an entry is made to transfer the amount in the "Deferred Tuition Income" liability account (debit) to tuition income (credit). This adjustment cancels the balance in the liability account and allows the fall tuition to be used for the fall semester. It would not be acceptable to hold the tuition payments that were collected in advance until after the beginning of the new fiscal year or to place them in an alternative income account, because this would not show the liability assumed by the organization when the advance payment is accepted.

Expenses Owed but Not Paid. There are times when an organization creates a debt in a current accounting period that will have to be paid in the next accounting period; for example, when the payroll at the end of the year spans two fiscal years or when interest is owed on a loan whose payment schedule includes two fiscal years. In both of these cases, an actual cash payment for the expenses incurred would be made not in the current period but in the next accounting period. For the actual charges to be properly matched against the proper budget, an adjustment would be made at the end of the year.

Consider the following example: An organization pays its employees every two weeks, and its fiscal year ends on December 31. The last salary period covers the last week in December, for which the institution owes $1,250, and the first week in January, at which time the institution will owe another $1,250 in salaries. Both amounts, or a total of $2,500, will be paid on January 6, with half ($1,250) to be charged to last year and the other half to the new year. In this case, an adjusting entry is made on December 31 to record the salary expense for the last week in December. This entry records a salary expense (debit) for $1,250 and creates a liability account, "Salaries Payable" (credit), for the $1,250 owed to the employees. The organization now shows the salary expense of $1,250 at the end of the fiscal year, and an obligation to pay $1,250 in salaries is recorded as a liability and carried over into the new year. On January 6, when the employees are paid, the entry decreases the cash account for $2,500 (credit), eliminates the "Salaries Payable" account balance of $1,250 (debit) carried over from the last accounting period, and records $1,250 in salary expense (debit) for the first week of the current accounting period.

Income Earned but Not Received. This adjustment is required when an organization earns money in one fiscal year but does not receive the cash until the next fiscal year; for example, when an organization earns interest income on an investment but the amount will not actually be drawn from the account until the next fiscal year, or possibly, not for two or more fiscal years. In such a case, the interest should appear on the financial statements at the end of the fiscal year in which it is earned.

In another example, an organization has completed a project at the end of the year. A final revenue payment of $5,000 is due as of June 30, the end of the fiscal year, but will not be received until after the final budget report is received and approved. Sixty days into the new fiscal year, the final budget report is filed, and then after another sixty days, the organization receives the final revenue payment for the project that ended last fiscal year. In this case, an adjusting entry is necessary to show that the final revenue payment was earned but not received on June 30. This adjusting entry records the amount in the revenue account as if it had actually been received (credit) and also records it in the asset account "Revenue Receivable" (debit). This asset account now carries the $5,000 owed over into the new year. When the revenue payment is finally received at the end of October, an entry is made to remove the $5,000 from the revenue receivable asset account (credit) and to increase the cash account for $5,000 (debit). In this situation, the only problem for the organization is that it must have a sufficient amount of cash on hand to cover the expenses until the revenue check is received.

Inventory: An Uncommon Adjustment

An accounting adjustment that is not common or often seen as relevant for public and nonprofit organizations is inventory. The reason inventory accounts are not often used by public and nonprofit organizations is that they are to represent unused raw materials bought for production purposes or leftover goods purchased for sale and are therefore often thought to be unnecessary or irrelevant for a public or nonprofit organization. This is not an accurate perception. Inventory accounts may be very important to an organization that has a self-support fund used to sell goods. If an inventory record is not maintained, the organization might be surprised to find too much inventory on hand, which could cause a cash-flow and profit problem, not to mention a concern about the security of the goods.

If an organization wants to determine the value of the supplies and materials purchased and sold in the current fiscal period and how much will be left over to benefit the next accounting period, an inventory is required. In a discussion of independent audits, Gross and Warshauer (1979, p. 373) point out that if a physical inventory is not conducted and reported, the auditors cannot state that an "examination has been made in accordance with generally accepted auditing standards."

The procedure for maintaining an inventory account for goods being sold by a self-supporting operation begins with a calculation of how much inventory is left at the end of the year; this is called the ending inventory. The ending inventory then becomes the beginning inventory in the new fiscal year. For example, at the end of the fiscal year, the amount of supplies on hand becomes the new ending inventory. Therefore, adding the supplies purchased over the fiscal year to the beginning inventory and subtracting the new ending inventory from the total yields the cost of the goods sold for the fiscal year, as shown below:

Beginning inventory (6/30/90)	$1,100	
Purchases 7/1/90 to 6/30/91	5,750	
Cost of goods for sale		$6,850
Ending inventory 6/30/91		950
Cost of goods sold		5,900

In this case there are accounts for both "inventory" and "purchases." The amounts shown for the cost of goods for sale and the cost of goods sold are important to the management of the operation. In a full income statement, the cost of goods sold would be subtracted from the sales, which would provide the amount of the gross profit. Subtracting the expenses from the gross profit yields the amount of the net profit of the operation.

Inventory Methods. The methods that may be used to maintain an inventory are called the "periodic" and "perpetual" methods. With both methods, the organization must note the date of purchase, what was bought, how many units were purchased, and the cost per unit. The perpetual method is more appropriate when the inventory includes large, expensive units, such as computers. With this method, when a unit is purchased, it is added to the inventory record. When the inventory unit is used, it is deleted from the inventory record. Thus, the number of units available can be determined at any time from the inventory record. Usually a physical count of the units is made periodically to verify the record.

With the periodic method, when a purchase is made, it is entered into the inventory record, but when a unit is sold, the inventory record is not changed; instead, inventory counts are taken periodically, and then the inventory record is adjusted and an accounting entry made. This inventory method is appropriate when a large number of small items is involved. For example, if an organization buys computer disks by the carton and each carton contains twenty-four boxes with ten disks per box, it would be more efficient to periodically count the boxes and then adjust the inventory than to adjust the inventory record each time a box of disks is distributed or sold.

Determining the Value of the Inventory. An important accounting concern is determining the cost to be assigned to units that have been removed from the inventory and those that remain in it. With the perpetual method, this is not usually a problem, because the purchase price of the specific unit being sold is known and therefore the specific price of each unit on inventory is known. With the periodic method, however, there may be a question as to whether the cost of the unit being sold should be calculated as the cost of the units most recently purchased or the cost of the oldest units on inventory. Public and nonprofit organizations typically use the cost of the oldest materials on record, even though this cost may not be close to the current market price. With consumable supplies, this may not be very important, but for an operation that buys and resells goods, makes a profit, and must pay taxes, it is indeed important.

There are three procedures that may be used to calculate the value of the inventory: first in–first out (FIFO), last in–first out (LIFO), and average cost. Most public and nonprofit organizations seem to prefer the FIFO method. Presented below is a description of the application of each inventory procedure to calculate the values of six cartons of paper in an end-of-year inventory where the beginning inventory and the purchases of paper for the year were as follows:

Inv. 7/1	4 cartons @ $6/carton	$ 24
Aug. 1	5 cartons @ $6/carton	$ 30
Nov. 10	8 cartons @ $7/carton	$ 56
Jan. 10	10 cartons @ $7/carton	$ 70
Apr. 18	5 cartons @ $8/carton	$ 40
Totals	32 cartons	$220

The FIFO method assumes that the first items bought (first in) were the first ones sold (first out), so that the cartons remaining are assumed to be the last ones that were bought. Thus, the price assigned to the six cartons in inventory at the end of the year would be five cartons at $8 each (purchased on April 18) plus one carton at $7 (purchased on January 10), for a total inventory value of $47. When this amount is subtracted from the total cost of the cartons in inventory at the beginning of the year and those purchased during the year, it is determined that the cost of the materials used or sold during the year was $173. With this method, the value given to the inventory is close to the current market price of $8 per carton, and the cost of the supplies used is less than the current market value.

With the LIFO method, the most recently purchased items (last in) are considered the first ones sold (first out); thus, the value of the inventory is calculated to be $36 (four cartons from the beginning inventory at $6 each and two cartons from the purchase on August 1 at $6 each). This is considerably less than the FIFO inventory value of $47. However, LIFO provides a higher cost of goods sold—$184, as compared to $173 with FIFO—which in turn lowers the amount of the taxable profit.

The average cost method determines the value of inventory by dividing the total cost of the materials purchased by the number of units available for use or sale. With thirty-two cartons purchased at a total cost of $220, the average cost is $6.875 per carton. Thus, the ending inventory is worth $41.25 (six cartons at $6.875 each), and the cost of goods sold is $178.75 (twenty-six cartons at $6.875 each). This method is a conservative, middle-of-the-road approach compared to the other two methods.

With a perpetual inventory, where items can be specifically identified when sold, the values assigned to the goods sold by a self-support operation as well as the goods in inventory are the actual costs. When the units sold can be specifically identified for a periodic inventory, this is called the "specific identification method."

Once a method of inventory valuation is selected, the operation should adhere to the "principle of consistency" and use that method only. The financial statements for the operation should indicate the method used; if different methods are used for different types of units being inventoried, each method should be indicated. When a taxable for-profit operation changes an inventory method, the change must be approved by the IRS and clearly reported in the financial statements.

Depreciation

One of the expenses incurred by both for-profit companies and by public or nonprofit organizations regards the use of their assets over a long period of time, such as buildings and equipment. The expense that recognizes this use is called depreciation expense, and should be disclosed on the organization's financial statements. Depreciation expenses reduce the value of the assets over the course of the years by entering the amount into a depreciation expense account (debit) at the end of the accounting period. At the same time, this journal entry records the amount of the expense in a contra account called accumulated depreciation (credit). The accumulated depreciation is then shown as a deduction against the appropriate fixed asset on the balance sheet. In for-profit operations, the amount of the depreciation expense is then subtracted from the income generated for the period, which means that it is quite important for tax purposes.

Depreciation is a controversial topic for public and nonprofit organizations. Many organizations do not include accounts for buildings and equipment in their accounting records, so that recognition of depreciation is not possible. Berne (1989, p. 316) explains that "not only are fixed assets and depreciation excluded from most funds in governments; inadequate accounting for fixed assets is also one of the most frequently cited exceptions to generally accepted accounting principles."

One argument against the inclusion of fixed assets and the use of depreciation is related to the way money is received for buildings and equipment. Because money is not received each year in the annual budget award but rather is received in special revenue awards, it is argued that depreciation expense should not be charged as an expense against the annual revenue receipts, since this would mean that an organization would make a greater claim for a revenue award than is needed for an annual operation. The argument continues that an annual award is not intended to be used over an extended period of years, even for the replacement of buildings and equipment—and that if depreciation were included as an annual cost, budgets would become excessively large—and that therefore it is not important to show the assets in the accounting records.

Some people counter this argument by saying that the way money is awarded should be changed and that organizations should be given an annual revenue allotment that can be set aside for the replacement of buildings and equipment. Since the large expenses incurred periodically to build buildings place an exceptionally large tax burden on those who happen to be the taxpayers at that time, they feel that this expense should be levied against annual awards, and the revenue should be laid aside so that the burden can be spread out over the years. In addition, the failure to include the depreciation of assets means that financial statements do not present a full disclosure of the costs of the operations. As a compromise, it has been suggested that depreciation should be entered into a separate fund, such as the fixed-asset fund. There have been various proposals of ways to implement this compromise, such as how depreciation expense can be recorded but not charged against the annual revenue award (or vice versa), but none has been universally accepted (Freeman, Shoulders, and Lynn, 1988; Gross and Warshauer, 1979; Henke, 1977; Scheps and Davidson, 1970).

This text recommends that depreciation be recognized in the fixed-asset fund, using the following procedure: When a building is built or equipment is bought, the asset is placed permanently in the set of accounts in that fund. It is recorded as an asset (debit), and at the same time the amount is added to the fund balance account (credit). When equipment and buildings are depreciated, entries are made to depreciation expense (debit) and accumulated depreciation (credit) accounts in the fixed-asset fund. The accumulated depreciation, which is a contra account, reduces the book value of the asset on the balance sheet for the fixed-asset fund. The charges to depreciation expense lower the fund balance when the expense accounts are closed at the end of the year. Therefore, the book value of the asset is updated, the fund balance represents the total book value of the fixed assets in the organization, and the expenses do not affect the annual operating budget award (this part of the procedure would not satisfy those who feel that revenue should be collected annually for building and equipment depreciation.) When the combined financial statements disclose the total costs, they would include the depreciation of the fixed assets. The financial statements for the fixed-asset fund would be useful for planning purposes and for raising money for new equipment and buildings. At the least they would provide hard evidence of costs and book values, so that managers would not have to rely on emotional appeals.

The following example illustrates how depreciation is calculated. A fire company purchases a truck for $11,000. The truck is estimated to have a life of ten years, with a salvage value of $1,000 at the end of the ten-year period. The truck is the only fixed asset in the fixed-asset fund. If the truck is bought on the first day of the accounting period, the fixed-asset fund records the asset "truck" into the accounts (debit) for an amount of $11,000 and into the fund balance (credit) for an amount of $11,000. The $1,000 salvage value is deducted from the total value of the truck, and the remaining $10,000 is depreciated equally over each of the ten years. Therefore, at the end of each year, there is a charge for the depreciation of the truck of $1,000. The journal entry records $1,000 for depreciation expense (debit) and places $1,000 in the accumulated depreciation account (credit), a contra account for the asset account "truck." The balance sheet at the end of the first year is shown in Exhibit 31. The $10,000 shown in the balance sheet for the truck is the book value—the purchase cost minus accumulated depreciation. The amount in the fund balance was reduced by $1,000 when the closing entries

Exhibit 31. Sample Fixed-Asset Fund Balance Sheet.

Blueberry Township
Fixed-Asset Fund
BALANCE SHEET
December 31, 1989

Assets

Truck	$11,000	
Less: accumulated depreciation	1,000	10,000

Liabilities and fund balance

Fund balance, 12/31/89		$10,000

were made. (If the truck had been purchased midway through the year, the depreciation would be calculated for six months of the first year, for a total $500; if it had been purchased ten months into the year, the depreciation would be calculated for two months and so on.)

The major points to be noted about depreciation are that (1) it is not a process used to present the market value of an asset, (2) it represents a book value that is adjusted for costs arising from use and obsolescence, (3) it does not represent cash being set aside for replacement purposes, (4) the cost of the asset may include some of the expenses paid to have the asset prepared and/or delivered for purchase, (5) there are several methods that can be used to compute depreciation, (6) the federal government provides regulations for depreciation for taxable for-profit operations, and (7) the depreciation rate and asset life may be adjusted during the use of the asset for repairs or if the life of the asset is extended. Because of these factors, particularly the fact that depreciation does not represent market value, depreciation should not be used for an annual budget award. For example, if an annual budget award includes an additional amount of money that was based on depreciation of an asset, that amount would not be likely to cover the cost of replacing the asset, simply because of inflation. The manager then would have to ask for more money in a special award to buy replacement equipment, and this request would probably not be understood or well received.

When an asset has not been depreciated and is no longer worth the amount shown on the balance sheet, the organization can "write down," or reduce, the value of the asset on the books. Write-downs are not popular because they incur a large expense for one of the accounting periods. This, in turn, creates an unusual charge to the fund balance and confuses the management system by allowing for an exception for the asset rather than recognizing use and obsolescence. If write-downs and depreciation are not used and an organization must remove an asset from the books, it has no accepted procedure for doing so—except to not list the assets!

Depreciation Methods. There are various methods available for computing depreciation, just as there are different methods for inventory valuation. Three of these methods are briefly described here. The first procedure is the straight-line method; this is the method that was used in the example given above involving a truck purchase. The $11,000 truck was estimated to have a useful life of ten years and a salvage value of $1,000. The equation used to calculate the depreciation was purchase price ($11,000) minus salvage value ($1,000) divided by years of life, which yields a depreciation of $1,000 each year for ten straight years.

The straight-line method is the most popular, particularly in public and nonprofit organizations, and the easiest to understand. The federal government permits operations to use the straight-line method for tax purposes; however, there are guidelines as to the number of years of estimated life that will be permitted for different types of equipment, and this number of years can be changed as deemed appropriate by the government. Moreover, in some cases, it is permitted to exclude a salvage value from the computation if this can be justified.

Another method for calculating depreciation is called the "units of production method." This method measures useful life in terms of units produced by a machine rather than in terms of years. It calculates the cost per unit by dividing the cost of the asset minus the salvage value by the number of units produced. The cost per unit is then multiplied by the number of units produced each year to arrive at the amount to be charged to depreciation. In the example of the truck, assume that the truck is estimated to have a useful life of 100,000 miles. The cost per mile, or unit, is then the purchase price ($11,000) minus the salvage value ($1,000) divided by the total number of miles (100,000), or $.10 per mile. If the truck is driven 8,500 miles in the first year, the depreciation is 8,500 miles times $.10 per mile, or $850. After the truck has been driven for 100,000 miles, it is fully depreciated, and the book value is the salvage value of $1,000.

For-profit companies are often interested in accelerating the depreciation of assets in order to increase the amount to be charged as depreciation expense against the gross profit of the company and to justify the purchase of newer equipment. In 1981, the federal government instituted a major change in the rules for depreciation by implementing the Accelerated Cost Recovery System (ACRS), which permits companies to speed up the depreciation of assets. As a result, a company can have a higher depreciation rate in the first several years, which decreases its taxable profit. This change was instituted by the government in order to encourage companies to buy new equipment more frequently to stimulate the economy. As noted above, this method may be used for tax purposes, but a company may opt to use the straight-line method in order to show larger profits on its public financial reports. This allows for larger returns on investments, which, in turn, attracts investors.

Equipment Inventory. Public and nonprofit organizations need to keep records on permanent equipment through inventory control records, which are tied into the accounting system when an equipment purchase is made, when depreciation is noted, and when equipment is sold or written off the books. This is part of the responsibility of the purchasing function, which provides control over all of the physical property of the organization (Scheps and Davidson, 1970).

With this system, an equipment inventory card is prepared for each piece of equipment at the time of its purchase. The information on this card includes the date of purchase, budget numbers, the purchase order number, the date the equipment was received, the date the existence of the equipment was verified or inventoried, the manufacturer's serial number, depreciation, and so on. In some cases, the equipment is given an identification number, which is recorded on the card, and a tag or sticker with the identification number on it is placed on the piece of equipment. When a physical inventory is taken, the verification date, as well as the condition of the equipment, is recorded on the inventory card. When equipment is sold or discarded, this is noted on the inventory card, which is then placed in a permanent file or in a computer record. A journal entry is then required to remove the equipment from the accounting records.

Summary

As public and nonprofit organizations become larger and more complex, the simple cash-basis method of accounting can no longer provide for the efficient management of resources and the preparation of accurate financial reports. The accrual method of accounting, which makes use of adjusting entries to allow the accounting system to allocate revenue receipts, income, and expenses to the proper accounting periods, provides for a more accurate system. In addition, as the profits of more self-supporting operations in public and nonprofit organizations become subject to taxation, the accrual method and adjustments have become more important and, in some cases, required by law.

The accrual method of accounting makes use of three types of adjustments: for revenues and expenses, for depreciation, and for inventory. Different methods may be used to calculate and record the amounts of these adjustments. No one method is inherently better than another, but managers should be knowledgeable of all of them, since there may be certain advantages or disadvantages in the use of a particular method for an organization.

There are four situations when adjusting entries for revenues and expenses may be required: when there is a payment of cash in the current period for goods or services to be received during a future accounting period; when cash is received in the current period for services or goods that will be delivered in a future period; when an expense is incurred that will not be paid until the next period; and when income is earned during the current period but will not be received until the next period.

Another adjustment involves the recognition of inventory for goods bought for resale in a for-profit operation. This adjustment ensures that the cost of the goods will be charged to the accounting period during which they are resold.

Depreciation may be the most controversial adjustment. Depreciation is a method that allows the cost of buildings and equipment to be allocated to the accounting periods when the assets will be used. It is a formal means to recognize the cost of the use of an asset and is not to be used to set money aside to replace the asset or to try to provide a market value for the assets in the accounting records.

11

Conducting Manager Audits and Analyses

This book would not be complete without a discussion of the importance of auditing and the analysis of financial information. This chapter presents a general introduction to these two topics (further information can be found in most textbooks on accounting and public finance). As emphasized throughout this book, the accounting and budgeting systems that have been described here provide the base on which a sound auditing and financial analysis program can be built. Without this base, managers will find it difficult to move their organizations into a more sophisticated sphere of operations.

An audit is an inspection of an organization's accounting and budgeting operations. Different audits may be made by different individuals associated with an organization, and they may include a review of the programs in relation to the revenue that was awarded for them, their management, the accomplishment of objectives, quality of services, and so on. Although audits are typically the domain of accountants, the managers and supervisors of operating units should also conduct audits. It is an old saying that "you don't get what you expect, you get what you inspect." Managers who do not establish a practice of inspecting the accounting and budgeting systems of their organizations may find that they get the unexpected.

Following the description of the auditing process, this chapter briefly addresses the analysis of financial information and explains the importance of the use of quantitative data in a planned analysis program. Three basic issues are involved in financial analysis: equity, efficiency, and effectiveness. *Equity* means the equitable distribution of expenditures and services to different budget units, services, geographical areas, and groups on the basis of income and race (Berne, 1989). Aristotle (Thomson, 1953, p. 166) explained that "equity, though just, is not the justice of the law courts but a method of restoring the balance of justice when it has been tilted by the law." When equity has been tilted by the practices of an organization, the balance must be restored. This is up to the manager.

Efficiency is a measure of the amount of work that was accomplished in relation to how much it cost; *effectiveness* is a measure of the quality of the services provided (Brown and Pyers, 1988). Of course, a manager cannot evaluate these factors if he or she does not have reliable and valid financial information or does not know what the numbers represent.

What Is an Audit?

A favorite description of auditing is provided by Finney and Miller (1957, p. 1), who explain that an audit is an "examination of accounting records and statements" conducted to "safeguard against fraud and error" and to ensure that the financial statements "have been prepared in accord with accepted accounting principles." They point out that there are two types of audits: one that is continuous and internal, which means it is conducted by the company's own accounting staff; and one that is periodic and conducted by public accountants who are not employees of the company (hence this may be called an external audit). Finney and Miller note that auditors express opinions, which means that the responsibility to act on audit findings falls on the management. Thus, management not only must personally act on the recommendations but also must ensure that the organization's accountants and bookkeepers act on them as well. There have been many cases where audit findings were not taken seriously or the recommendations were not followed, to the financial disadvantage of an organization.

Audits may also be categorized according to when they are conducted. In a preaudit, the balance in an expenditure category is checked before an expenditure is processed against that category. Preaudits should be a daily operation in the management of the budget and may be conducted automatically by a computer program. Postaudits are conducted after expenditures are made; often this is after the end of a fiscal year, but it may be an unannounced review held at any time during the year (Freeman, Shoulders, and Lynn, 1988).

Some large organizations have auditing staffs responsible for conducting the internal continuous audits. These auditors report directly to top management and/or the governing board (Freeman, Shoulders, and Lynn, 1988). After a survey of 284 for-profit companies, Macchiaverna (1978) concluded that the scope of the internal continuous audit was expanding to include a broader range of activities. The internal auditors were devoting almost as much time to nonfinancial audits of such matters as compliance with policies and procedures, controls, and so on as to financial audits. As Courtemanche (1986, p. 19) puts it, the internal audit is a "control over other controls." This is particularly relevant to public and nonprofit organizations because of the importance of the budgeting system activities in such organizations. Macchiaverna's (1987) survey also found that internal auditors were interacting more frequently with senior-level managers and that companies were investing resources in the upgrading of their internal auditing staffs. Both of these findings should be considered seriously by public and nonprofit organizations.

Of course, many organizations, particularly smaller ones, do not have the resources to support a staff of internal auditors or even to hire someone temporarily to conduct an internal audit. In fact, many organizations have to stretch their dollars to afford the often required external auditor. In some cases, the external audit is conducted by the accounting firm that handles the organization's cash and prepares its financial reports. This is not usually a source of problems, but in some cases it could be a little like hiring the fox to guard the henhouse.

Because of the financial restrictions of small organizations, they may tend to ignore issues of audit control; however, they still need to have internal auditors examine accounts, budgets, procedures, controls, financial reports, programs, and so on. In these cases the organization may establish an internal auditing committee, including the manager or managers and a member or members of the governing board, to conduct reviews in lieu of a full-time staff of auditors (Gross and Warshauer, 1979). This internal auditing team can expand its examination to include the utilization of resources, such as buildings and equipment, program outcomes in relationship to the use of the resources, the techniques used to manage a budget, methods used to prepare the budget, and adequacy of the records used for management decisions (these may not all be reviewed in any one audit). The findings of an internal audit should be compared to those of the external audit (this may keep the external auditors on their toes).

Manager Audits

In addition to the audits described above, the manager of the organization, the manager of an operating unit, or the supervisor of several operating units should take time to conduct audits of the budgeting and accounting systems as well as the activities associated with these systems, such as policies and procedures. These audits need not be lengthy, but they can be quite valuable. For example, in a case where a bookkeeper was caught embezzling money, she declared that it was really the manager's fault, since her books and records were never checked, and the temptation had been just too great. The staff of internal auditors remedied the situation quickly. The manager audit also offers an opportunity to collect data that can be used in an ongoing financial analysis program.

The design of an audit conducted by a manager or an internal audit committee varies by organization and type of operating unit. It must take into consideration the organization's accounting and budgeting system, its management structure, and the financial activities, documentation, and program in the manager's unit or section of the organization. For example, the audits in a school district, a police department, a church, a professional association, a city arts commission, a public library, a township, and a university would have considerably different designs because of the organizations' different budget systems, funds, policies and procedures, control forms, missions, activities, outcome measures, and so on. And within an organization, the design will vary according to the operating unit or fund's source of revenue, number of personnel, and activities; for example, a program department that provides services and collects cash from people outside the organization would require an audit design different from that appropriate to a personnel department that provides services to people inside the organization.

Whatever the specific design, however, all manager audits will use the same basic methods and examine the same elements, such as accounting forms, budget forms, budget plans, authorization and approval practices and procedures, budget reports, inventory records, inventory reports, petty cash receipts, and financial statements, and so on. All of these elements cannot and should not be examined each time an audit is conducted; rather, selections should be made in advance.

Another point for a manager to consider is that the word *audit* often conjures up an image that an investigation is being conducted because someone is stealing. Although this is sometimes the reason for an audit, such cases are rare. Rather, the main objectives of most manager audits should be to determine whether the unit or organization can improve its operations by acting on the findings revealed by the audit, such as changes taking place in the organization, in new technologies, in the services provided, in policies and procedures, and so on. This audit is an excellent opportunity to identify "traditional" practices that are no longer relevant, appropriate, or necessary and that may have become a barrier to the implementation of new programs. For example, when a new program with excellent potential was proposed by the professional managers of one organization, it could not be implemented because of the traditional accounting practices. The accountants strenuously resisted the changes that would be required for the implementation of the new program, and the managers who had proposed it were forced to make compromises that severely limited its effectiveness.

The Audit Trail. The key technique in any audit is to follow the audit trail. The audit trail begins with the original source document used to enter a business transaction into the accounting records. For example, if the transaction was a purchase, the auditor will examine the purchase order form to make sure that it has the proper authorization signatures as specified by the organization's policies and procedures and that it has an approval signature indicating that a preaudit was conducted. Then the trail leads to an entry in a journal. After the entry has been verified, the trail then splits into two paths. One path follows the delivery of the materials purchased, the corresponding accounting entries, and the records on the budget reports. The other path traces the posting of the journal entry for the purchase order to the general ledger and possibly the subsidiary ledger. As the audit follows the trail, it makes a check on the records maintained by each office, such as the use of the budget reports and the security of the records (especially personnel reports).

In conducting an audit, a manager or internal auditing committee should select one or more transactions from a file and then follow the trail for each of them through the organization. The transactions selected should (1) represent different types of expenditures, such as wages, supplies, equipment purchase, and travel reimbursement; (2) use different forms, such as a purchase order, a requisition, and a travel reimbursement; and (3) involve different types of receipts, such as cash or checks received at the operational level and checks for a budget award received in a central office. The review will determine whether the proper forms are being used, the information is being recorded correctly, the signatures are original (signature stamps are not recommended, as they pose a security risk), proper office records are being maintained for each form, the security practices are realistic, cash in the office is protected, the elapsed time to process the different forms is appropriate, and so on.

As the documents are traced through the organization, the audit should check for the proper use of journals, ledgers, internal transaction documents (such as vouchers, receipts, cash transmittal forms, internal purchase orders, and cash deposit forms), receiving slips, invoices, monthly reports, bank reconciliation statements, and financial reports. When these documents are examined, the budget numbers, receipt numbers, names of vendors or customers, and other information required by the policies of the organization or unit should be checked and recorded on an audit form.

The audit should compare the dollar amounts on the budget forms, accounting forms, records in the different offices, budget reports, receipts, receiving slips, invoices, vouchers, canceled checks, cash transmittal forms, and bank statements. When an audit is tracing transactions, other documents should be randomly selected and checked; for example, when a purchase order is being checked in the audit trail, other purchase orders should be examined (not traced) for accuracy. If petty cash is drawn from the budget being reviewed, the amount on hand must be counted, and the receipts on file plus the cash on hand should equal the amount withdrawn from the cash account for the petty cash fund.

Finally, at the last level of the organization where checks are written and deposits are made, the total of the receipts and expenditures should be checked for each category against the budget award. The amounts on the selected source documents, receipts, and invoices should be followed to the canceled checks, deposit slips, and bank statements. At this time, the amount of the budget expenditures, the budget award, and the actual cash received should be checked against the bank statements and budget reports.

As an audit progresses through the levels of the organization, a form or a checklist should be used to establish a formal set of written records to be submitted with the audit report. This form should indicate, for example, the offices included in the audit, the number and type of documents reviewed, internal numbers on the forms, dates and amounts on the source documents, places where the transactions were traced or checked, and copies of any documents deemed to be inappropriate. A second audit form should be used to record the expenditures in the different records from different offices. A superficial check of the records at each level in the process cannot provide an in-depth analysis of the system because it would not disclose any possible lack of agreement between the records at the different levels and the budget reports. Such a lack of agreement could indicate a problem with the system or the security of funds.

If the organization uses a computer system, the documents should be checked up to the point of entry into the computer and then confirm the output. Two sets of test entries should be entered into the computer, particularly if remote stations are used. Both sets of entries should represent the typical types of entries usually entered into the system, but the entries in one set should be free of errors, while those in the other set should be incorrect. The computer outputs on both should then be examined to determine whether the system is working properly. For example, if the computer system is designed to disallow an overexpenditure in a budget category, a test entry would be made for an expenditure greater than the amount of the budget balance to see whether the computer rejects it. When batch processing is used, the internal computer logs should also be examined in relation to the documents being traced. Tests of the computer system may be made at any time, not just when an audit is being conducted, and should be unannounced.

Financial Statements. An audit should not stop with the examination of the internal operations of the organization but should include a review of the financial statements. This review would ask questions such as the following: Do the financial statements properly and clearly disclose the financial operations of the organization? If different funds are used, do each fund's financial statements properly exhibit the purpose and activities for which the fund has been established? When combined statements are used, are these statements confusing? Do the assets, liabilities, fund balance, revenue, and expenditures agree with the data collected in the audit of the internal operations? The approved and adopted budgets should be compared with the opening and closing entries as well as with the financial statements. Do the amounts agree? For example, do the revenue award, the revenue receipts, and cash reported in the financial statements agree? Do the authorized budget expenditures agree with the actual expenditures? How does the difference between the revenue and expenditures relate to the excess (or deficit) shown in the fund balance?

Review of Budget Procedures. An audit affords an excellent opportunity to review the procedures related to the preparation and management of the budget. For example: Are the same budget preparation methods being used throughout the organization? Do the personnel involved in the preparation and management of the budget at the different levels have a clear understanding of the procedures? Do they understand the objectives of the budget preparation procedures of the organization? What documents are used to prepare a budget, and how are they used?

The lines of communication throughout the unit or organization should be checked. How long does it take for the information to be processed through the system to activate the budget at the operational levels? How long does it take to implement budget allocations, supplements, and amendments? Are the allocations, supplements, and amendments accurately recorded? Are the methods and records used to manage the budget appropriate? Are the budgets managed according to organizational policies?

Finally, the procedures for approving the budget proposals, amendments, supplements, and final reports must be examined carefully. What personnel are involved in the decision-making process and in the authorization process? How are these processes recorded and reported in the different offices? Do the different levels involved with processing budget transactions actually review the requests and reports, or is a rubber-stamp approval used?

Program Reveiw. An audit should review the method used to prepare the budget, such as program budgeting or zero-based budgeting, and compare the program proposal with the program accomplishments. This review should ask questions such as the following: Were the proposed activities or services delivered? Can the expenditures be justified in terms of these activities and services? This part of an audit does not require that judgments be made regarding program quality; this is the responsibility of the supervisors of the unit and professionals in the field when a program evaluation is conducted. Rather, the objective of the program review in the audit is to deter people from gutting the program budget for personal professional benefit, such as using program funds to pay for travel to a meeting that is unrelated to the program but is a great place to look for jobs. While there are laws to protect revenue and assets from abuse for personal financial gain, it is not a criminal offense to use program funds for personal professional gain, and such use is difficult to prove. The only method that can hope to protect the public against such abuse is the examination of the use of money in relation to the purposes for which the funds were provided. If abuse is found or suspected, a revelation through an audit should discourage further indiscretions.

Fund Balances. An audit of an organization must include an examination of the balances in the funds to determine whether the revenues in a fund are being used as intended. For example: Are the restricted funds used according to the restrictions placed on them? Are the unrestricted funds used as intended by the governing board? Are there unused fund reserves? How are the excesses in the income funds handled? What are the conditions and use of fund reserves in a debt fund, investment fund, or endowment fund? When the fund balance section is reviewed, particular attention should be given to transfers between funds, including a check that the proper accounting terms are used for a transfer and a trace of the money to ensure that it is not transferred and subsequently spent improperly.

The Audit Report. After an audit has been completed, a report on it should be presented to top management and the board. The report should have four parts: the objective, the findings, the conclusions, and the recommendations of the auditors (Courtemanche, 1986). The conclusions and recommendations should refer to the findings, particularly the quantitative data accumulated by the auditors. Upon the review and reaction by the board, the audit report should be prepared for full disclosure. Preferably, it will be reviewed personally with the people responsible for the records that were audited. Without a disclosure or review with the people responsible for the audited budget, future internal audits will likely not be taken seriously. Any action recommended and approved by the governing board as a result of the audit should be taken immediately. A plan for the changes should be developed and implemented before further risks or new developments take effect and create complications.

The Financial Analysis

A common criticism of the bugeting process used by public and nonprofit organizations is that the budgets are not forward-looking but are oriented to the past. In many cases, this may be true. For example, an organization that each year simply adjusts the amount of a budget request upward by 5 percent to cover salary adjustments and then slates a surplus, if any, for program development or new ideas is ensuring that its future will be limited and lifeless. Another backward approach is to base new budget allocations on past expenditures. To cut the allocation of an operating unit that has not used all of its past year's budget allotment is to encourage surplus spending by unit managers at the end of the year to avoid having their budgets cut in the new year. At the other end of the spectrum are organizations that compliment and reward managers who save money, which may cause them to go to extra lengths to avoid spending their allotments. This may lead to a decrease in program quality and the overall effectiveness of the organization. As Brown and Pyers (1988) point out, an organization needs an integrated financial management system that provides more information than just how much was spent in relation to how much was budgeted.

An evaluation of the equity, efficiency, and effectiveness of an organization's utilization of resources is a key component of the process of using an organization's past to help plan its future. This evaluation requires more than merely making budget comparisons; it requires an analysis that addresses past financial and program data as well as future goals. Only thus can an organization determine how its operations may be revised.

The planned analysis may consider the cost and quality of all the organization's activities, total and unit costs in terms of geographical region and personal characteristics of clients (such as income, race, and sex), the effectiveness and efficiency of revenue utilization, and a myriad of other internal measures. The analysis should not, however, be limited to data on operations within the organization but must also take into consideration the environment in which the organization operates. For example, it should consider the potential impact on revenue awards of factors affecting the local, national, and international economy, such as the gross national product (GNP), lending rates, trade deficits, and so on; potential new sources of revenue; trends affecting the relative advantages of different types of investments, such as savings accounts, money market funds, corporate stocks, bonds, and real estate; the market values of assets in relation to the book values; and asset-liability ratios in regard to potential revenues.

If the analysis is not preplanned and backed up by formal hard data, its details could become endless and overwhelming, or it might evolve into just an interesting informal discussion. Thus, the plan should include not merely the collection and review of data but also the quantitative comparisons that will be used. In a discussion of the use of quantitative methods in analyses conducted by for-profit companies, Brown (1987, p. 1) notes that the analyst must "come to grips with the increasing complexity and specialization of the financial markets." He warns, however, that "quantitative illiteracy or careless application of these methods puts one at a serious disadvantage in a very competitive environment and can lead to disastrous results." The same advice can be given to managers of public and nonprofit organizations. The quantitative methods that Brown recommends include the use of present values; a perpetuity formula; different rate-of-return measures; descriptive statistics, such as measures of central tendency (mean, median, mode) and measures of dispersion (for example, variance and ranges); and the establishment of hypothetical tests. Albeit public and nonprofit organizations do not typically enjoy the luxury of having a staff of statisticians, they often do have the luxury of having a working governing board. The statistical methods are not outside the range of capabilities of most managers and many board members in public and nonprofit organizations. They do, however, require a commitment of time.

While a for-profit company concentrates on costs and profit margins, public and nonprofit organizations must focus on expenditures and revenue. For example: What are the expenditure patterns? What are the revenue patterns? What are the patterns of the relationships between expenditures and revenues? How are they related to the future economy? The first requirement, as Coombs and Hallak (1987, p. 40) point out, is to know where and "how to get the basic data and how to judge the reliability of different sources." Once the data are acquired, a breakdown of expenditures into recurrent and capital costs may be necessary. A breakdown of revenue by sources is also important in the pattern analysis. Do the financial records provide this information? If so, is the information valid and reliable?

Finally, it must be determined whether the analysis will make use of the cost-benefit or the cost-effectiveness method. Guthrie, Garms, and Pierce (1988) explain the differences between these two methods and their relative advantages and disadvantages. A cost-benefit analysis evaluates the benefits of a program in relation to the costs of offering it. The problem with this approach is arriving at the dollar value of the benefit. How does one measure the dollar value of the benefits provided by a police department, school, or hospital? The cost-effectiveness approach does not establish a benefit cost but examines alternative program costs in relation to each other to arrive at the least expensive alternative. This assumes that the benefit is worth the cost and that the objective is to find the least expensive way to provide it, and so it may not take into consideration the important issues of quality and equity.

Summary

While there is no substitute for an external audit conducted by a third party, the external audit cannot provide the needed assurances that an organization's financial resources are secure during the year. For this reason, internal audits should be conducted as a supplement to the external audits. Many organizations cannot afford an internal auditing staff and so should use an internal auditing team composed of managers and board members. This team can conduct a regular, inexpensive examination of the organization's accounting and budgeting systems and a review of its activities. Even these audits, however, regardless of their format, should be backed up by a manager's audit.

The key element in an audit is the audit trail, which begins with the selection of source documents and then traces the transactions and forms related to these documents through the organization. When the audit trail is being followed, a review should also be conducted of other areas, such as the process used to prepare the budget, the techniques used to manage budgets, and the compatibility of the records and procedures in the system. The audit should include a review of the preparation and approval of the final report of the budget in the budgeting system and, in the accounting system, should examine the journals, general ledger, subsidiary ledger, trail balance, assets, liabilities, and fund balance, continuing through to the financial statements.

One of the important features of an internal audit is that it can examine the relationship between the proposed program activities and services for which the budget was awarded and the actual cost and delivery of services. In a private company, the net profit can be compared to the expenditures made to generate the profit. However, in a public or nonprofit organization, the program outcomes and expenditures must be balanced against the proposed program financed by the budget award. The internal audit should also examine the balances in the funds and the transfers between funds. The improper use of fund reserves can be a serious problem.

Finally, the auditors should be careful to document their work for the audit report. This report must be accurate and should provide as much quantitative data as possible. When an audit has been completed and presented to management and the board, a full report of the findings should be provided to all parties involved, and if actions are recommended, they should be taken at once.

A planned financial analysis should address the issues of the equity, efficiency, and effectiveness of the operations of the organization; an examination of these and other questions requires reliable and valid financial and program data. An important objective of such an analysis is to keep the organization looking toward the future. Thus, its design should be relevant to the mission of the organization.

References

American Institute of Certified Public Accountants. *Hospital Audit Guide.* (5th ed.) New York: American Institute of Certified Public Accountants, 1986.

Anthony, R. "Closing the Loop Between Planning and Performance." In R. E. Brown (ed.), *Accounting and Accountability in Public Administration.* Washington, D.C.: American Society for Public Administration, 1988.

Arthur Andersen & Company. *Sound Fiscal Management in the Public Sector.* New York: Arthur Anderson & Company, 1976.

Bailey, L. P. *Governmental GAAP Guide 1990.* San Diego, Calif.: Harcourt Brace Jovanovich, 1989.

Berne, R. "Accounting for Public Programs." In J. L. Perry (ed.), *Handbook of Public Administration.* San Francisco: Jossey-Bass, 1989.

Bowsher, C. A. "Sound Financial Management: A Federal Manager's Perspective." In R. E. Brown (ed.), *Accounting and Accountability in Public Administration.* Washington, D.C.: American Society for Public Administration, 1988.

Breneman, D. W., and Nelson, S. W. *Financing Community Colleges: An Economic Perspective.* Washington, D.C.: Brookings Institution, 1981.

Brown, R. E. "Control Aspects of Accounting." In R. E. Brown (ed.), *Accounting and Accountability in Public Administration.* Washington, D.C.: American Society for Public Administration, 1988.

Brown, R. E., and Pyers, J. B. "Putting Teeth into the Efficiency and Effectiveness of Public Services." In R. E. Brown (ed.), *Accounting and Accountability in Public Administration.* Washington, D.C.: American Society for Public Administration, 1988.

Brown, S. J. "Introduction to Quantitative Methods." In S. J.

Brown and M. P. Kritzman (eds.), *Quantitative Methods for Financial Analysis.* Homewood, Ill.: Dow Jones–Irwin, 1987.

Brueningsen, A. F. "SCAT—A Process of Alternatives." *Management Accounting,* Nov. 1976, p. 56.

Chatfield, M. *A History of Accounting Thought.* Hinsdale, Ill.: Dryden Press, 1974.

Coombs, P. H., and Hallak, J. *Cost Analysis in Education.* Baltimore, Md.: Johns Hopkins University Press, 1987.

Cope, G. H. "Municipal Budgetary Practices." *Baseline Data Report,* 1986, *18* (3), 1–13.

Cope, G. H. "Budgeting Methods for Public Programs." In J. L. Perry (ed.), *Handbook of Public Administration.* San Francisco: Jossey-Bass, 1989.

Courtemanche, G. *The New Internal Auditing.* New York: Wiley, 1986.

Finney, H. A., and Miller, H. E. *Principles of Accounting.* (5th ed.) Englewood Cliffs, N.J.: Prentice-Hall, 1957.

Freeman, R. J., Shoulders, C. D., and Lynn, E. S. *Governmental and Nonprofit Accounting: Theory and Practice.* (3rd ed.) Englewood Cliffs, N.J.: Prentice-Hall, 1988.

Governmental Accounting Standards Board. *Codification of Governmental Accounting and Financial Reporting Standards.* Stamford, Conn.: Governmental Accounting Standards Board, 1987.

Gross, M. J., Jr., and Jablonsky, S. F. *Principles of Accounting and Financial Reporting for Nonprofit Organizations.* New York: Wiley, 1979.

Gross, M. J., Jr., and Warshauer, W., Jr. *Financial and Accounting Guide for Nonprofit Organizations.* (3rd ed.) New York: Wiley, 1979.

Guthrie, J. W., Garms, W. I., and Pierce, L. C. *School Finance and Educational Policy: Enhancing Educational Efficiency, Equality and Choice.* (2nd. ed.) Englewood Cliffs, N.J.: Prentice-Hall, 1988.

Hartman, W. T. *School District Budgeting.* Englewood Cliffs, N.J.: Prentice-Hall, 1988.

Henke, E. O. "Fund Accounting—Nonprofit Organizations." In S.

Davidson (ed.), *Handbook of Modern Accounting*. New York: McGraw-Hill, 1970.

Henke, E. O. *Accounting for Nonprofit Organizations*. (2nd ed.) Belmont, Calif.: Wadsworth, 1977.

Hyatt, J. A., and Santiago, A. A. *Financial Management of Colleges and Universities*. Washington, D.C.: National Association of College and University Business Officers, 1986.

Kam, V. *Accounting Theory*. New York: Wiley, 1986.

Kehoe, E. "Educational Budget Preparation: Fiscal and Political Considerations." In R. C. Wood (ed.), *Principles of School Business Management*. Reston, Va.: Association of School Business Officials International, 1986.

Knezevich, S. J. *Program Budgeting (PPBS)*. Berkeley, Calif.: McCutchan, 1973.

Kuhn, R. H. "Fund Accounting—Governmental." In S. Davidson (ed.), *Handbook of Modern Accounting*. New York: McGraw-Hill, 1970.

Lee, G. A. "The Coming of Age of Double Entry: The Giovanni Farolfi Ledger of 1299–1300." In C. Nobes (ed.), *The Development of Double Entry*. New York: Garland, 1984a.

Lee, G. A. "The Development of Italian Bookkeeping: 1211–1300." In C. Nobes (ed.), *The Development of Double Entry*. New York: Garland, 1984b.

Lee, G. A. "The Florentine Bank Ledger Fragments of 1211: Some New Insights." In C. Nobes (ed.), *The Development of Double Entry*. New York: Garland, 1984c.

McCaffery, J. L. "Strategies for Achieving Budgetary Goals." In J. L. Perry (ed.), *Handbook of Public Administration*. San Francisco: Jossey-Bass, 1989.

Macchiaverna, P. *Internal Auditing*. New York: Conference Board, 1978.

McNamara, R. S. *The Essence of Security: Reflections in Office*. New York: Harper & Row, 1968.

Mansfield, R. "The Financial Reporting Practices of Government: A Time for Reflection." In R. E. Brown (ed.), *Accounting and Accountability in Public Administration*. Washington, D.C.: American Society for Public Administration, 1988.

Matkin, G. W. *Effective Budgeting in Continuing Education: A*

Comprehensive Guide to Improving Program Planning and Organizational Performance. San Francisco: Jossey-Bass, 1985.

Meigs, W. B., and Meigs, R. F. *Accounting: The Basis for Business Decisions.* (6th ed.) New York: McGraw-Hill, 1984.

Meisinger, R. J., Jr., and Dubeck, L. W. *College and University Budgeting: An Introduction for Faculty and Academic Administrators.* Washington, D.C.: National Association of College and University Business Officers, 1984.

Merewitz, L., and Sosnick, S. H. *The Budget's New Clothes.* Chicago: Markham, 1971.

Millar, B. "Non-Profits Charge That Overhaul of Accounting Rules Would Distort Financial Situation of Many Charities." *Chronicle of Philanthropy,* 1990, *2* (16), 1, 23-24.

Moscove, S. A., and Simkin, M. G. *Accounting Information Systems: Concepts and Practice for Effective Decision Making.* (3rd ed.) New York: Wiley, 1987.

Municipal Finance Officers Association of the United States and Canada. *Governmental Accounting, Auditing, and Financial Reporting.* Chicago: Municipal Finance Officers Association of the United States and Canada, 1968.

National Association of College and University Business Officers. *A College Planning Cycle.* Washington, D.C.: National Association of College and University Business Officers, 1975.

National Association of College and University Business Officers. *College and University Business Administration.* (4th ed.) Washington, D.C.: National Association of College and University Business Officers, 1982.

National Committee on Governmental Accounting. *Municipal Accounting and Auditing.* Chicago: Municipal Finance Officers Association, 1951.

National Committee on Governmental Accounting. *Governmental Accounting, Auditing, and Financial Reporting.* Chicago: National Committee on Governmental Accounting, 1968.

Needles, B. E., Jr. *Financial Accounting.* Boston: Houghton Mifflin, 1983.

Novick, D. "The Origins and History of Program Budgeting." *California Management Review,* Fall 1968, pp. 1-12.

Oakerson, R. "Governance Structures for Enhancing Accountability and Responsiveness." In J. L. Perry (ed.), *Handbook of Public Administration*. San Francisco: Jossey-Bass, 1989.

Robbins, S. P. *The Administrative Process*. (2nd ed.) Englewood Cliffs, N.J.: Prentice-Hall, 1976.

Scheps, C., and Davidson, E. E. *Accounting for Colleges and Universities*. (Rev. ed.) Baton Rouge: Louisiana State University Press, 1970.

Schick, A. "Contemporary Problems in Financial Control." In R. E. Brown (ed.), *Accounting and Accountability in Public Administration*. Washington, D.C.: American Society for Public Administration, 1988.

Skousen, K. F., Langenderfer, H. Q., and Albrecht, W. S. *Principles of Accounting*. (2nd ed.) New York: Worth, 1983.

Sorter, G. H., and others. "Range of Potential Parameters." In J. J. Cramer and G. H. Sorter (eds.), *Objectives of Financial Statements*. New York: American Institute of Certified Public Accountants, 1974.

Thomson, J.A.K. *The Ethics of Aristotle*. Baltimore, Md.: Penguin Books, 1953.

Welsch, G. A., Hilton, R. W., and Gordon, P. N. *Budgeting: Profit Planning and Control*. (5th ed.) Englewood Cliffs, N.J.: Prentice-Hall, 1988.

Williams, J. J. "A New Perspective in the Evolution of Double Entry Bookkeeping." In C. Nobes (ed.), *The Development of Double Entry*. New York: Garland, 1984.

Yamey, B. S. "The Functional Development of Double Entry Bookkeeping." In C. Nobes (ed.), *The Development of Double Entry*. New York: Garland, 1984.

Index